THE AMSTERDAM
ADDRESS BOOK

Text:	Martin Cleaver
Editor:	Phil Harriss
Layout:	Cristina Silva
Photography:	Jon Davison
Cartography:	Falk-Verlag

We would like to thank the following for their invaluable help in preparing this guide: Anthony Akerman, Marlies Bommike, Gemma Coumans, Hugh Esten, Marijn Helle, Irma Hesp, Annet Neve, Stan Rijven, José van der Voort, Anneke Vreeburg, the VVV: Amsterdam Tourist Bureau.

Your opinion matters. If you find a change, or a gem of a place we should know about, our editor would be happy to hear from you. Be sure to include your name and address, since in appreciation for a useful suggestion, we'd like to send you a free travel guide.

COPYRIGHT© 1993 by Berlitz Publishing Ltd., London Road, Wheatley, Oxford OX9 1YR, Great Britain.

All rights reserved. No part of this book may be reproduced or transmitted in any form or by any means, electronic or mechanical, including photocopying, recording or by any information storage and retrieval system without permission in writing from the publisher.

Berlitz Trademark Reg. U.S. Patent Office and other countries—Marca Registrada.
Printed in Switzerland by Weber S.A., Bienne.

CONTENTS

INTRODUCTION	7
HISTORY	8
SIGHTS	**13**
Historic Buildings	13
Business, Civic and Domestic Architecture	18
Churches	20
Parks, Gardens and Courtyards	23
Squares	25
Canal Houses	27
Cemeteries	29
MUSEUMS	**31**
Art Museums	31
History, Science and Thematic Museums	34
ART GALLERIES	**43**
Art Dealers and Sales Galleries	43
Antique Dealers	49
Crafts Galleries	50
SHOPPING	**53**
Department Stores	53
Fashion	54
Shoes	57
Jewellery	58
Home Furnishings	59
Gifts	60
Markets	62
Flowers	63

CONTENTS

Bookshops	64
Music	68
Gourmet Foods	70
Evening Shopping	72
Healthcare	72
Tatoo Artist	73
Stationery	73

4 RESTAURANTS — 75

Extravagant	75
Economical	78
Dutch	79
Late-Night Places	82
Ethnic	83
Fish	94
Lunch/Snacks	95
Vegetarian	97

NIGHTLIFE — 99

Bars	99
Cinema	107
Theatre	108
Classical Music, Dance and Opera	112
Pop and Rock Concerts	114
Jazz Cafés	114
Discos and Nightclubs	115
Red-Light District	117
Gay	117

CONTENTS

HOTELS	**121**
Campsites	121
Youth Hostels	122
Budget Hotels	123
Medium-Price Hotels	126
Deluxe Hotels	129
Top-Price Hotels	130
CHILDREN	**133**
Attractions	133
Excursions Outside Amsterdam	135
Restaurants	136
Shops	137
Babysitters	139
WALKS, TOURS AND DAY TRIPS	**141**
City Sightseeing Tours	141
Canal Boat Trips	143
Day Trips Outside Amsterdam	144
PRACTICAL INFORMATION	**155**
Airport	155
Climate	155
Consulates	155
Crime and Petty Theft	155
Customs and Immigration	155
Disabled Visitors	156
Driving in Amsterdam	156
Drugs	157
Electric Current	157
Emergencies	157

CONTENTS

Festivals	158
Libraries	159
Medical Care	159
Money Matters	160
Newspapers and Magazines	160
Post Offices	160
Public Holidays	161
Public Lavatories	161
Telephone	161
Tipping	161
Tourist Information	161
Transport	162
Water	162

MAP SECTION	**163**

INDEX	**183**

INTRODUCTION

*A*fter the big three—Rome, London and Paris—Amsterdam is the most popular tourist city in Europe. While other European capitals awe the visitor with their massive squares and boulevards, the intimate, human scale of Amsterdam's streets and houses make even the first-time visitor soon feel at home here and it's a rare traveller who is content with only one visit.

Though Amsterdam remains, as ever, a centre of international commerce, the city retains the cosy warmth of a society that was once smaller and less hurried. For centuries, the traders of the world have met here to exchange goods, yet the city on the Amstel retains its unique character as the capital of a small, peaceful and prosperous country.

The streets themselves invite you to wander freely. The water flows serenely through the long, curving canals; the trees grow tall and green beside the water; and, while ambling over the gently sloping bridges, you'll experience a relaxing sense of freedom unlike that found in any other capital.

Paradoxically, this freedom is enjoyed among tightly-packed rows of houses, some of them the narrowest in the world. Amsterdammers' minds are apparently as broad as their houses are narrow. Perhaps it was the centuries of living on top of each other that taught them their patient tolerance for the bewildering ways of others. Whatever the reason, Amsterdam has always prided itself on the friendly welcome it gives to strangers.

This book was created to complement the Berlitz Travel Guide to Amsterdam and to help you find your own way through this fascinating city while enjoying the art treasures of its museums, the easy conviviality of its pubs and cafés and the astounding variety of its entertainments and nightlife.

Whether the traveller's whims lead to serene contemplation of the Dutch Masters in the halls of the Rijksmuseum, or to a late-night stroll through the famous Red Light District; to an afternoon of classical music in the Concertgebouw, or to all-night dancing in the newest discotheque: nothing that is human is foreign to Amsterdam.

HISTORY

Few cities illustrate their own history as well as Amsterdam. From its beginnings as a medieval fishing village, its rise to city status with the damming of the Amstel, through the Golden Age with its graceful expansion along a network of canals, to the monuments and housing developments of later centuries—each stage of the city's history has left a plainly visible mark. The people of the city have, for the time being, set sensible limits on its growth, but where the city will finally end, no one can say. The question of where it began is more simple.

The Dam on the Amstel

There was a time when the waters of the River Amstel flowed directly into the River IJ and out to the Zuider Zee. But the fishermen who lived on the sandbanks at the mouth of the Amstel knew that fierce storms could send sea water rushing into the river to flood the countryside. By 1275, these enterprising folk had diked the river's banks and diverted its waters into a network of canals. A dam was built across the Amstel on the site occupied today by Dam Square, the location of the Royal Palace and the Nieuwe Kerk.

By 1300, the settlement of Amstelredamme (or Amstelodam: old spellings vary) was officially chartered as a city. A protective wall was built around this city and a deep moat dug around the wall. Today the wall is gone but the moat, known as the Singel, remains. A reported miracle in 1345 attracted religious pilgrims and the city prospered as a trading centre through the late Middle Ages. After a devastating fire in 1425, brick construction was made compulsory and the city began to acquire its characteristic look. By this time, the Low Countries, roughly equivalent to the confederation now known as Benelux, had fallen under the rule of the Duke of Burgundy. The prosperous Duchy passed, by marriage, into the hands of the Hapsburg dynasty and what is now The Netherlands became part of the Holy Roman Empire in 1506.

The 80 Years' War

Amsterdam in the 1500s was a centre of exchange not only of goods, but of ideas. Sephardic Jews, expelled from Portugal and Spain, found refuge there, as did the Protestant Huguenots fleeing persecution in France. It was the spread of the Protestant Reformation in the Amsterdam region that eventually brought the Dutch into conflict with their Habsburg rulers.

When the Hapsburg Emperor Charles V retired, he divided his Empire. Amsterdam fell within the western half of this division, inherited by Charles' son, Philip II, King of Spain. Philip sent Spanish troops into the region to suppress the Protestant Reformation, provoking the Dutch to armed revolt. The ensuing conflict, known here as the 80 Years' War, resulted in the independence of the United Netherlands. William the Silent, Prince of Orange, led the military effort against Spain and his sons continued the struggle after his death. Although the new nation was a republic, the House of Orange continued to play a decisive role in affairs of state and in time became the royal family of The Netherlands.

The Golden Age

The 17th century is rightly remembered by the Dutch as their Golden Age. It was the century of Rembrandt and Vermeer, of Huygens and Leeuwenhoek. The Dutch led Europe in the arts and sciences, in exploration and commerce, and set an example of tolerant self-government during an age of absolutism. Prior to the war, Antwerp had been the commercial capital of the region, but with the Spanish occupation of that city, international commerce moved north. Amsterdam became the financial capital of the world and celebrated its new prosperity with the construction of a magnificent Town Hall (today's Royal Palace) on Dam Square.

As Amsterdam expanded, the old city wall was torn down and three concentric canals were dredged around the Singel moat. It is this *grachtengordel*, the ring of canals comprising the Herengracht, the Keizersgracht and the Prinsengracht (the Gentlemen's, Emperors' and Princes' Canals, respectively) that provides the most readily recognizable picture of Amsterdam today. At this time, houses were taxed by the breadth of their canal frontage, encouraging the construction of the tightly-packed narrow houses for which the city is famous. Unable to advertise their wealth with the broad façades favoured in other European cities, well-to-do Amsterdammers crowned their houses with flamboyant ornamental gables, one of the city's most celebrated features.

When leaders of the Dutch Reformed Church first gained control of Amsterdam, they tried to suppress the public practice of other religions. The hidden Catholic Church of the Amstelkring dates from this period. But, as the city prospered, these strictures were eased and Jews, Catholics and Protestants all built impressive houses of worship in Amsterdam.

An early addition to the layout of the city was the Jordaan. Originally the French quarter of the city (the name is derived from *jardin*), its narrow streets became home to the working people of Amsterdam and it remains the city's most distinctive neighbourhood. The venerable "brown" pubs of the Jordaan are now joined by boutiques and galleries, while its crooked houses shelter a lively community of artists.

HISTORY

French Domination
The 18th century saw a decline in Amsterdam's fortunes. The rise of British naval power enabled London to supplant Amsterdam as a financial centre and the military power of France threatened Dutch independence. The French Revolution spilled over into The Netherlands in 1795. Dutch revolutionaries joined French forces to establish the short-lived Batavian Republic.

When Napoleon Bonaparte became Emperor of the French, he installed his younger brother Louis as King of The Netherlands. The City Hall became, for the first time, the Royal Palace. When Louis fled in 1810, he left behind a fine collection of Empire furniture still displayed in the Palace. It was the French who introduced numbered street addresses to The Netherlands. Prior to that time, the tradesmen of Amsterdam had marked their homes with colourful signs advertising their professions. Many of these are still visible in the city centre.

Kingdom of The Netherlands
With the collapse of Napoleon's empire, The Netherlands became an independent kingdom. The constitution of 1848 limited the powers of the monarch and insured the primacy of elected government. Although the national government conducts its day-to-day business in The Hague and the Royal Family maintains its principal residence there, the constitution requires that the monarch be crowned in Amsterdam.

The Industrial Revolution came slowly to The Netherlands, but at the end of the 19th century Amsterdam expanded rapidly. New neighbourhoods were built, with long rows of brick apartment houses to accommodate the growing population. Although the new blocks were built on a larger scale than those of the centre, the city retained its intimacy. The top floors of the newer buildings are not out of touch with the life of the street.

The 19th century was also a period of monumental civic architecture in Amsterdam. Many great public buildings date from this period, including the Rijksmuseum, the Concertgebouw and the Central Station (which gave the city one of its noblest landmarks, but blocked the view of the harbour).

Between the World Wars, public works projects produced two great parks, the Vondelpark in the centre of town and the Amsterdamse Bos which lies between Amsterdam and nearby Amstelveen. The innovative style of architecture known as the Amsterdam School also produced many distinguished projects, particularly in the south of the city. This was encouraged by a left-wing council that was willing to spend large amounts on public housing, including embellishments.

HISTORY

World War II and After

The German occupation of 1940–1945 inflicted great suffering on Amsterdam, virtually annihilating the age-old Jewish community. The terror of those years is recorded in the extraordinary diary kept by Anne Frank who, with her family, hid from the Nazis for two years in the attic of a house on Prinsengracht. The hardships of occupation were aggravated by the harsh winter of 1944–45, a time of shortages and hunger throughout The Netherlands, but especially in Amsterdam.

With liberation, the task of rebuilding the devastated Dutch economy began and the expansion of Amsterdam continued along carefully planned lines. The redevelopment of the Nieuwmarkt, the massive office and housing projects of the Bijlmermeer and new satellite towns such as Almere all provide valuable object lessons for the student of city planning.

The post-war years also brought the loss of The Netherlands' overseas colonies and a fresh wave of immigration. Some came from the former colonies of Indonesia and Surinam, others (principally from Turkey and Morocco) first entered as guest workers. While a chronic housing shortage and persistent high unemployment have placed a strain on the much-admired Dutch social services and caused some friction between natives and immigrants, the new arrivals have clearly enriched the city's culture and cuisine. The sounds of Caribbean and North African music can now be heard alongside the traditional street organ and carillon; Indonesian restaurants and Turkish bakeries have become an indispensable feature of the city.

The youth revolution of the 1960s took an especially vivid form in Amsterdam, where radical movements have long found fertile soil. From the Reformation of the 16th century, the Batavian revolution of the 1790s and the Labour movement of the 19th and 20th centuries, to the Provos' and squatters' movements of the 1960s, '70s and '80s, Amsterdammers have always been quick to take their grievances to the streets.

As the unification of Europe draws nearer and Amsterdam's seventh century comes to a close, the city continues to renew and adapt itself. Amsterdam goes about its modern-day business while preserving its historic legacy and sets the world an example of pragmatic tolerance and humane planning.

SIGHTS

Amsterdam is more a village than a city. A capital without a government, monarch or even major broadcasting facilities, it retains the charm of ages past in its canals, alleyways and historic buildings. Modern edifices of architectural interest also share the limelight. The most interesting attractions range from courtyards to cemeteries, from 20th-century housing estates to canal houses. Styles in the city's long and eventful history criss-cross in an apparently random fashion as ancient constructions acquire a more modern function.

We have divided the city's sights into seven categories: HISTORIC BUILDINGS; ARCHITECTURE; CHURCHES; PARKS, GARDENS and COURTYARDS; SQUARES; CANAL HOUSES; and CEMETERIES. Entries are in alphabetical order within each category.

HISTORIC BUILDINGS

BEURS VAN BERLAGE 8 B1   tram 4, 9, 14, 16, 24, 25
Damrak 243 (1012 ZJ); tel. 6265257. Daily 11 a.m.-5 p.m. only during exhibitions, or to attend concerts.
The Beurs was designed in 1896 and built only in 1903 after much argument. The controversy at its birth may explain the two maxims on the tower: *Duur uw Uur* ("take your time"); and *Beidt uw Tijd* ("bide your time"). In Holland, Hendrik Petrus Berlage and his Exchange Building have become synonymous with the advent of modern architecture. The building marks the transition from art nouveau to New Realism, from fantasy and romance to rationalism. The work served as an example to both the architects of the Amsterdam School and the Modernists. Berlage's Exchange was not designed purely for business. It was also intended as a monument to the working people of the world; a monument that also attempted to unite the arts and sciences. This is reflected in the ornate tiling and decoration.

The Stock Exchange itself has long moved on to new premises, but the main hall has been in use since 1984 for exhibitions. The other two halls have been converted into large and small concert halls for the Netherlands Philharmonic Orchestra and the Dutch Chamber Orchestra (see NIGHTLIFE: CLASSICAL MUSIC, DANCE AND OPERA). In this way, Berlage's Exchange Building now serves the purpose for which he intended it: as a palace of the arts.

Illuminated bridges over the Leliegracht, one of Amsterdam's main canals, show the natural beauty of this city.

SIGHTS

BLAUWBRUG 11 C2   tram 4, 9, 14. Ⓜ Waterlooplein
Over River Amstel by Muziektheater.
Like the Hogesluis over the Amstel at Sarphatistraat, the "Blue Bridge" was inspired by the bridges of Paris. It was designed in 1884 by W. Springer and B. de Greef. All the elements such as the lanterns and abutments, are dedicated to Navigation and Shipping (just take a look over the railing).

BURGERWEESHUIS   10 A1   tram 1, 2, 4, 5, 9, 16, 24, 25
Kalverstraat 92 (1012 PH).
This unexpected haven of rest adjacent to Kalverstraat was built in 1570. The boys' courtyard of the orphanage dates from 1632. It has a loggia with 14 Doric columns. The girls' courtyard, dating from 1634, currently houses the Amsterdam Historical Museum.

14

BUS- OF TUIGHUIS   10 A1   tram 1, 2, 5
Singel 423 (1012 WP).
Designed in 1606 by Hendrick de Keyser, this richly decorated trapezium-shaped gable has volutes, triglyph pilasters, lions' masks, scrolls and a straight cornice with orbs. It was a modern façade for its time, owing to the lack of string courses. Formerly used as a store for gunpowder and arms, the Tuighuis is now part of the University of Amsterdam Library.

CENTRAL STATION   9 C1   tram 1, 2, 4, 5, 9, 13, 16, 17, 24, 25
Stationsplein (1012 AB).
The Central Station was completed in 1889 by P.J.H. Cuypers, A.L. van Gendt and L.J. Eymer and is set on an island between Amsterdam and the River IJ. While the building now shields the city from the water, its neo-Renaissance façade still provides a reminder of Amsterdam's sea-faring heritage. There's a clock on one tower and a wind-vane on the other.

FORMER MAIN POST OFFICE   9 A2   tram 13, 14, 17
Nieuwezijds Voorburgwal 182 (1012 SJ).
Derived from the late-Gothic chancellery in Leeuwarden, this is C.H. Peters' largest, if not his most subtle, building in the "post-office Gothic" style. Built from 1895 to 1899, it was vacated by the post office a couple of years ago and is now a major new shopping precinct.

HISTORIC BUILDINGS

FORMER RIJKS-ENTREPÔT **12** A2 tram 9, 14
Kadijksplein (1018 AD).
Seen from the Plantage Doklaan, this is an impressive row of traditional Amsterdam warehouses, mostly dating from the 19th century. They were recently gutted and converted into showpiece apartments with restaurants and small-business accommodation. An ideal combination of new and old for the architecture buff.

HOLLANDSE SCHOUWBURG **12** A2 tram 9, 14
Plantage Middenlaan 24 (1018 BE); tel. 6224308. Daily 10 a.m.-4 p.m. Admission free.
Once a theatre in the heart of Amsterdam's former entertainment area (the district has now become the rustic Plantage suburb), the Hollandse Schouwburg was used during the war as a congregation point for Jews, before they were transported to concentration camps. It is now a memorial to the thousands of Dutch Jews who died.

IMPERIAL CONTINENTAL GAS ASSOCIATION **6** A1 tram 10
Haarlemmerweg 10 (1014 BE).
The gas works on the road to Haarlem is one of Amsterdam's most spectacular examples of 19th-century architecture. The complex's picturesque brick and wood gables belie its function and ensure its place in history. A park is now spreading around the building and there are plans to convert the one remaining gasometer into a music or theatre venue.

KONINKLIJK PALEIS **8** A2 tram 1, 2, 4, 5, 9,
(ROYAL PALACE) 13, 16, 17, 24, 25
Nieuwezijds Voorburgwal 147 (1012 RJ); tel. 6248698. Mid-June to early September: daily 12.30-5 p.m. Admission: adults f 5, 4-12s f 1.50.
Opened as the City Hall in 1655 in the prosperous Golden Age, the building was converted into a palace by Louis Bonaparte, the Emperor's brother, during his brief sojourn as king in Amsterdam (1806-1810). Today, the Dutch Royal Family uses the palace only occasionally and it is open to the public when they are not in residence. The entrance is hard to find behind the seven arches embellishing the façade. The story goes that the doorway was made as unobtrusive as possible to protect the City Hall from attack. The interior of the palace is well worth a visit. The Council Room, Throne Room and Royal Apartments are adorned with majestic pillars, ornate carvings and lavish decorations and furnishings. Check the opening hours by phone, as the building is often used for state functions.

SIGHTS

MAAGDENHUIS   10 A1   tram 1, 5
Spui 21 (1012 WX).
This accommodation for Roman Catholic orphan girls was built from 1783 to 1787 by Abraham van der Hart. The aim was for it to be "free of pomp and adornment but sound and strong". It is now the administrative centre of the University of Amsterdam and was the heart of Dutch student protests in the late 1960s. It faces the Lievertje, a statue of a little boy which became the focus of the hippy/Provo revolution of the period.

MONTELBAAN TOWER   9 D2   tram 1, 2, 4, 5, 9, 13, 16, 17, 24, 25
Oude Schans 2 (1011 KX).
The lower part of the Montelbaan Tower dates from 1512 and was part of the city's defences along the Oude Schans. It was completed in 1606 by Hendrick de Keyser, who added an octagonal tower and a timber steeple (also known as Mallejan), which resembles the tower of the Oude Kerk. The building now houses the offices of the Amsterdam Water Authority.

MUIDERPOORT   12 B2   tram 9, 14
Alexanderplein (1018 BZ).
Once one of the gates to the city, the Muiderpoort was built in 1770 by Cornelis Rauws. A classical construction facing the Tropical Museum, it has a central dome and lantern and is topped by a relief of the Amsterdam coat of arms by A. Ziesenis.

NEDERLANDSE   tram 16, 24, 25
HANDELSMAATSCHAPPIJ/ABN
Vijzelstraat 30-34 (1017 HL).   **10** B2
K.P.C. de Bazel's masterpiece uses a variety of bricks and stone to achieve a feeling of movement. The commonest criticism of the building is that it is too large in relation to the adjoining canal houses which are pushed aside by the enormous mass of brick and stone.

OLYMPIC STADIUM   15 D2   tram 16
Stadionplein 20 (1076 CM).
The stadium was built for the 1928 Olympic Games in Amsterdam. The architecture by J. Wils, C. van Eesteren and G. Jonkheid unmistakeably reveals the influence of Frank Lloyd Wright. The stadium was extended and restored in 1937, but now faces demolition to make way for housing development. If this is allowed to happen, it will be the first Olympic Stadium in the world to be destroyed.

HISTORIC BUILDINGS

OOSTINDISCH HUIS   11 C1   Ⓜ Nieuwmarkt
Oude Hoogstraat 24 (1012 CE).
Built in 1605 by architect Hendrick de Keyser. The richly detailed entrance is constructed from cushion blocks and includes a round window over a door surrounded by volutes. It is flanked by cross-windows, above which the tympana have volutes and masks. The crown is a rarity: an ensemble of volutes, scrolls, stone-dressed window openings and a balustrade.

OUDEMANHUISPOORT   10 B1   Ⓜ Nieuwmarkt/Weesperplein
Kloveniersburgwal (1012 CN).
This gateway was constructed in about 1601 and, as the name suggests, was the entrance to a Home for Old Men and Women that was once situated here. It now provides access to the university building and to a second-hand book market. The sculpture by Ziesenis portrays a maiden offering a cornucopia to two aged figures. The gate on the Oudezijds Achterburgwal (1754) has an arched pediment with a pair of spectacles symbolizing old age.

ST. ANTONIESPOORT (WAAG BUILDING) 9 C2   Ⓜ Nieuwmarkt
Nieuwmarkt 4 (1012 CR).
St. Antoniespoort was built in 1488 and was altered by Alexander Paqualini and Willem Dirksz in 1545. Until the 17th century it was used as a fortification. In 1617 it was converted to the Waag (Public Weighhouse), where produce was weighed before being sold at the city markets. In 1691 the building housed the dissecting room of the Guild of Surgeons and so provided the scene for Rembrandt's famous painting *Dr Tulp's Anatomy Class*. The main building is flanked by heavy round towers. The city side has octagonal staircase towers. Until 1986, St. Antoniespoort housed the Jewish Historical Museum, but it now faces an uncertain future atop Amsterdam's baldest square on the edge of the Red Light District (see also Nieuwmarkt, p 26).

SCHEEPVAARTHUIS 9 D2   tram 1, 2, 4, 5, 9, 13, 16, 17, 24, 25
Prins Hendrikkade 108-114 (1011 AK); open office hours as public transport ticket centre.
Built in 1916, the Scheepvaarthuis was constructed to house the offices of six shipping companies. It is generally regarded as the first building to be completed entirely in the style of the Amsterdam School. The building is more ornate than later examples of the style, which is best known for its social housing projects. This is primarily thanks to the architects De Klerk and Kramer, who were working in Van der Mey's office at that

SIGHTS

time. This magnificent building is crowned by its geometrically-ornamented central well. It recently became the headquarters of Amsterdam's public transport service.

SCHREIERSTOREN 9 D1   tram 1, 2, 4, 5, 9, 13, 16, 17, 24, 25
Prins Hendrikkade 94-95 (1012 AE).
One of the defensive towers of the first city walls. The windows, doors and plaques are later additions. A characteristic feature is the round-arched frieze on which the battlements were formerly placed. Ships used to arrive and depart from here, hence the name: "the Weeping Tower".

WESTINDISCH HUIS/KLEINE VLEESHAL 7 D1   18, 22
Haarlemmerstraat 75 (1013 EL); tel. 6247280.
In 1623 this building was rented to the Dutch West India Company to which it owes its present name. In 1647 the Nieuwezijds Men's Lodging House was established here. The building was rebuilt to house the Lutheran Orphanage in 1826. It has recently been restored and was used for a while as the Registry Office for weddings. Only the elevations of the courtyard retain their 17th-century appearance.

WILLEMSPOORT 6 B1   tram 3, 18, 22
Haarlemmerplein 50 (1013 HS).
A neo-classical gatehouse once used for the assessment and collection of local taxes. It was restored and converted to dwellings in 1986.

BUSINESS, CIVIC AND DOMESTIC ARCHITECTURE

BETONDORP 19 D2   tram 9, Ⓜ Amstel Station
Duivendrechtselaan, Onderlangs, Middenweg, (1097 TW).
In the early 1920s, when the housing shortage in Amsterdam rose to 20,000, the city organized a competition for prefabricated housing units to be built in the rural area of Watergraafsmeer. The ten winning entries used eight different systems, all based on concrete—hence the estate's name: Betondorp (Concrete Village). The abodes were designed by J.B. van Loghem, D. Greiner, W. Greve and J. Gratama. Between 1923 and 1928, 900 units were built. In 1979 the city authorities decided to renovate Betondorp. The suburb has acquired fame thanks to the extraordinary number of talented individuals from all walks of life who grew up in the village. They include politicians, scientists, writers, film-makers and soccer legend Johan Cruyff.

BUSINESS, CIVIC AND DOMESTIC ARCHITECTURE

INTERNATIONAL INSTITUTE 13 C2
FOR SOCIAL HISTORY
🚌 22

Cruquiusweg 31 (1019 AT); tel. 6685866. Monday to Friday 9.30 a.m.-5 p.m., Saturday 9.30 a.m.-1 p.m. (by appointment only). Admission: free.
The conversion of the concrete warehouse, King Willem I, was undertaken in 1987 by Atelier Pro from The Hague. The building now houses the famous archives of the International Institute for Social History (including Karl Marx's personal effects and writings). It is also home to the Dutch Press Museum (see MUSEUMS: THEMATIC MUSEUMS).

NMB BANK HEAD OFFICE
Ⓜ Bijlmer

Bijlmerplein 888 (1102 MG); tel. 5639111. Two open days are planned for 1992, the 2nd Sundays in June and September.
The most spectacular and—according to some—significant new building in Holland. It was designed in the tradition of architectural expressionism; the designers would like to be regarded as organic architects. The building is in tower-like clusters around green courtyards and is divided into working units for groups of 40. Instead of air-conditioning, there is an air-circulation system with solar collectors, heat-recovering equipment and water reservoirs. In the interior, plants ensure the right humidity. Designed to save energy.

PENTAGON
Ⓜ Nieuwmarkt

Zuiderkerkhof/St. Antoniesbreestraat.
The Nieuwmarkt area was ravaged in the late 1970s to make way for Amsterdam's metro line. To build an underground railway in sandy soil, it is necessary to construct the tunnel on the surface and then sink it into position. Everything in the path of the tunnel has therefore to be demolished. This practice met with widespread local opposition and the protests are commemorated on the walls of Nieuwmarkt metro station. However, the opposition appears to have motivated the planners into doing their best to replace what was lost. The Pentagon is a fine example of thoughtful urban development from the early 1980s.

WESTELIJK ENTREPÔTDOK 12 A2
tram 9, 14

Westelijk Entrepôtdok (1018 AD).
Urban renewal with social housing is now to be found in the 17th-century warehouses in the Western Entrepôt Dock. The warehouses are so deep that the blocks have been cut in half, with an inner courtyard and dwellings front and back. The architect was Joop van Stigt, from Amsterdam.

SIGHTS

CHURCHES

AMSTEL CHURCH 10 B2 tram 6, 7, 10
Amstelveld 10 (1017 JD); tel. 6383409. Church can be viewed by appointment and during concerts.
The Amstel Church dates from 1670 and is the only wooden church in the city. After its recent restoration, it has become a venue for cultural activities and also houses a beautiful bar/restaurant offering a view of Amstelveld.

ENGLISH CHURCH 10 A1 tram 1, 2, 5
Begijnhof 48 (1012 WV); tel. 6249665. Monday to Friday 2-4 p.m.
The uncomplicated design of this medieval church fits in admirably with the rustic atmosphere of the Begijnhof courtyard. The interior contains several old English memorial plaques and pulpit panels designed by the young Piet Mondrian. The church is often used for concerts.

JOHANNES AND URSULA 10 A1
BEGIJNHOF CHURCH tram 1, 2, 5
Begijnhof 29 (1012 RM); tel. 6233565. Daily 8 a.m.-5 p.m.
This church was built in 1665 in secret, to hold Catholic church services during the period of Protestant domination heralded by the Reformation in 1587. It is situated in the quiet Begijnhof and the peace of the square is reflected in the building itself. Guided tours by "Mee in Mokum" include a visit to the church (see Amsterdams Historisch Museum, p.35).

MOSES AND AARON CHURCH 10 C1 tram 9, 14
Waterlooplein 205-207 (1011 PG); tel. 6221305. Open by appointment, or during exhibitions.
By the mid-19th century, the authorities in the north of Holland started turning a blind eye to the construction of Catholic churches. Many Dutch cities were then graced with large neo-classical buildings that were not immediately recognizable as churches. The Moses and Aaron Church is one successful example.

NIEUWE KERK 8 B2 tram 1, 2, 4, 9, 14, 16, 24, 25
Dam (1012 NL); tel. 6268168. Daily 11 a.m.-5 p.m.
Despite the name (New Church), it dates from 1408. After fires in 1421 and 1452, the Iconoclasm of 1566 and the great fire of 1645, little remains of the original building. The present cross-shaped basilica with Renaissance furnishings dates from soon after 1645. Admiral Michiel de

CHURCHES

Ruyter and the poets P.C. Hooft and Joost van den Vondel are buried here. From 1815 onwards, all the Dutch kings and queens were inaugurated in this "national" church. The Nieuwe Kerk is currently used for cultural events, as well as providing a venue for regular organ concerts.

NOORDERKERK 6 B1   tram 3, 10, 🚌 22
Noordermarkt 48 (1015). Sunday during services. Often open on Saturday for visitors to the adjacent market.
While it is not usually possible to see the interior, this church is well worth a visit. It dominates the Noordermarkt. Designed in 1620 by Hendrick Staetsen and Hendrick de Keyser as a precursor to the Westerkerk, it has withstood the tests of time despite a lack of maintenance. Its grandeur is largely thanks to the sobriety and serenity evoked by its exceptional form.

OOSTERKERK   🚌 22, 28
Kleine Wittenburgstraat 1 (1018 LS); tel. 6272280. Monday to Friday 9 a.m.-2 p.m.
A 17th-century church built by Daniel Stalpaert to serve the growing population of the islands to the east of the city centre. Today this old area of ship-building wharfs has become a new neighbourhood and the church is now a social and cultural centre.

OUDE KERK 9 C2   Ⓜ Nieuwmarkt
Oude Kerksplein 23 (1012 GX); tel. 6258284/6249183. Monday to Saturday 11 a.m.-5 p.m., Sunday 1.30-5 p.m.
Amsterdam's oldest church was a wooden chapel on this site, built in 1306. Between 1330 and 1571 a series of alterations and additions resulted in the building as we know it now. During the Reformation, the decorations disappeared, but the 15th-century paintings on the wooden roof were preserved. The stained-glass windows date from the 16th and 17th centuries. The bells and the large organ are renowned. Rembrandt's wife Saskia was buried here in 1642.

OUDE LUTHERSE KERK 10 A1   tram 1, 2, 5
Handboogstraat 4 (1012 XM); tel. 6231572. Guided tours by appointment. Admission free.
The Old Lutheran Church and its inventory date from 1633; the wedding hall from 1885. It houses a permanent exhibition on 400 years of Lutheranism in Amsterdam. The building is now part of the Ramada Renaissance Hotel and is used for congresses and concerts.

SIGHTS

PORTUGEES ISRAELISCHE GEMEENTE SYNAGOGE   11 D1
tram 9, 14
Mr Visserplein 3 (1011 RD); tel. 6245351. Sunday to Friday 10 a.m.-12.15 p.m. and 1.30-4 p.m.
The synagogue of the Portuguese Jewish community was completed in 1675 by separatist Jews who had fled the Inquisition in Spain and Portugal. In its time it was the world's largest synagogue. Taking photographs inside is forbidden.

ST. NICHOLAS CHURCH   9 C1
tram 1, 2, 4, 5, 9, 13, 16, 17, 24, 25
Prins Hendrikkade 73 (1012 AD); tel. 6248749/6227942. 1 April to 15 October: Tuesday to Saturday 11 a.m.-4 p.m., Sunday 10 a.m.-1 p.m. 16 October to 31 March: Saturday 11 a.m.-4 p.m., Sunday 10 a.m.-1 p.m.
As you emerge from Central Station, the cathedral-like silhouette of the St. Nicholas Church dominates the skyline. It was built in 1887 to replace the clandestine Amstelkring Chapel and became Amsterdam's most important Catholic church. St. Nicholas is the patron saint of sailors and the red illuminated cross on the roof was the first sight that sailors used to get of the city as they approached Amsterdam from the sea.

WAALSE KERK   11 C1
Ⓜ Nieuwmarkt
Oudezijds Achterburgwal 157-159 (1012 DH); tel. 6232074. Admission free; report to the verger.
Built in the 17th century for the Wallonian community of French-speaking Protestants, this church still offers a peaceful sanctuary in the Red Light District. The fine acoustics and the famous organ are often used for concerts.

WESTERKERK   6 B1
tram 13, 14, 17
Prinsengracht 281 (1016 GW); tel. 6247766. Monday to Saturday 10 a.m.-4 p.m. Tower: June to 15 Sept. Tuesday, Wednesday, Friday and Saturday 2-5 p.m.
Hendrick de Keyser, also responsible for the Noorderkerk and the Zuiderkerk, carried out his most famous work in the Westerkerk. The imposing tower 85 metres (283 feet) high is topped with a crown modelled on that of Emperor Maximillian of Austria. It has dominated the Amsterdam skyline since 1631. The climb to the top is well worth it for the amazing panoramic view of the city. In the neo-classical interior, the grand organ (1680), painted by Lairesse, is especially noteworthy. Rembrandt was buried in the Westerkerk, in a pauper's grave. His grave has never been located. The grave of his son Titus, however, was recently discovered during excavations.

PARKS, GARDENS AND COURTYARDS

ZUIDERKERK 11 C1   tram 9, 14. Ⓜ Nieuwmarkt
Zandstraat 5 (1011 HJ); tel. 6222962. Monday to Friday 12.30-4.30 p.m. Admission f 1 (by prior arrangement). Tower: 1 June to 15 October Wednesday, Thursday 2-5 p.m., Friday 11 a.m.-2 p.m., Saturday 11 a.m.-4 p.m.
This was Amsterdam's first Calvinist church. De Keyser's design was completed in 1614. Rembrandt may have painted the *Night Watch* in part of the church: he used to hire the building because the canvas would not fit in his house. The church is now used for exhibitions, mainly on urban planning and architecture.

PARKS, GARDENS AND COURTYARDS

AMSTELPARK   8, 48, 49, 60, 158, 173
Close to the RAI Conference Centre. Daily dawn to dusk. Admission free.
This park was laid out in 1972 for the second Floriade, a massive garden festival organized in a different location every ten years. A superb rose garden and spectacular rhododendron area are reminders. The chic Rosarium Restaurant and the Glasshouse Gallery are among the attractions, but Amstelpark also provides plenty of facilities for children: pony rides, farm animals and a miniature train.

AMSTERDAMSE BOS   170, 171, 172
Main entrance: Van Nijenrodeweg. Daily 24 hours. Admission free.
Covering 800 hectares (1,977 acres), the Amsterdamse Bos is the largest area of greenery in the city. It was laid out in the 1930s as part of a work-project for the unemployed. A broad spectrum of recreational facilities are now provided here. The 1-kilometre (0.6-mile)-long stretch of water, called the Bosbaan, is used for rowing and canoeing. There are many activities for children, 14 jogging routes, ice skating and other sports facilities. It is even the home of the Amsterdam Cricket Club. There are also several restaurants, the Bos Museum (see MUSEUMS: THEMATIC MUSEUMS), a buffalo and bison reserve and an open-air theatre. From May to October bicycles can be hired at the main entrance, to ride on the 40 kilometres (25 miles) of bicycle paths.

BEATRIXPARK 16 B2   tram 5
Next to the RAI Exhibition Centre. Daily dawn to dusk. Admission free.
The attraction of this park is its lack of recreational facilities and the resulting haven of peace and quiet in the bustle of south Amsterdam. Only the ducks and geese cause any commotion.

SIGHTS

BEGIJNHOF 10 A1   tram 1, 2
Spui. Daily dawn to dusk. Admission free.
The city's best-kept secret is this courtyard, in an enclave hidden away between Spui, Kalverstraat and Nieuwe Zijds Voorburgwal. In the 14th century, it was the site of a residence of the Begijntjes, unmarried women or widows who lived in a religious sisterhood according to strict rules, but who were not nuns. Most of the houses were "modernized" in the 17th and 18th centuries. The house with the wooden façade at No.34 dates from about 1475 and is said to be the oldest preserved wooden house in all of Holland. There were big city fires in 1421 and 1452; after 1521 it was forbidden to build wooden houses.

VAN BIENENHOFJE 6 B1   tram 13, 14, 17
Prinsengracht 89-133 (1015 DN). Daily dawn to dusk. Admission free.
The largest courtyard in Amsterdam, apart from the Begijnhof, was completed in 1804 to provide "relief and shelter for those in need". An inscription saying so is written above the entrance.

CLAES CLAESZHOFJE 6 B1   tram 13, 14, 17
1e Egelantierdwarsstraat, opposite No.4 (1015 RW). Daily dawn to dusk. Admission free.
Two adjoining courtyards, both dating from the early 17th century. A striking wooden tower dominates the place.

FRANKENDAEL 19 C2   tram 9
Middenweg 72 (1097 BS). Daily dawn to dusk. Admission free.
Frankendael is both the name of a fine 18th-century mansion (closed to the public) and a shady park surrounding it. Part is in use as a city nursery.

HORTUS BOTANICUS 12 A2   tram 7, 9, 14
Plantage Middenlaan 2 (1018 DD); tel. 6258411. October to March: Monday to Friday 9 a.m.-4 p.m., Saturday, Sunday 11 a.m.-4 p.m. April to September: Monday to Friday 9 a.m.-5 p.m., Saturday, Sunday 11 a.m.-5 p.m. Admission f 5, under-14s f3.
Started in 1638 by the University of Amsterdam, the Hortus is one of Holland's oldest gardens. Among the 6,000 species of plant is the world's oldest (400 years) and probably largest, pot plant.

HUISZITTEN WEDUWEHOF 6 B1   tram 3
Karthuizersstraat 89-51 (1015 LN). Daily 24 hours. Admission free.
Constructed in 1650 by Daniel Stalpaert. Complete restoration and intensive occupation have had a deleterious effect on the peaceful atmosphere of this garden, but it remains impressive.

SQUARES

OOSTERPARK 18 B1   tram 3, 9
Oosterpark/Mauritskade. Daily 24 hours. Admission free.
Situated in the midst of a 19th-century working-class neighbourhood, this green haven in the east of the city provides recreation for the local inhabitants. It was inspired by the English landscape parks.

RAEPHOFJE 6 B1   tram 3
Palmgracht 26-38 (1015 HM). Daily dawn to dusk. Admission free.
An intimate spot hidden among the tall trees of Palmgracht (*gracht* means canal, but the name in this case is misleading: there has been no water along here for years).

ST. ANDRIES HOFJE 6 B1   tram 13, 14, 17
Egelantiersgracht 105-141 (1015 RG). Daily dawn to dusk. Admission free.
One of the oldest (1617) and most charming courtyards in Amsterdam. Worthy of mention is the age-old and subtly ornamented, tiled wall at the entrance.

VONDELPARK 16 A1   tram 1, 2, 3, 5, 6, 12
Stadhouderskade, close to Leidseplein. Daily 24 hours. Admission free.
Named after Holland's best-known poet and playwright, Joost van den Vondel (born 1587, died 1679), the Vondelpark was laid out in 1865 in English style. Despite its location in the thick of the city, this green lung provides an oasis of rest. Lakes, attractive cafés (especially at the Film Museum) and meandering foot and cycle paths give the park a unique character. Open-air concerts are organized in the summer from Thursday (evenings) to Sunday (afternoons).

ZON'S HOFJE 6 B1   tram 13, 14, 17
Prinsengracht 157-171 (1015 DR). Daily dawn to dusk. Admission free.
A less spectacular courtyard than nearby Van Bienenhofje (see above).

SQUARES

AMSTELVELD   tram 4
Amstelveld (1017 JD).
A surprisingly attractive square bordered by Prinsengracht and Reguliersgracht. The white wooden Amstelkerk adds to the peaceful atmosphere and the new café-restaurant provides an ideal meeting place. On Monday, the silence is broken by the flower market (10 a.m.-3 p.m.) reviving the original market function of the square.

SIGHTS

DAM 8 B2
tram 1, 2, 4, 9, 14, 16, 24, 25
Dam (1012 NP).
This is the site of a 13th-century dam in the River Amstel. The fishing village which sprung up around it became in 1275 the heart of the town of Amstelredam. Until the 19th century, ships were able to sail from the River IJ to Dam Square. With the construction of the City Hall (now Royal Palace) in the 17th century and the presence of the Nieuwe Kerk, the function of this square as town-centre was established. On 4 May, the National Monument (designed by J.J. Oud) is the site of the annual memorial service to the victims of World War II. At 8 pm on that day, all traffic stops throughout the country for two minutes' silence.

LEIDSEPLEIN 6 B2
tram 1, 2, 5, 6, 7, 10
Leidseplein (1017 PT).
An entertainments centre par excellence. Within 200 metres are at least seven theatres, 18 cinemas, two rock venues, dozens of bars and as many international restaurants. Throughout the year, open-air entertainment in the square is provided by jugglers and musicians. In the winter there is a diminutive ice rink. The area has been recently extended through the old prison (now completely renovated and unrecognizable) to Max Euweplein, with its fountain, cafés and exclusive shops.

MUNTPLEIN 10 B2
tram 4, 9, 16, 24, 25
Muntplein (1012 WR).
This square is actually a bridge, 68-metres (227-feet) wide, stretching across the Singel. The Munttoren (mint tower, 1620), was built on the remains of the old city wall. It acquired the name from the building next to it, where gold and silver coins were minted from 1672.

NIEUWMARKT 9 C2
tram 9, 14. Ⓜ Nieuwmarkt.
Nieuwmarkt (1012 CR).
A large square around the Waag Building (also known as the St. Antoniespoort, see above: HISTORIC BUILDINGS). The square is barren and wind-swept. Don't park around the edge. It looks inviting, but is a favourite venue for police tow-truck drivers.

NOORDERMARKT 6 B1
🚌 18, 22
Noordermarkt (1015 MV).
A characteristic corner of the Jordaan, alongside the imposing Noorderkerk. Quiet most of the time, the area is disturbed on Monday mornings by the flea and cloth market and on Saturday by the bio-dynamic and bird markets.

CANAL HOUSES

REMBRANDTSPLEIN 10 B2   tram 4, 9, 14
Rembrandtsplein (1017 CV).
This square is famous for its nightlife and cabaret. It is one of the nicest places in which to sit and drink a cool beer in the summer.

WATERLOOPLEIN 11 D1   tram 9, 14
Waterlooplein (1011 NV).
Once the heart of the Jewish quarter, the Waterlooplein is now dominated by the Stopera (1985): the City Hall and Opera rolled into one. Much of the original character has now been lost, but the flea market (Monday to Saturday, see SHOPPING: MARKETS) retains something of the old flavour.

CANAL HOUSES

BROUWERSGRACHT WAREHOUSES 8 B1   18, 22
Brouwersgracht. No admission.
These warehouses were built in the Golden Age for the storage of colonial wares such as spices, porcelain, silk and tobacco, imported by the East and West India Companies from all over the world. They fell into disrepair in the 19th century, but in the last 20 years have found a new function as up-market housing.

DRIE GRACHTENHUIS 10 B1
(HOUSE ON THREE CANALS)   tram 4, 9, 16, 24, 25
O.Z. Voorburgwal 249/Grimburgwal/O.Z. Achterburgwal (1012 EZ). No admission.
A fine 17th-century house, built in 1610 by Claes Adrianszoon. It is renowned for its unique location, on the corner of three canals (Oudezijds and Nieuwezijds Achterburgwal and Grimburgwal).

FELIX MERITIS 6 B2   tram 1, 2, 5
Keizersgracht 324 (1016 EZ); tel. 6231311.
Napoleon was received here during his visit to Amsterdam. This robust neo-classical building (built in 1787 by Jacob Otten Husky) was a centre for the sciences and arts until the late 19th century. From 1960 to 1980 it was known as the Shaffy Theatre, which made a name for itself as a centre for innovative drama. It is now in use as the Amsterdam Summer University, but sporadic theatre and dance shows are still performed here (see NIGHTLIFE: CLASSICAL MUSIC, DANCE AND OPERA).

SIGHTS

DE GOUDEN BOCHT 10 A2
(THE GOLDEN BEND)
tram 1, 2, 5, 16, 24, 25
Herengracht 441-513 and 426-480. No admission.
Between Leidsestraat and Vijzelgracht are a row of patrician houses known as the Golden Bend. The double staircases and decoration of the façades compete in beauty and opulence.

MUSEUM VAN LOON 10 B2
tram 16, 24, 25
Keizersgracht 672 (1017 ET); tel. 6245255. Monday 10 a.m.-5 p.m., Sunday 1-5 p.m. Admission f 5.
The painter Ferdinand Bol was one of the first inhabitants of the canal house built in 1672. With its huge collection of family portraits, style rooms and French Garden, this stately mansion is a fine indication of the wealth of Amsterdam merchants.

NARROWEST HOUSE 8 B1
tram 1, 2, 4, 5, 9, 13, 16, 17, 24, 25
Singel 7 (1012 VC). No admission.
The narrowest house in Amsterdam is only as wide as its front door and is jammed between two 17th-century buildings. Taxes were once paid according to the number of windows of a house and the width of its frontage. This is one reason why canal houses are often so narrow yet deep.

TRIPPENHUIS 11 C1
Ⓜ Nieuwemarkt
Kloveniersburgwal 29 (1011 JV). No admission.
Built in 1662 by Justus Vingboons, the Trippenhuis's Corinthian columns and frieze make it one of the most impressive canal houses in the city. It was inhabited for many generations by the Trip family, one of the merchant clans of Amsterdam's Golden Age. The building is so large that it was able to house the complete collection of the Rijksmuseum in the 19th century.

WILLET-HOLTHUYSEN MUSEUM 11 C2
tram 4, 9, 14
Herengracht 605 (1017 CE); tel. 5231822. Daily 11 a.m.-5 p.m. Admission f 2.50.
An original and completely furnished Patrician house, built in 1689 in Louis XV - and neo-Louis XVI-style. It houses the glass and porcelain collection of Abraham Willet. Behind the house is a fine 18th-century French-style garden.

CEMETERIES

NIEUWE OOSTERBEGRAAFPLAATS 19 C2 tram 10
Kruislaan 126 (1097 GA); tel. 6940074. Daily dawn to dusk.
While not exclusively Jewish, this cemetery forms an important memorial to victims of World War II. There is an urn containing ashes of Amsterdam Jews who died in Buchenwald concentration camp and a glass memorial to the victims of Auschwitz.

ZEEBURG JEWISH CEMETERY 19 D1 tram 10
Kramatweg near Flevopark. Daily dawn to dusk.
Zeeburg used to be the most important cemetery for poor Jews, but only very few graves remain today.

ZORGVLIED 148
Amsteldijk 273 (1079 LL); tel. 6445236. Daily dawn to dusk.
Opened in 1867 on the banks of the River Amstel, this most sentimental of cemeteries contains many well-known figures from the arts and culture.

MUSEUMS

One of the main attractions of Amsterdam, rain or shine, is its wealth of museums. Some trace the history of the city, covering its position as a trade and finance centre and its role as a haven for refugees and exiles from all corners of the globe. Others range from the sublime (the Six Collection) to the ridiculous (piggy banks).

Three museums form an essential part of any tour itinerary: the Rijksmuseum, Van Gogh Museum and Anne Frank House. Yet there are so many more. Anyone planning to visit more than half a dozen would be well advised to invest in a Dutch Museum Year Card. This provides free admission to 400 museums throughout Holland for one year from the date of purchase, although there may sometimes be an extra charge for special exhibitions. The *Museum Jaarkaart* (MJK) costs *ƒ* 40 and is obtainable over the counter (you must also supply a passport photo) from most museums and tourist offices. Young people under 26 can also obtain reduced admission to museums with a Youth Card. If a museum (or other cultural venue) offers reductions for holders of the CJP (*Cultureel Jongeren Passport*), it should also accept most foreign youth cards.

ART MUSEUMS

Amsterdam has been, at one time or another, home to many of the greatest of European artists. Rembrandt lived most of his life in the city and even Vincent Van Gogh spent an unhappy year lodging at the naval base (adjacent to the Maritime Museum) where his uncle was commander, before deciding that academic study was not for him. (The VVV tourist office sells an excellent folder detailing a walk that passes many of his haunts.)

Amsterdam belies its size as a major centre of contemporary art. In addition to the museums listed below, much can also be seen in the city's countless commercial galleries. See p.43 ART GALLERIES.

The great 17th-century sailing ship Amsterdam *is moored at the quayside as part of the collection of the Nederlands Scheepvaartmuseum.*

MUSEUMS

FODOR MUSEUM　　**10** A2　　　　　　　　　　　　tram 16, 24, 25
Keizersgracht 609 (1017 DS); tel. 6249919. Daily 11 a.m.-5 p.m. Closed 1 January. Admission: adults f 1, children under 6 free, 6-to-16s and over-65s f 0.50.
The Fodor Museum, opened in 1863 and hence the oldest contemporary art museum in Holland, is still a premier public venue for contemporary Dutch art. It is a great place to catch up with the latest work by Amsterdam's most interesting artists. The museum's large and quiet garden provides a fine backdrop to the sculpture on show there. It is soon to lose its old function and house the Dutch Design Museum.

MUSEUM VAN LOON　　**10** A2　　　　　　　　　　tram 16, 24, 25
Keizersgracht 672 (1017 ET); tel. 6245255. Monday 10 a.m.-5 p.m. Admission: f 5, over-65s f 4.
This 18th-century canal house was bought by Hendrik van Loon in 1884 for his newly-wed son. Its present owners, the Van Loon Foundation, maintain it in its late-18th, early-19th century style. The house also accommodates about 50 family portraits from the 17th to 19th centuries, providing a unique picture of patrician families at the time of the Dutch Republic.

REMBRANDTHUIS　　**11** C1　　　　　　　　　　　　tram 9, 14
Jodenbreestraat 4-6 (1011 NK); tel. 6249486. Monday to Saturday 10 a.m.-5 p.m., Sunday and holidays 1-5 p.m. Admission: adults f 6.50, children under 10 free, 10-to-15s f 3.50, over-65s f 5.
Around the corner from the famous Flea Market in the heart of the old Jewish quarter is the house where Rembrandt lived and worked. It now provides a home for a priceless collection of 250 of the master's drawings and etchings, as well as paintings by his teachers and pupils. An informative exhibition details the etching process as practised by Rembrandt.

RIJKSMUSEUM　　**16** B1　　　　　　　　　　tram 6, 7, 10, 16, 24, 25
Stadhouderskade 42 (1071 ZD); tel. 6732121. Tuesday to Saturday 10 a.m.-5 p.m., Sunday and holidays 1-5 p.m. Admission: adults f 6.50, children under 5 free, 6-to-17s and over-65s f 3.50.
The heart and soul of Holland. The exterior of the Rijksmuseum is a spectacle in itself, while the inside holds a treasure of 15th- to 19th-century art and crafts. Rembrandt's *Night Watch* (the original title is *The Company of Captain Frans Banning Cocq and Lieutenant Willem van Ruytenburch*) may be the most famous work in this enormous collection,

ART MUSEUMS

but other Golden Age jewels include the marvellously intimate domestic scenes by Jan Vermeer; luminous landscapes by Jacob van Ruisdael; Jan Steen's boisterous tavern scenes; spirited portraits by Frans Hals; not to mention other masterpieces by Rembrandt van Rijn. While the Rijksmuseum's collection of 17th-century Dutch Masters is unequalled, it is not the Museum's only strength. There is a vast array of Dutch painting from the centuries before and after this period. The evolution of painting in Holland can be traced from the Middle Ages onwards, a fascinating progression. But the Rijksmuseum's collection is not limited to Dutch art. There is a generous selection from foreign schools (French, Italian and Flemish), an entire museum of Asian art, art from the Islamic world, porcelain, dolls houses, furniture and excellent exhibitions on Dutch history.

SIX COLLECTIE   **11** C2   tram 4, 9, 14
Amstel 218 (1017 AJ); tel. 6732121. Monday, Wednesday, Friday 10 a.m.-noon. Admission free.
The extraordinary art collection in the private home of the Six family can only be seen by arrangement on a guided tour. There are two tours a day, one at 10 a.m. and one at 11 a.m. Admission is free, but you must obtain a ticket in advance at the Rijksmuseum. It is necessary to show your passport as identification before taking the tour. The furnishings and porcelain are reason enough to pay a visit to this stately canal house, but the jewel of the collection is Rembrandt's portrait of Jan Six himself.

STEDELIJK MUSEUM   **16** B1   tram 2, 3, 5, 12   🚍 63, 170
Paulus Potterstraat 13 (1071 CX); tel. 5732911/5732737 (recorded message in Dutch). Daily 11 a.m.-5 p.m. Closed 1 January and 5, 24 and 31 December. Admission: adults f 7, children under 7 free, 7-to-16s and over-65s f 3.50.
One would hardly guess from the ornate 19th-century exterior that the Stedelijk is the home of modern art in Amsterdam, but it is. The light and spacious interior is a pleasant surprise, but the art on the walls is something more. Not only are all the great names of modern art here, but the works shown are among their best. Picasso, Matisse, Cézanne, Chagall, Kandinsky, Van Gogh, Mondrian and the world's greatest collection of Malevich's work are among the highlights. Yet one of the greatest pleasures of the Stedelijk is discovering the many fine Dutch artists of the modern period whose works are too little known outside Holland. And then there are the multi-media installations of the rising generation. At lunchtime, the restaurant is a favourite spot for local office workers and shoppers from the P.C. Hooftstraat.

MUSEUMS

VAN GOGH MUSEUM　**16** B1　　　　　　　　　tram 2, 3, 5, 12
Paulus Potterstraat 7 (1071 CX); tel. 5705200. Monday to Saturday 10 a.m. to 5 p.m., Sunday and holidays 1-5 p.m. Admission: f 10, children under 6 free, 6-to-17s and over-65s f 5.
This monument to De Stijl, bearing a striking resemblance to the later work of Piet Mondrian, was based on a design by the great Dutch architect, Gerrit Rietveld. It houses a stunning assortment of work by Vincent Van Gogh, collected by his long-suffering brother Theo. As Vincent hardly sold anything and left everything to his brother, Theo's collection was formidable. Every phase of the remarkable career is present, from the brooding peasant scenes of his early work, to the fiery landscapes and self-portraits of the last year in Arles. Paintings by Vincent's friends and contemporaries are also displayed here, as are examples of the Japanese art that influenced him so profoundly, most of them from Vincent's own collection.

HISTORY, SCIENCE AND THEMATIC MUSEUMS

AGNIETENKAPEL　**10** B1
(ST. AGNES' CHAPEL)　　　　　　　　　tram 4, 9, 14, 16, 24, 25
Oudezijds Voorburgwal 231 (1012 EX); tel. 5253341. Monday to Friday 9 a.m.-5 p.m. Admission: f 1.50.
St. Agnes's Chapel houses the historical museum of the University of Amsterdam. The permanent display relates the history of the University. Temporary exhibits illustrate modern scientific developments, with an emphasis on research carried out at the University itself. Ring the bell for admission.

ALLARD PIERSON MUSEUM　**10** B1　　　tram 4, 9, 16, 24, 25
Oude Turfmarkt 127 (1012 GC); tel. 5252556. Tuesday to Friday 10 a.m.-5 p.m., Saturday, Sunday 1-5 p.m. Admission: adults f 3.50, over-65s f 2.
An archaeological museum, located in a neo-classical building which once housed the Netherlands Bank (built 1869). The collection comprises ancient relics from the Egyptian, Middle Eastern, Greek, Etruscan and Roman civilizations.

HISTORY, SCIENCE AND THEMATIC MUSEUMS

AMSTERDAMS HISTORISCH   **10** A1
MUSEUM   tram 1, 2, 4, 5, 9, 14, 16, 24

Kalverstraat 92 (1012 PH); tel. 5231822. Daily 11 a.m.-5 p.m. Closed 1 January. Admission: adults f 5, children under 6 free, 6-to-16s and over-65s f 2.50.

Located in the former Burgerweeshuis (Citizens' Orphanage), this beautiful 17th-century building with its spacious courtyard holds an extraordinary collection of artifacts illustrating the history of Amsterdam. Art treasures are also exhibited, including a hall of militia portraits from the Golden Age. Just past the entrance, an automated display demonstrates the growth of the city and its population. You can go on to stroll through the history of the city, from its founding in the Middle Ages, through the revolt against Spain, the Golden Age, the Batavian Revolution, the rise of the monarchy and the colonial empire and on to the present.

    All this is illustrated with paintings, weapons, household objects and an elegant 18th-century interior. Captions for most exhibits are in Dutch only, but you can borrow an English-language guide book at the front desk. When you're ready for a break, sit down and inspect the David and Goliath statues in the restaurant. On leaving, don't miss having a good look at the St. Luciënsteeg entrance, where 22 old city gablestones have been restored and set into the wall.

ANNE FRANKHUIS   **6** B1   tram 13, 14, 17, 🚌 21, 170

Prinsengracht 263 (1016 DW); tel. 6264533. June to August: Monday to Saturday 9 a.m.-7 p.m., Sunday and holidays 10 a.m.-7 p.m. September to May: Monday to Saturday 9 a.m.-5 p.m., Sunday and holidays 10 a.m.-5 p.m. Closed 1 January and Yom Kippur. Admission: adults f 6, children under 10 free, 10-to-17s f 3, over-65s f 2.50.

Those already familiar with Anne Frank's story through her book, or the films and plays made from it, may still be unprepared for the experience of the sliding bookcase and the secret staircase that leads to the tiny rooms where the Frank and Van Damm families lived for two years before they were betrayed to the Nazis.

    Pictures of film stars of the period are still pasted to the walls of Anne's room, where she left them in 1944 when she and her family were captured. Besides maintaining the hiding place of the Frank family as a permanent memorial, the Anne Frank Institute is vigilant in monitoring the activities of neo-Nazi groups in Holland and abroad. The adjoining museum houses exhibitions documenting the continuing struggle against anti-Semitism and racism.

35

MUSEUMS

AVIODOME (NATIONAL
AVIATION MUSEUM)   train to Schiphol, from Central Station
Westelijke Randweg 1 (1118 AA) Schiphol-Centrum; tel. 6041521. April to October: Monday to Friday 10 a.m.-5 p.m., Saturday, Sunday noon-5 p.m. November to March: closed Monday. Admission: adults f 6, 4- to-12s f 4.50.
Tickets available at Central Station include the price of a return train trip, coffee and apple pie and admission to the Aviodome. The museum provides a permanent show on the development of aviation and space exploration, with more than 35 planes, various satellites and technological curiosities. Highlights include a Fokker Spin (1911) and a World War II Spitfire.

BIJBELS MUSEUM (BIBLE MUSEUM)   6 B2   tram 1, 2, 5
Herengracht 366 (1016 CH); tel. 6242436. Tuesday to Saturday 10 a.m.-5 p.m., Sunday 1-5 p.m. Admission: adults f 3, 4-16s and over-65s f 2.
Occupying two fine old canal houses, the Bible Museum provides a survey of the background to the Good Book based on archaeological finds, antique Bibles, prints ancient and modern, models and a slide-show. Notice the stone tablet which portrays a crooked piece of wood; this is a reference to the building's first resident, Jacob Cromhout (meaning "crooked-wood").

BOSMUSEUM   tram 16 to Haarlemmermeerstation or Sneltram to Amstelveen
Koenenkade 56 (1081 KG); tel. 6431414. Daily 10 a.m.-5 p.m. Admission: free.
A permanent exhibition about the use and maintenance of the Amsterdamse Bos, a tranquil woodland area to the south of the city. The Bosmuseum was created in the 1930s as part of a work project for the unemployed. From both Amstelveen and Haarlemmermeerstation there is a 1.5km (1 mile) walk to the Bosmuseum.

GEELS & CO,   9 C1
COFFEE AND TEA MUSEUM   tram 1, 2, 4, 5, 9, 24, 25
Warmoesstraat 67 (1012 HX); tel. 6240683. Friday, Saturday noon-5 p.m.
The museum is to be found in a tasting room and historic shop. It includes old coffee roasters, tea machines and coffee mills.

GEMEENTEARCHIEF
(AMSTERDAM MUNICIPAL ARCHIVES)   tram 3, 4
Amsteldijk 67 (1074 HZ); tel. 6646916. Monday to Friday 8.45 a.m.-4.45 p.m., Saturday 9 a.m.-12.15 p.m.

HISTORY, SCIENCE AND THEMATIC MUSEUMS

Amsterdam's municipal archives house a permanent exhibition of posters and photographs pertaining to the history of the city.

HASH INFO MUSEUM   **9** C2   Ⓜ Nieuwmarkt
Oudezijds Achterburgwal 148 (1012 DV); tel. 6235961. Tuesday to Sunday noon-6 p.m.
Information on the worldwide cultivation and use of cannabis over the centuries, with a colourful display of comics, labels, T-shirts and other paraphernalia associated with marijuana in more recent times. There is also a reference library of books, videos and tapes.

JOODS HISTORISCH MUSEUM   **11** D2
(JEWISH HISTORICAL MUSEUM)   tram 9, 14. Ⓜ Nieuwmarkt
Jonas Daniel Meyerplein 2-4 (1011 RH); tel. 6269945, info line 6254299. Daily 11 a.m.-5 p.m., closed on Yom Kippur. Admission: adults ƒ 7, children under 10 free, 10-to-14s and over-65s ƒ 3.50.
This museum, opened in 1987, documents the history of Jews in Holland from the arrival of the first refugees from the Spanish Inquisition in the 16th century. Exhibits include religious objects, portraits of Jews who were influential figures in Dutch history and views of the old Jewish quarter of Amsterdam. Letters, newspapers, photographs and government documents tell, in chilling detail, the story of the Nazis' attempt to annihilate Dutch Jews. The Museum is closed on Yom Kippur, the Day of Atonement, which usually falls in September. The Museum is also keeper of the complete work of artist Charlotte Salomon.

KATTENKABINET   **10** A2   tram 16, 24, 25
Herengracht 497 (1017 BT); tel. 6265378. Tuesday to Sunday noon-5 p.m. only during shows. Admission: ƒ 7.50.
A bizarre and select collection of paintings, prints and objects focusing on Amsterdam's favourite pet, the cat. The Cabinet is in a 17th-century canal house with rooms decorated in a 19th-century style.

MADAME TUSSAUD'S   **8** B2
SCENERAMA   tram 1, 2, 4, 9, 13, 14, 24, 25
Dam 20 (1012 NP); tel. 6229239. September to June: daily 10 a.m.-6 p.m. July, August: daily 9 a.m.-7 p.m.
A new look to an old attraction. This is Madame Tussaud's only venue outside Britain. In what is known as an "audio-animatronic-show", light, sound, temperature, wax models and moving puppets are used to provide a survey of past, present and future. The Scenerama focuses on Dutch history, but also caters for the foreign visitor.

MUSEUMS

MAX EUWE CENTRUM
tram 1, 2, 4, 9, 13, 14, 24, 25
Max Eueweplein 30A (1017 MA); tel. 6257017. Tuesday to Friday (and 1st Saturday of the month) 10.30 a.m.-4 p.m. Admission free.
A look at the history, spread and development of chess, concentrating on the career of Max Euwe, the first and only Dutch world chess champion.

MUSEUM AMSTELKRING   9 C1
tram 1, 2, 4, 5, 9, 24, 25
Oudezijds Voorburgwal 40 (1012 GE); tel. 6246604. Monday to Saturday 10 a.m.-5 p.m., Sunday and holidays 1-5 p.m., closed 1 January. Admission: f 4.50, under-15s and over-65s f 3.
Although Amsterdam's tolerance of religious diversity has been proverbial since the 1500s, there was a notable lapse in this policy in the early 17th century, when public practice of the Catholic faith was prohibited. Amsterdam's Catholics attended mass in concealed churches at this time, one of which has been lovingly preserved in the Amstelkring Museum. Hidden behind three houses, *Ons' Lieve Heer Op Solder* (Our Dear Lord in the Attic) is a fascinating place. There is an ingenious economy of space at work in this clandestine chapel: note the hinged pulpit and the priest's wall-bed. The church remained in use even after the prohibition of public Catholic worship was lifted.

NATIONAAL SPAARPOTTENMUSEUM   8 A2
(NATIONAL PIGGY BANK MUSEUM)
tram 13, 14, 17
Raadhuisstraat 12 (1016 DE); tel. 5567425. Monday to Friday 1-4 p.m. (and by appointment). Admission: adults f 1.50, under-13s f 1.
More than 2,000 piggy banks from all parts of the world find a home here. Exhibits include 500-year-old examples from Indonesia and mechanical porkers.

NEDERLANDS FILMMUSEUM   16 B1
tram 1, 2, 3, 5, 6
Vondelpark 3 (1071 AA); tel. 5891400. Tuesday to Saturday 11 a.m.-5 p.m. (library); daily from 5 pm (film shows).
The Film Museum is located in the Vondelpark Pavilion (1880) and looks at the history and development of film. Exhibitions and shows are organized on various themes and personalities from the film world. In the two cinemas, films are screened from the museum's own extensive collection. One auditorium has been fitted with the exquisite 75-year-old interior of the Parisien, a porn cinema near Central Station that was demolished to make way for an extension to the Victoria Hotel. The Film Museum has one of the finest outdoor bars in the city and on summer evenings there are occasionally outdoor screenings.

HISTORY, SCIENCE AND THEMATIC MUSEUMS

NEDERLANDS PERSMUSEUM   13 C2
(DUTCH PRESS MUSEUM)   tram 6, 10, 🚌 22
Cruquiusweg 31 (1019 AT); tel. 6685866. Monday to Friday 9.30 a.m.-5 p.m., Saturday 9.30 a.m-1 p.m. (by appointment only). Admission free.
A collection focusing on the Dutch press, including journals, 17,000 titles from 1600 to the present, archives of and about journalists, curios and political cartoons. The museum is in an old converted cocoa warehouse which also houses the International Institute for Social History.

NEDERLANDS PIANO   6 B1
EN PIANOLA MUSEUM   tram 18, 22
Westerstraat 106, (1015 MN); tel. 6279624. Phone for opening times.
The museum has a collection of mechanical pianos, including reproductions from the period 1903–1935. There are also some pianolas.

NEDERLANDS SCHEEPVAART MUSEUM   12 A2
(MARITIME MUSEUM)   🚌 22, 28
Kattenburgerplein 1 (1018 KK); tel. 5232222. Tuesday to Saturday 10 a.m.-5 p.m., Sunday and public holidays 1-5 p.m., closed 1 January. Admission: adults f 10, children under 6 free, 6-to-16s and over-65s f 7.50.
The Maritime Museum has organized an imposing and delightful survey of Dutch maritime history. The model ships inside are fun, but the real thing waiting for you outside is even better. Take the kids.

NEDERLANDS THEATERINSTITUUT   8 A2
(THEATRE MUSEUM)   tram 13, 14, 17
Herengracht 168 (1016 BP); tel. 6235104. Tuesday to Sunday 11 a.m.-5 p.m.
This fine 17th-century canal house houses a permanent exhibition on theatre, including set designs, masks, costumes, models, miniature theatres and puppets. Regular exhibitions are held and there is a documentation centre and library.

NINT MUSEUM OF TECHNOLOGY   17 D2   tram 3, 4
Tolstraat 129 (1074 VJ); tel. 6754211. Monday to Friday 10 a.m.-5 p.m., Saturday, Sunday noon-5 p.m. Admission: adults f 7.50, 6-13s f 5.
See and experience modern technology at work. Exhibitions are devoted to science, technology, building, computers and energy. Great for children.

MUSEUMS

OPEN HAVEN MUSEUM
(OPEN HARBOUR MUSEUM)
🚋 28

KNSMlaan 311 (1019 LE); tel. 6205522. Wednesday to Friday, Sunday 1-5 p.m. Admission: f 3.50, under-18s, over-65s f 2.50.
These were once the premises of the Royal Dutch Steamship Company. As well as putting on exhibitions of its own, including a permanent collection about the Eastern Harbour area (1880–1920), the Museum also stages art shows and events.

SCHRIFTMUSEUM J.A. DORTMOND   10 A1
tram 1, 2, 5

Singel 425 (1012 WP); tel. 5252284. Monday to Friday 9.30 a.m.-1 p.m. and 2-4.30 p.m.
A collection of handwriting and calligraphic accessories illustrating the history of writing from 3000 BC to the present, from hieroglyphics to ball-point pens.

SEX MUSEUM   9 C1
tram 16, 24, 25

Damrak 18 (102 LH); tel. 6228376. Daily 10 a.m.-11 p.m.
Erotic art through the centuries.

SURINAAMS HISTORISCH MUSEUM   13 C2
tram 10, 6   🚋 22

Zeeburgerdijk 21 (1093 SK); tel. 6632942. Monday to Saturday 10 a.m.-5 p.m., Sunday and holidays noon-5 p.m. Admission: f 5.
Photos, paintings, books, prints and etchings illustrate the history of Surinam, the former Dutch colony (Dutch Guyana) on the north-east coast of South America.

TRAMLIJNMUSEUM   15 D2
(ELECTRIC TRAM MUSEUM)
tram 6, 16

Amstelveenseweg 264 (1075 XV); tel. 6737538. April to June and September, October: Sunday 10.30 a.m.-5.30 p.m. July, August: Sunday 10.30 a.m.-5.30 p.m., Tuesday to Thursday, Saturday 1-2 p.m. Closed November to March. Admission: adults f 4, 4-12s f 2.
Not so much a museum as a collection of working antique trams which run along a special line into the Amsterdamse Bos.

TROPENMUSEUM (TROPICAL MUSEUM)   18 B1
tram 3, 9, 10

Linnaeusstraat 2 (1092 CK); tel. 5688200. Monday to Friday 10 a.m.-5 p.m., Saturday, Sunday noon-5 p.m. Admission: adults f 7.50, under-18s f 4.
A semi-permanent exhibition covering Africa, Latin-America, Oceania, the Middle East and South-East Asia. This award-winning museum provides a refreshing look at the Third World.

HISTORY, SCIENCE AND THEMATIC MUSEUMS

VERZETSMUSEUM   17 D2
(RESISTANCE MUSEUM)   tram 4, 12, 25   🚌 15
Lekstraat 63 (1079 EM); tel. 6449797. Tuesday to Friday 10 a.m.-5 p.m., Saturday, Sunday and holidays 1-5 p.m., closed 1 January and 25 December. Admission: adults f 3.50, children under 7 free, 7-to-16s and over-65s f 1.75.
The newly renovated Verzetsmuseum commemorates the heroism of those who resisted the Nazi occupation of 1940–45. The permanent collection comprises photographs, documents and memorabilia. The museum occasionally hosts visiting exhibitions on other resistance struggles of the 20th century.

VROLIKMUSEUM   Ⓜ Holendrecht
Meibergdreef 15 (AMC building, 1105 AZ); tel. 5664664. Groups only and by appointment only.
Embryological and anatomical models and preparations form the bulk of the Vrolikmuseum's exhibits. There is also a collection of old bones, dating from 1770.

WERF 'T KROMHOUT (KROMHOUT WHARF)   12 B2   🚌 22, 28
Hoogte Kadijk 147 (1018 BJ); tel. 6276777. Monday to Friday 10 a.m.-4 p.m. Closed on public holidays. Admission: adults f 3.50, children under 15 and over-65s f 1.75.
This working boatyard is also a museum of Dutch shipbuilding. A guided tour of the wharf in English illustrates the history of the yard, which has been in business at this location since 1680. The tour includes demonstrations of steam and diesel engines. Boat-makers give an explanation of their craft.

WERKSPOOR MUSEUM   12 B2   🚌 22, 28
Oostenburgergracht 77 (1018 NC); tel. 6251035.
This museum, formerly a factory for railway train engines, can be seen by appointment only and is closed in the month of July. Models of steam and diesel engines, together with pictures, tell the story of the factory from its founding in 1827.

ZOOLOGICAL MUSEUM   12 B2   tram 7, 9, 14
Plantage Middenlaan 38-40 (1018 CZ); tel. 5233400. Daily 9 a.m.-5 p.m.
This museum is part of Artis, the oldest zoo in Holland. It comprises a collection of stuffed animals. A slide show provides impressions of animal life on the Dutch coast. See also CHILDREN: ATTRACTIONS.

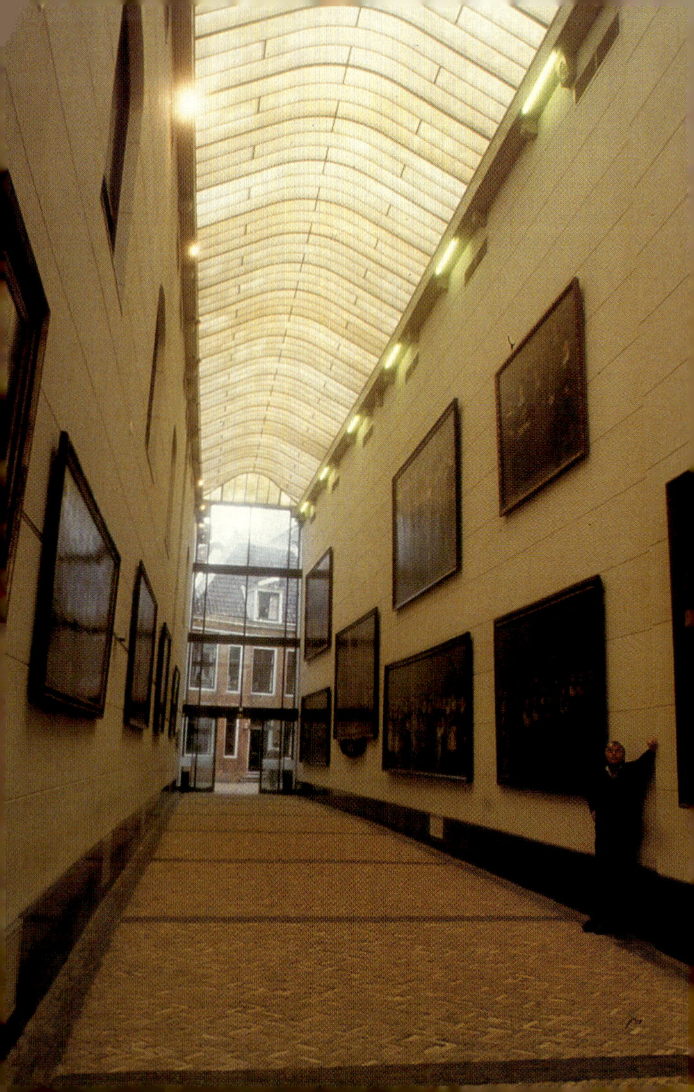

ART GALLERIES

The fine arts in Amsterdam are certainly not restricted to the confines of the Stedelijk, Rijks- and Van Gogh Museums. With about 250 art dealers and 1500 working artists, the city plays a prominent role in world art. Antiques and curios are similarly well represented. And between the two extremes of fine-art and bric-à-brac, you will find the lively and diverse world of arts and crafts.

Three factors contribute to this flourishing arts world. Since the 17th century, Amsterdam has drawn artists from home and abroad with its open and tolerant society. City fathers, wealthy merchants and ecclesiastical authorities were the first customers. At the same time, Amsterdam was spreading its trading contacts world-wide and acquiring refined articles from the Middle and Far East in particular. This cosmopolitan character is still reflected today in the range of international art on offer and in the presence of many foreign artists.

A third factor is formed by the grants available to artists since World War II, guaranteeing them an income. The independent "Artoteeks" set up to lend out paintings, drawings and sculptures have also given art a prominent position in Amsterdam life.

In the eighties, the free-market mechanism gained in importance as the grants were cut. The number of active artists dropped but the range of art galleries has been maintained. Some dealers just buy and sell art, while others act as agent for certain artists.

The list that follows is a reliable cross-section of Amsterdam's most important galleries, art dealers, crafts and curio shops.

ART DEALERS AND SALES GALLERIES

AKINCI **8** B1 tram 1, 2, 4, 5, 9
Singel 74 (1015 AC); tel. 6380480. Tuesday to Saturday noon-6 p.m. and by appointment.
Abstract work by Dutch artists is the primary attraction, but there's also an international collection focussing on Europe.

Portraits of the first city fathers can be found in the Civic Guard Gallery next to the Amsterdam Historisch Museum.

ART GALLERIES

AMAZONE **8** B1   tram 1, 2, 4, 5, 9
Singel 72 (10015 AC); tel. 6279000. Tuesday to Friday 10 a.m.-5 p.m., Saturday 1-5 p.m.
Contemporary art by women artists.

**AMSTERDAMS
BEELDHOUWERS COLLECTIEF**   🚌 18, 22
Zeilmakersstraat 15 (1013 DJ); tel. 6256332. Wednesday to Sunday 1-6 p.m. and by appointment.
The Amsterdam Sculptors' Collective provides space for figurative and abstract sculptures, objects and installations, mainly by Dutch artists.

PAUL ANDRIESSE **6** B1   tram 13, 14, 17
Prinsengracht 116 (1015 EA); tel. 6236237. Tuesday to Friday 10 a.m.-1 p.m. and 2-6 p.m., Saturday 2-6 p.m.
The very latest two- and three-dimensional work by Dutch and foreign artists.

ANIMATION ART **5** B2   tram 13, 14, 17
Berenstraat 19 (1016 GG); tel. 6277600. Tuesday to Friday 11 a.m.-6 p.m., Saturday 11 a.m.-5 p.m.
Specializes in original drawings from animation films.

DE APPEL **7** C1   🚌 22, 28
Prinseneiland 7 (1013 LL); tel. 6255651. Tuesday to Saturday 1-5 p.m.
A very famous Amsterdam arts centre. The exhibitions are from an art-history perspective. Films and lectures are also on the bill.

APUNTO **9** C1   tram 14, 16, 24, 25
Damrak 30 (1012 LJ); tel. 6204384. Tuesday to Saturday 1-5 p.m. and by appointment.
Figurative, realistic and conceptual work by Dutch artists is shown; also foreign work, especially from Germany, Canada, Italy and Austria.

ART GALLERY COMIC SENSE **10** A1   tram 1, 2, 5
Singel 417 (1012 WP); tel. 6222313. Monday to Saturday 1-6 p.m.
Work by comic-strip artists, cartoonists and illustrators is on display.

ARTI ET AMICITAE **10** B1   tram 14, 16, 24, 25
Rokin 112 (1012 LB); tel. 6232092. Tuesday to Sunday noon-5 p.m.
Two- and three-dimensional work (also photography and video) mainly by Dutch artists. The building is also the venue for the oldest artists' club in Holland.

ART DEALERS AND SALES GALLERIES

ASSELIJN 6 B2   tram 1, 2, 5
Lange Leidsedwarsstraat 189-200 (1017 NR); tel. 6249030. Tuesday to Saturday noon-5 p.m. and by appointment.
Figurative and abstract work by Dutch artists.

SUZANNE BIEDERBERG GALLERY 8 B2   tram 9, 16, 24, 25
Oudezijds Voorburgwal 223 (1012 EX); tel. 6245455. Wednesday to Saturday 2-6 p.m. and by appointment.
Two- and three-dimensional work from both Dutch and international artists.

PIETER BRATTINGA PRINT GALLERY 7 C2   tram 16, 24, 25
Prinsengracht 628 (1017 KT); tel. 6224265. Monday to Friday 1-4.30 p.m. and by appointment.
Series of graphic experiments are sold.

BRINKMAN AMSTERDAM 6 B2   tram 13, 14, 17
Rozenstraat 59 (1016 NN); tel. 6227493. Tuesday to Saturday noon-6 p.m., every 1st Sunday in the month and by appointment.
Focuses on contemporary avant-garde work by Dutch and foreign artists.

CANON IMAGE CENTRE 10 A2   tram 1, 2, 5
Leidsestraat 79 (1017 NX); tel. 6254494. Tuesday to Friday noon-5.45 p.m., Saturday 11 a.m.-4.45 p.m.
A photography gallery where pictures are sold. Photo courses are run and there is also a bookshop.

D'EENDT 8 A2   tram 1, 2, 5
Spuistraat 270/272 (1012 VW); tel. 6265777. Wednesday to Saturday noon-6 p.m., Sunday 2-6 p.m.
Figurative, realistic and abstract work by Dutch and European artists. Photographs and video art are also on display.

ESPACE 10 A2   tram 16, 24, 25
Keizersgracht 548 (1017 EL); tel. 6386034. Tuesday to Saturday noon-5.30 p.m. and by appointment.
One of Amsterdam's first commercial galleries of modern art (established in 1956). The collection is mainly of 20th-century and contemporary art by Dutch artists.

DE EXPEDITIE 8 A2   tram 13, 14, 17
Leliegracht 47 (1016 GT); tel. 6204758. Wednesday to Saturday 1-5 p.m.
Wide-ranging shows with no particular speciality.

ART GALLERIES

BARBARA FARBER 6 B1   tram 13, 14, 17
Keizersgracht 265 (1016 EC); tel. 6276343. Tuesday to Saturday 1-6 p.m. and by appointment.
The accent here is on international contemporary art, with displays of photography, video, objects and installations.

FORUM GALERIE 8 A2   tram 13, 14, 17
Onder de Torensluis/Singel 165a (1012 VK); tel. 6265207. Tuesday to Saturday 1-6 p.m. and by appointment.
Abstract work by Dutch and foreign artists, mainly from France, India, Israel and the U.S.A.

VAN GELDER   tram 3
Planciusstraat 9a (1013 MD); tel. 6277419. Tuesday to Saturday 1-5.30 p.m.
Formal art and art derived from conceptualism is Van Gelder's forte.

INSTITUTE OF CONTEMPORARY ART 10 A2   tram 1, 2, 5
Nieuwe Spiegelstraat 16 (1017 DE); tel. 6201260. Tuesday to Sunday 11 a.m.-5 p.m., Thursday 11 a.m.-9 p.m. Admission f7, (Tuesday, Thursday 5-9 p.m. admission free).
A major gallery, vast by Amsterdam standards, which puts on shows by prominent international artists.

JURKA 10 B1   tram 1, 2, 4, 5, 9
Singel 2-8 (1015 AA); tel. 6266733. Wednesday to Saturday 12.30-5.30 p.m. and by appointment.
Two- and three-dimensional work mainly by Dutch artists. Photography is a sideline.

THE LIVING ROOM 6 B2   tram 13, 14, 17
Laurierstraat 70 (1016 PN); tel. 6258449. Tuesday to Saturday 2-6 p.m.
Figurative and abstract work mainly by Dutch artists.

MONTEVIDEO 8 A1   tram 13, 14, 17
Singel 137 (1012 VJ); tel. 6237101. Tuesday to Saturday 1-6 p.m.
Montevideo is both an organization of media artists and a gallery showing work that has some link with electronic media, photography and installations.

PETIT 8 A2   tram 1, 2
Nieuwezijds Voorburgwal 270 (1012 RS); tel. 6267507. Tuesday to Saturday noon-5 p.m. and by appointment.

ART DEALERS AND SALES GALLERIES

Displays figurative work by Dutch artists, including prints, drawings, watercolours, sculpture and ceramics.

PRINTSHOP **17** C1 tram 4
Prinsengracht 845 (1017 KB); tel. 6251656. Monday to Saturday 11 a.m.-5.30 p.m.
Abstract work (prints, drawings, watercolours, gouaches) mainly by Dutch artists.

PULITZER ART GALLERY **6** B2 tram 13, 14, 17
Prinsengracht 325 (1016 GZ); tel. 5235235. Daily 24 hours.
Two- and three-dimensional work in the courtyard of the Pulitzer Hotel, with the emphasis on foreign art.

REFLEX MODERN ART GALLERY **16** B1 tram 7, 10
Weteringschans 83 (1017 RZ); tel. 6272832. Tuesday to Saturday 10.30 a.m.-5.30 p.m. and by appointment.
Cobra—an anarchic, abstract school of Dutch art started in the 1950s—is well-represented here, as is *nouveau realisme*.

DE SELBY 22, 28
Nieuwe Teertuinen 16 (1013 LV); tel. 6250990. Wednesday to Saturday 1-5 p.m. and by appointment.
Two- and three-dimensional work with an international flavour.

SIAU **6** B2 tram 13, 14, 17
Keizersgracht 267 (1016 EC); tel. 6267621. Tuesday to Saturday 11 a.m.-5.30 p.m., Sunday 2-5 p.m.
Figurative, realistic and abstract work by contemporary Dutch artists.

SIGNAAL tram 7, 10
Zieseniskade 23-24 (1017 RT); tel. 6247533. Wednesday to Saturday noon-5 p.m., Sunday 1-5 p.m.
Russian, Georgian and Iranian artists have been featured alongside the Dutch collection at Signaal. Figurative and abstract work are the strengths.

STEENDRUKKERIJ AMSTERDAM **6** B2 tram 7, 10, 17
Lauriergracht 80 (1016 RM); tel. 6241491. Wednesday to Saturday 1-5.30 p.m. and by appointment.
Most of the conceptual and experimental prints on display here have been printed on the premises. The work is mainly abstract and mainly by Dutch artists.

ART GALLERIES

STELTMAN 8 A2   tram 1, 2
Spuistraat 330 (1012 VX); tel. 6228683. Tuesday to Saturday 11 a.m.-6 p.m.
Work from Spain, Italy and the U.S.A. is featured strongly among the 20th-century art held at Steltman.

SWART 16 A1   tram 2
Van Breestraat 23 (1071 ZE); tel. 6764736. Wednesday to Saturday 2-6 p.m. and by appointment.
Art from the 1980s, selected by the doyen of the Amsterdam gallery scene, Riekje Swart.

TORCH 6 B1   tram 13, 14, 17
Prinsengracht 218 (1016 HD); tel. 6260284. Thursday to Saturday 1-6 p.m., 1st Sunday in the month 1-5 p.m. and by appointment.
Torch is good at keeping up with contemporary trends, especially in photography/video and installations.

VLAAMS CULTUREEL CENTRUM (BRAKKE GROND)   tram 4, 9, 16, 24, 25
De Brakke Grond-Nes 45 (1012 KD); tel. 6229014. Tuesday to Saturday 10 a.m.-8.30 p.m., Sunday 1-5 p.m.
A centre for Flemish culture, with two galleries where all disciplines of art (including interior design) are on show.

NANKY DE VREEZE 8 B1   tram 1, 2, 4, 5, 9
Singel 37 (1012 VC); tel. 6273808. Monday to Saturday 10 a.m.-5.30 p.m. and by appointment.
Twentieth-century and contemporary art, figurative and abstract work by Dutch artists form the bulk of the collection at Nanky de Vreeze, but there is also a place for spacial design and architecture.

FONS WELTERS 6 B2   tram 13, 14, 17
Bloemstraat 140 (1016 LJ); tel. 6227193. Tuesday to Saturday 2-6 p.m. 1st Sunday in the month 1-5 p.m. and by appointment.
Probably the best selection of modern Dutch sculptures in the city is gathered together by Fons Welters. Abstract pieces, objects/installations and spacial design are all on display.

WETERING GALERIE 6 B1   tram 7, 10
Lijnbaansgracht 288 (1017 RM); tel. 6236189. Wednesday to Saturday 12.30-5.30 p.m. and by appointment.
Drawings, acrylic/oil paintings, sculpture and spacial design by Dutch artists.

ANTIQUE DEALERS

ANTIQUE DEALERS

VAN DREVEN TOEBOSCH ANTIQUAIRS   **10** A2   tram 7, 10
Nieuwe Spiegelstraat 68 (1017 DH); tel. 6252732. Monday to Saturday 11.30 a.m.-5.30 p.m.
An art dealer who specializes in clocks, barometers and music boxes.

EBLE/AZIATICA   tram 7, 10
Spiegelgracht 31 (1017 JP); tel. 6278443. Tuesday to Saturday 11 a.m.-6 p.m.
Japanese art from 1600 to 1900 is displayed at this gallery. The collection is changed every six months.

DE HAAS ART NOUVEAU-ART DECO   **10** A2   tram 1, 2
Kerkstraat 155 (1017 GG); tel. 6265952. Tuesday to Saturday 11 a.m.-5.30 p.m.
As the name suggests, De Haas specializes in the styles of art that dominated the period from the late-19th century to 1930.

TOTH IKONEN   **10** A2   tram 7, 10
Nw Spiegelstraat 34 (1017 DG); tel. 6253371. Tuesday, Thursday noon-6 p.m.; Friday, Saturday 11 a.m.-6 p.m.
Toth Ikonen exhibits antique Russian icons painted on wood, together with collections of bronze travelling icons.

ITALIAANDER GALLERIES   **6** B2   tram 1, 2
Prinsengracht 526 (1017 KJ); tel. 6250942. Daily noon-5.30 p.m.
Primitive art from all parts of the world, including ethnic jewellery and textiles.

KALPA ART   **10** A1   tram 1, 2
Wijde Heisteeg 9 (1016 AS); tel. 6221989. Wednesday to Saturday 12.30-6 p.m.
Traditional African art, made in and imported from, that continent.

KUNSTHANDELAAR EN ANTIQUAIR   **10** A2
FRIDES LAMERIS   tram 7, 10, 16, 24, 25
Nieuwe Spiegelstraat 55 (1017 DD); tel. 6264066. Monday to Friday 10 a.m.-6 p.m., Saturday 10 a.m.-5 p.m.
Both works of art and antiques are sold by this dealer.

ART GALLERIES

LEMAIRE 10 B2 — tram 7, 10
Reguliersgracht 80 (1017 LV); tel. 6237027. Monday to Friday 10 a.m.-5.30 p.m., Saturday 11 a.m.-2 p.m.
Lemaire houses a permanent exhibition of primitive art, ethnographical objects and exotic textiles. It also holds a collection of Tibetan artefacts and primitive jewellery.

DE LOOIER ANTIQUE MARKET 6 B2 — tram 7, 10, 17
Elandsgracht 109 (1016 TT); tel. 6249038. Sunday to Wednesday 11 a.m.-5 p.m., Thursday 11 a.m.-9 p.m.
An extensive covered market, with a varied collection of curios, records, glass, silver and toys.

THOM AND LENNY NELIS ANTIQUES 6 B2 — tram 1, 2
Keizersgracht 541 (1017 DP); tel. 6231546. Tuesday to Saturday 11 a.m.-5 p.m.
Medical instruments and pharmacy are the chosen subjects of these art and antiques dealers.

VAN ROSSUM & CO 7 C2 — tram 1, 2
Herengracht 518 (1017 CC); tel. 6221010. By appointment only.
This historic canal mansion now houses a very exclusive antiques business. Rooms are furnished with artefacts from several periods, spanning the Golden Age of Dutch antiques and art.

CRAFTS GALLERIES

ART UNLIMITED 6 B2 — tram 1, 2
Keizersgracht 510 (1017 EJ); tel. 6248419. Monday 11 a.m.-6 p.m., Tuesday to Friday 10 a.m.-6 p.m., Thursday 10 a.m.-9 p.m., Saturday 10 a.m.-5 p.m.
Art Unlimited's postcards have found their way all over Europe and this Amsterdam-based operation has two outlets in the city. One on the Keizersgracht, the other on the new Max Euweplein behind the Lido.

ATELIER ARTIGLAS 17 C1 — tram 7, 10
Weteringschans 257 (1017 XJ); tel. 6235460. Tuesday to Friday 11 a.m.-5.30 p.m., Saturday 10 a.m.-4 p.m.
Glass handicrafts, with Tiffany a speciality.

CRAFTS GALLERIES

ANDRE COPPENHAGEN   **6** B2   tram 13, 14, 17
Bloemgracht 38 (1015 TK); tel. 6243681. Tuesday to Friday 9 a.m.-5.30 p.m., Saturday 9 a.m.-5 p.m.
Coppenhagen's is noted for its unique and extensive collection of beads.

DROOMDOOS   tram 13, 17
Leliestraat 1 (1012 BD); tel. 6201075. Wednesday to Friday 11 a.m.-6 p.m., Saturday 11 a.m.-4 p.m.
Martine Both turned from publishing to making exquisite and ornately decorated boxes in all shapes and sizes.

GUNTUR HOLLAND   **17** C2   tram 3
Ceintuurbaan 67 (1072 EV); tel. 6628813. Monday 1-6 p.m., Tuesday to Friday 9 a.m.-6 p.m., Saturday 9 a.m.-5 p.m.
Indonesian arts and crafts.

MATELSKI MUZIEK GALERIE   **17** C2   tram 3
Sarphatipark 74 (1073 EA); tel. 6646450. Monday to Saturday 10 a.m.-5 p.m.
Matelski trades in old musical instruments—mainly stringed—and musical curios.

OUT OF AFRICA   **6** B2   tram 13, 17
Herengracht 215 (1016 BG); tel. 6234677. Monday to Friday 10 a.m.-6 p.m., Saturday 10 a.m.-5 p.m.
African arts and crafts.

VAN PARIDON BROTHERS   **8** A2   tram 1, 2
Nieuwezijds Voorburgwal 361-365 (1012 RM); tel. 6235911. Monday 1-5.30 p.m.; Tuesday, Thursday, Saturday 9.30 a.m.-5.30 p.m.; Wednesday, Friday 10.30 a.m.-5.30 p.m.
Religious sculpture, icons, rosaries and other religious artefacts.

PEBBLE ROCK SHOP   **10** A2   tram 1, 2
Reguliersdwarstraat 121 (1017 BL); tel. 6261986. Monday to Friday noon-6 p.m., Saturday noon-5 p.m.
Minerals and precious stones, both loose and in jewellery are sold. Expert advice is given on the wearing of precious stones.

RA SIERADEN   **10** B2
Vijzelstraat 80 (1017 HL); tel. 6265100. Tuesday to Friday noon-6 p.m., Saturday 11 a.m.-5 p.m.
Work by Dutch jewellers and goldsmiths is displayed. Documentation about the artists is also available.

NAUTIC CLUB
50 STUKS
EXTRA MILD
12.50

...IEDING!
...TAS
50
LICHT
OP

ORIGINEEL
SUMATRA

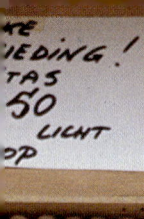

★

50 STUKS
17.50

WILDE HAVANA
WH 36
50 SIGAREN 5908

Brasil
is lichter
dan u denkt

senoritas
50 SIGAREN 1193

50 BR
16

Tabakshuis

1ᵉ KLAS
SUMATR

SHOPPING

Amsterdam has been spared the blight of hypermarkets, so still has a wide range of shops large and small in the centre. There are supermarkets for food in the suburbs and a few furniture giants dotted around the surrounding industrial estates, but Amsterdam must be one of the few major cities in Europe where you can still meet your daily needs at the local shops. Some Amsterdammers are even lucky enough to have a milkman knock on their door.

The best-known shopping streets are Nieuwendijk and Kalverstraat (straddling Dam Square, but largely dominated by mediocre boutiques), P.C. Hooftstraat (near the Van Gogh Museum) and Beethovenstraat in the heart of Amsterdam's up-market area called Nieuw Zuid. However, the back streets between Singel and Prinsengracht towards the Jordaan can provide some of the most interesting surprises. They harbour a profusion of little shops specializing in everything from toothbrushes to postcards, art nouveau furnishings and 1950s' lamps.

Shops in Amsterdam are generally open from 9 a.m. to 6 p.m., except for Mondays (1-6 p.m.) and Saturdays (9 a.m-5 p.m.). Many in the centre and on the main shopping streets are also open on Thursday evenings from 7-9 p.m. There are some rather esoteric exceptions such as butchers, who open Monday mornings instead of Monday afternoons. Bakers, of course, tend to close early every day and fish shops are usually closed all day on Mondays. All shops are obliged to have a yellow and white card in the window indicating the opening hours on a bar chart.

DEPARTMENT STORES

DE BIJENKORF   **8** B2   tram 4, 9, 14, 16, 24, 25
Dam 1 (1012 JS); tel. 6218080. Monday 11 a.m.-6 p.m., Tuesday, Wednesday, Friday 9 a.m.-6 p.m., Thursday 9 a.m.-9 p.m., Saturday 9 a.m.-5 p.m.
Amsterdam's largest department store, with an international reputation and a vast assortment of clothes, a delicatessen, furnishings and books. There's plenty to browse through when the weather is bad and it's a pleasant place to take a break for coffee and a snack.

World-famous Dutch cigars are not expensive and range from miniature versions to those of Churchillian proportions.

SHOPPING

HEMA 8 B1   tram 4, 9, 14, 16, 24, 25
Nieuwendijk 174 (1012 MT); tel. 6234176. Monday 1-6 p.m., Tuesday to Friday 9 a.m.-6 p.m., Thursday till 9 p.m., Saturday 9 a.m.-5 p.m. Also at Reguliersbreestraat 10 (1017 CN); tel. 6246506.
Hema is like a penny bazaar, but with more style. You'll find anything from lamps and stationery to its traditional, hot, Dutch smoked sausage. Prices are low.

MAISON DE BONNETERIE 10 B1   tram 4, 9, 16, 24, 25
Rokin 140 (1012 LE); tel. 6262162. Monday 1-5.30 p.m., Tuesday to Friday 9.30 a.m.-5.30 p.m., Thursday till 9 p.m., Saturday 9.30 a.m.-5 p.m.
The most exclusive, distinguished and expensive department store in Amsterdam. It has an old-fashioned layout and concentrates on fashion, perfume and accessories.

METZ & CO 6 B2   tram 13, 14, 17
Keizersgracht 455 (1017 DK); tel. 6248810. Monday 11 a.m.-6 p.m., Tuesday to Friday 9 a.m.-6 p.m., Tuesday till 9 p.m., Saturday 9 a.m.-5 p.m.
Furniture, designer-goods, lamps and some clothing constitute the stock at Metz. On the roof is a wonderful penthouse designed by Gerrit Rietveld (1888-1964). Once a showroom for furniture, it now houses a coffee shop with a spectacular view over the city.

VROOM & DREESMAN 10 A1   tram 4, 9, 14, 16, 24, 25
Kalverstraat 201 (1012 XC); tel. 6220171. Monday 1-6 p.m., Tuesday to Friday 9 a.m.-6 p.m., Thursday till 9 p.m., Saturday 9 a.m.-5 p.m.
A modest department store, with a wide range of goods at reasonable prices. Though not the most fashionable chain, it is the biggest, with branches throughout The Netherlands.

FASHION

501 11 C1   tram 14, 9
St. Antoniesbreestraat 136/138 (1011 HB); tel. 6247300. Monday 1-6 p.m., Tuesday, Wednesday, Friday 9.30 a.m.-6 p.m., Thursday 9.30 a.m.-9 p.m., Saturday 9.30 a.m.-5 p.m.
New and second-hand clothes, with brands such as Jeans, Diesel, Levis and Donovan.

FASHION

AMERICA TODAY **17** C2 tram 3, 6
Sarphatistraat 34 (1018 GM); tel. 6383337. Monday 1-6 p.m., Tuesday, Wednesday, Friday 10 a.m.-6 p.m., Thursday 7-9 p.m., Saturday 9 a.m.-5 p.m.
Fashionable jeans and clothing are imported from the U.S.A. by America Today for less than the official importer likes to see. A second branch has now opened in Bilderdijkstraat.

ASIAN FASHION SHOP HIMALAYA **7** C1 tram 1, 2, 5, 17
Haarlemmerstraat 103 (1013 EM); tel. 6382963. Tuesday to Friday 11 a.m.-6 p.m., Saturday 11 a.m.-5 p.m.
Hand-woven woollen shawls from the Himalayas, caps, jackets, accessories and jewellery.

BOETIEK BELLE FLEUR **6** B1 tram 13, 17
2e Egelantiersdwarsstraat 3 (1015 SB); tel. 6278586. Monday to Friday noon-6 p.m., Saturday noon-5 p.m.
Clothes made from authentic African fabrics.

CLASSIC WESTERN HOUSE **10** A1 tram 4, 9, 14, 16, 24, 25,
Kalverstraat 154 (1012 XE); tel. 6223329. Monday 11 a.m.-6 p.m., Tuesday to Friday 10 a.m.-6 p.m., Thursday 10 a.m-9 p.m., Saturday 9.30 a.m.-5.30 p.m.
Vendors of Western clothing, jewellery, posters and even cowboy and Indian statues. Wild.

55

DUTCH DESIGN IN FASHION **8** A2 tram 1, 2, 5, 13, 17
Singel 182 (1012 AJ); tel. 6232638. Monday 1-6 p.m., Tuesday to Friday 10 a.m.-6 p.m., Saturday 10 a.m.-5 p.m.
Women's fashion, designed in The Netherlands.

THE ENGLISH HATTER **10** A1 tram 1, 2, 5
Heiligeweg 40 (1012 XS); tel. 6234781. Monday 1-5.30 p.m., Tuesday to Friday 9 a.m.-5.30 p.m., Saturday 9 a.m.-5 p.m.
English and Irish hats are sold here in an appropriate atmosphere.

FRANK GOVERS **6** B2 tram 1, 2, 5
Keizersgracht 500 (1017 EH); tel. 6228670. Tuesday to Saturday 10 a.m.-6 p.m.
Frank Govers is Holland's best known fashion designer and ipso facto the most expensive. Haute couture, pret-à-porter and perfumes are sold in his shop. Very exclusive.

SHOPPING

HATSHOP CHAPEAU! 8 A2
tram 1, 2, 5
Spuistraat 185 A (1012 VN); tel. 6202845. Tuesday to Friday noon-6 p.m., Saturday noon-5 p.m.
Hats and accessories. The collection is made up of special designs by a variety of designers.

LADY DAY 6 B2
tram 17, 14, 13
Hartenstraat 9 hs (1016 BZ); tel. 6235820. Monday 1-6 p.m., Tuesday, Wednesday, Friday 10 a.m.-6 p.m., Thursday 10 a.m.-9 p.m., Saturday 10 a.m.-5 p.m.
New and second-hand American clothing.

MATELOOS 6 A2
tram 13, 17
De Clerqstraat 17 (1053 AA); tel. 6832384. Monday 1.30-6 p.m., Tuesday, Wednesday, Friday 11 a.m.-6 p.m., Thursday 11 a.m.-9 p.m., Saturday 9 a.m.-5 p.m.
This shop doesn't beat about the bush and subtitles itself "fashion for fat women". It means clothing for young women from size 46 (20).

DE PAPILLON 10 B1
tram 4, 9, 14, 16, 24, 25
Rokin 104 (1012 KZ); tel. 6230648. Monday 1-6 p.m., Tuesday, Wednesday, Friday 10 a.m.-6 p.m., Thursday 10 a.m.-9 p.m., Saturday 10 a.m.-5 p.m.
So small you might easily miss it, Papillon has a wide range of clothing for ballet and theatre.

RICHFIELD FOR PRESTIGE 16 A2
tram 2, 5, 12
P C Hoofstraat 58 (1071 CA); tel. 6756203. Monday 1-6 p.m., Tuesday, Wednesday, Friday 10 a.m.-6 p.m., Thursday 10 a.m.-9 p.m., Saturday 10 a.m.-5 p.m.
High-class women's and men's clothing is sold from this boutique, sited in one of Amsterdam's most exclusive shopping streets.

SISTERS 6 B2
tram 10, 17
Lauriergracht 110 (1016 RP); tel. 6268593. Monday 1-6 p.m., Tuesday to Friday 11 a.m.-6 p.m., Saturday 10 a.m.-5 p.m.
Fashion from the 1960s and 1970s, including jewellery and shoes, new and second-hand.

SPETTERS KINDERMODE 17 C2
tram 3
1e V.d. Helststraat 58 (1072 NX); tel. 6716249. Monday 10 a.m.-5 p.m., Tuesday to Saturday 9 a.m.-5 p.m.
In close proximity to Albert Cuypstraat Market, Spetters Kindermode sells fashionable denim clothes for children at a reasonable price.

SHOES

DR. ADAMS 8 B2   tram 4, 9, 14, 16, 24, 25
Oude Doelenstraat 7 (1012 ED); tel. 6223734. Monday 12.30-6 p.m., Tuesday, Wednesday, Friday 10 a.m.-6 p.m., Thursday 10 a.m.-9 p.m., Saturday 9.30 a.m.-5 p.m.
Dr. Adams is best known for its Western boots and its excellent service. Contemporary foot-wear is also in stock.

BALLY FOR MEN 10 A2   tram 1, 2, 5
Leidsestraat 41 (1017 NV); tel. 6248862. Monday 1-5.30 p.m., Tuesday, Wednesday, Friday 9 a.m.-5.30 p.m., Thursday 9 a.m.-9 p.m., Saturday 9 a.m.-5 p.m. Also at Mixed Bally's: Leidsestraat 8 (1017 PA); tel. 6222888 and P.C. Hooftstraat 130 (1071 CE); tel. 6754171.
The men's department of this internationally-renowned shoe shop has stock that is wide ranging, pricey, but well made.

BIG SHOE 8 A2   tram 7, 13, 14
Leliegracht 12 (1015 DE); tel. 6226645. Tuesday, Wednesday, Friday 10 a.m.-6 p.m., Thursday 10 a.m.-9 p.m., Saturday 10 a.m.-5 p.m.
Women's shoes from size 42 to 46 ($8^1/_2$ to $11^1/_2$) and men's from 46 to 50 ($11^1/_2$ to $13^1/_2$). There's a large selection at a reasonable price.

FRED DE LA BRETONNIERE 10 A1   tram 1, 2, 5
St Luciensteeg 20 (1012 PM); tel. 6234152. Monday 1-6 p.m. Tuesday, Wednesday, Friday 9.30 a.m.-6 p.m., Thursday 9.30 a.m.-9 p.m., Saturday 10 a.m.-5 p.m.
Exclusive leather bags and shoes are designed in-house.

CINDERELLA SCHOENEN 10 A1   tram 1, 2, 4, 9, 14, 16, 24, 25
Kalverstraat 177 (1012 XB); tel. 6233617. Monday noon-6 p.m., Tuesday to Friday 9.30 a.m.-6 p.m., Thursday 9.30 a.m.-9 p.m., Saturday 9.30 a.m.-5 p.m.
Cinderella has a colourful selection of shoes, mostly Italian.

PUNCH 10 C1   tram 14, 9
St. Antoniesbreestraat 73 (1011 HB); tel. 6266673. Monday 11 a.m.-6 p.m., Tuesday, Wednesday, Friday 10 a.m.-6 p.m., Thursday 10 a.m.-9 p.m., Saturday 10 a.m.-5 p.m.
Punch specializes in shoes and clothes from England, especially leather shoes.

SHOPPING

SHOEBALOO 10 A2 tram 1, 2, 5
Koningsplein 7 (1017 BB); tel. 6267993. Monday noon-6 p.m., Tuesday, Wednesday, Friday 10 a.m.-6 p.m., Thursday 10 a.m-9 p.m., Saturday 10 a.m.-5 p.m.
An all-round modern shoe shop for young and old.

STEPHAN KELIAN 16 A2 tram 2, 5, 12
P.C. Hooftstraat 99 (1071 BR); tel. 6734022. Monday 1-6 p.m, Tuesday, Wednesday, Friday 10 a.m.-6 p.m., Thursday 10 a.m.-9 p.m., Saturday 10 a.m.-7 p.m.
Exclusive shoes are designed by Stephan Kelian to be sold from his shop in Amsterdam's most exclusive street.

JEWELLERY

CHERUBIJN 6 C1 18, 22
Prinsengracht 16 (1015 DV); tel. 6273799. Monday 11 a.m.-2 p.m., Tuesday to Friday 11 a.m.-6 p.m., Saturday 11 a.m.-5 p.m.
Old and antique jewellery from Africa and Asia.

PAUL LIJFERING 10 B1 tram 4, 9, 14, 16, 24, 25
Oudemanhuispoort 1A (1012 CN); tel. 6380296. Tuesday to Friday 10.30 a.m.-6 p.m., Saturday 10.30 a.m.-5 p.m.
Watches and pens made before 1965 and large silverware are the two specialities of Paul Lijfering. Repairs to gold and silverware are undertaken.

SCHILLING JUWELIER 10 A2 tram 16, 24, 25
Nw Spiegelstraat 23 (1017 DB); tel. 6239366. Monday 1-6 p.m., Tuesday to Friday 10 a.m.-6 p.m., Saturday 10 a.m.-5 p.m.
Silver and gold jewellery and silver utensils.

Diamonds

COSTER DIAMONDS 16 B1 tram 3, 16, 12, 24
Paulus Potterstraat 2-4 (1071 CZ); tel. 6762222. Monday to Saturday 9 a.m.-5 p.m.
Staff at this merchant's provide an interesting, free guided tour of their establishment, taking you past replicas of the British Crown Jewels and a 181-carat black diamond, the Kollinan, which has not been cut. Coster

HOME FURNISHINGS

Diamonds is situated conveniently between the Rijksmuseum and the Van Gogh Museum.

VAN MOPPES DIAMONDS 16 C1 — tram 4, 16, 24, 25
Albert Cuypstraat 2-6 (1072 CT); tel. 6761242. Monday to Saturday 8.30 a.m.-5 p.m. Closed from 24 Dec to 1 Jan.
This diamond merchant is sited in an inconspicuous corner of the city, near Albert Cuypstraat Market. Free demonstrations are given and the building is accessible to wheelchairs.

REUTER DIAMONDS 10 A2 — tram 1, 2, 5
Singel 526 (1017 AZ); tel. 6249715. Monday to Friday 9.30 a.m.-5.30 p.m., Saturday 9.30 a.m.-5 p.m.
Free demonstrations of cutting and polishing diamonds are given from Monday to Saturday 10 a.m.-5 p.m. Reuter also has a branch in Kalverstraat.

HOME FURNISHINGS

ECHHARDT & LEEUWENSTEIN 8 A2
Spuistraat 281 (1012 VR); tel. 6261340. Tuesday to Friday 9 a.m.-6 p.m., Saturday 10 a.m.-5 p.m.
Very modern furniture, with a baroque twist.

EDHA INTERIEUR 16 A1 — tram 2, 3, 5, 12
Willemsparkweg 5-9 (1071 GN); tel. 6732401. Tuesday to Friday 9 a.m.-6 p.m., Saturday 10 a.m.-5 p.m.
An exclusive furniture and lamp shop near the Stedelijk Museum. Amsterdam's only establishment for reproduction Shaker furniture.

FROZEN FOUNTAIN 11 C2 — tram 4
Utrechtsestraat 101 (1017 VK); Tuesday to Friday 9 a.m.-6 p.m., Saturday 10 a.m.-5 p.m.
Exotic painted furniture, much of it older than it looks.

DE KASSTOOR 6 B2 — tram 13, 14, 17
Rozengracht 204-210 (1016 NL); tel. 6239093. Monday 1-6 p.m., Tuesday, Wednesday, Friday 9.30 a.m.-6 p.m., Thursday 7-9 p.m., Saturday 9.30 a.m.-5 p.m.
Stunning and exclusive modern furniture and accessories. There's a separate Italian section.

SHOPPING

STUDIO 19C **8** A2 tram 13, 14, 17
Oude Leliestraat 3 (1016 BD); tel. 6201687. Monday 1-6 p.m., Tuesday to Friday 9 a.m.-6 p.m., Saturday 10 a.m.-5 p.m.
Modern svelt plywood furniture, made locally.

WONEN 2000 **6** B2 tram 13, 14, 17
Rozengracht 215-225 (1016 NA); tel. 6234865. Monday 1-6 p.m., Tuesday, Wednesday, Friday 9.30 a.m.-6 p.m., Thursday 7-9 p.m., Saturday 9.30 a.m.-5 p.m.
The less exclusive brother to De Kasstoor (see above), which is opposite.

GIFTS

ABAL **17** C2 tram 3
Ceintuurbaan 238 (1072 GE); tel. 6641083. Monday 1-6 p.m., Tuesday, Wednesday, Friday 10 a.m.-6 p.m., Thursday 10 a.m.-6 p.m., and 7-9 p.m., Saturday 10 a.m.-5 p.m.
Crafts from Third World countries. Goods include African musical instruments, shawls and belts.

ART SHOP RULOT **10** A2 tram 1, 2, 5
Kerkstraat 163 (1017 GG); tel. 6278290. Monday noon-5.30 p.m., Tuesday to Friday 10.30 a.m.-5.30 p.m., Saturday 10.30 a.m.-5 p.m.
A commercial shop selling hand-made jewellery for a reasonable price. The art on the wall is for sale too.

DE ASP **10** A2 tram 1, 2, 5
Kerkstraat 135 (1017 GE); tel. 6231630. Monday to Wednesday, Friday 10.30 a.m.-5 p.m., Saturday noon-5 p.m.
Hand-painted ceramics are made and sold by De Asp.

CHRISTMAS WORLD **8** A2 tram 1, 2, 5, 13, 17
Nieuwezijds Voorburgwal 137-139 (1012 RJ); tel. 6227047. Monday to Saturday 9 a.m.-6 p.m.
Christmas World sells articles for the Christmas tree all year round. Much of the stock is imported from the U.S.A.

GIFTS

COLLECTORS **11** D1   tram 9, 7, 14
Muiderstraat 21 (1011 PZ); tel. 6383045. Tuesday to Saturday 9.30 a.m.-5 p.m.
Collectors specializes in 1950s nostalgia. You might find anything from a juke-box to a Dinky Toy here. There's even a genuine American limo.

FOCKE & MELTZER **8** B2   tram 4, 9, 14, 16, 24, 25
Rokin 124 (1012 LK); tel. 6231944. Monday to Friday 9 a.m.-5.30 p.m., Thursday 9 a.m.-9 p.m., Saturday 9 a.m.-5 p.m.
Lead crystal from Leerdam, earthenware from Makkum, porcelain and hand-painted Delft Blue. Not the cheapest place to buy them, but certainly the best.

GIFTSHOP TENDENZ **10** A2   tram 1, 2, 5
Singel 540 (1017 AZ); tel. 6222410. Monday to Saturday 10 a.m.-6 p.m. April to September: also on Sunday 11 a.m.-6 p.m.
One of the most expensive and best of Amsterdam's giftshops. Chrome is the forte.

VAN GOGH GIFTSHOP **10** A2   tram 1, 2, 5
Leidsestraat 81 (1017 NX); tel. 6208644. Daily 1-6 p.m., Thursday till 9 p.m.
All the Van Gogh souvenirs you could ever wish to see (and some you'd probably rather not), from T-shirts to ties.

INPAKWINKEL **17** C1   tram 6, 7, 10, 16, 24, 25
2e Weteringdwarsstraat 35 (1017 SR); tel. 6255511. March to September: Tuesday to Saturday 10 a.m.-6 p.m; October to February: Tuesday to Saturday 11 a.m.-5 p.m.
There are plenty of original ways to wrap your gifts at the "Wrap Shop".

'T JAPANSE WINKELTJE **8** A2   tram 1, 2, 5, 13, 14, 17
Nieuwezijds Voorburgwal 177 (1012 RK); tel. 6279523. Monday 11 a.m.-6 p.m. Tuesday to Friday 9.30 a.m.-6 p.m., Saturday 9.30 a.m.-5 p.m.
The Japanese Shop sells Japanese curios, kimonos, porcelain, travel guides and postcards.

HET KANTENHUIS **17** C1   tram 4, 9, 24, 24, 26
Kalverstraat 124 (1012 PK); tel. 6248618. Monday 11.45 a.m.-6 p.m., Tuesday, Wednesday, Friday 9.15 a.m.-6 p.m., Thursday 9.15 a.m.-9 p.m., Saturday 9.15 a.m.-5 p.m.
Paradise for lace lovers: it is sold by the metre or as a tablecloth. The second floor has a collection of hand-fans from different countries, made from a variety of materials.

SHOPPING

VAN DER LAAN'S 8 B2
(DELFTS BLAUW)
tram 4, 9, 16, 24, 25
Nieuwedijk 24 (1012 ML); tel. 6273974. Monday 1-6 p.m., Tuesday to Friday 9 a.m.-6 p.m., Saturday 9 a.m.-5 p.m.
Hand-painted Delft Blue in a souvenir shop bursting at the seams.

MUSIKADO 10 A1
tram 1, 2, 5
Spui 13 (1012 WX); tel. 6261990. Tuesday to Friday 10.30 a.m.-5.30 p.m., Saturday 11 a.m.-5 p.m.
Gifts that bear some relation to music fill the shelves at Musikado. There are lots of musical boxes, statuettes and miniature instruments.

ROSENTHAL STUDIO-HAUS 10 A1
tram 1, 2, 5
Heiligeweg 49-51 (1012 XP); tel. 6245865. Monday 1-6 p.m., Tuesday to Friday 9.30 a.m.-6 p.m., Saturday 9.30 a.m.-5 p.m.
A design shop that stocks vases, crockery and cutlery from Rosenthal and Feninie and the like.

MARKETS

ALBERT CUYPMARKT 17 C1
tram 4, 16, 24, 25
Albert Cuypstraat (1072 CT). Monday to Saturday 9 a.m.-5 p.m.
Amsterdam's longest and best-known street market, serving the local and immigrant population. Food, clothing, plants and fabrics: Old Dutch alongside the exotic.

DAPPERMARKT 18 B1
tram 3, 6, 10
Dapperstraat (1093 BT). Tuesday to Saturday 10 a.m.-3 p.m.
Amsterdam's archetypal working-class market, for fruit and veg, cheese, fish, cheap clothing and shoes.

FLOWER MARKET 10 B2
tram 4, 9, 14, 16, 24, 25
Singel near Muntplein (1017 AX). Monday to Wednesday, Friday, Saturday 9 a.m.-5 p.m., Thursday 9 a.m.-9 p.m.
A major tourist attraction, the flower market is a colourful mix of flowers, bulbs, and even pot plants.

NOORDERMARKT 6 B1
tram 3, 10
Westerstraat (1015 MV). Monday 8 a.m.-1 p.m.
In the heart of the Jordaan, the textile market on Monday morning draws crowds from far and wide for bargains in cloth and clothing.

POSTZEGELMARKT   **8** A2   tram 1, 2, 5
Nieuwezijds Voorburgwal 294 (1012 RT). tel. 6258806. Wednesday, Saturday 7 a.m.-4 p.m.
The market for coins and stamps, with many philatelist shops nearby (e.g. in the Rosmarijnsteeg). It has become an eldorado for young stamp collectors, especially those willing to get up very early.

TEN KATEMARKT   **6** A2   tram 7, 17
Ten Katestraat (1053 CE). Monday to Saturday 9.30 a.m.-5 p.m.
A small and very friendly market by Kinkerstraat, one of Amsterdam's major suburban shopping streets, in a cosmopolitan area of the city. Turkish and Moroccan stalls are alongside those selling Dutch produce. There are herrings and Vietnamese snacks to eat on the spot.

WATERLOOPLEINMARKT 11 D1   tram 9, 14, Ⓜ Waterlooplein
Waterlooplein (1011 NV). Monday to Saturday 9 a.m.-4 p.m.
The legendary flea market has lost some of its charm after moving from its old location in the heart of the Jewish quarter, to a wind-swept square nearby and now back into the shadow of the City Hall. But it is still a popular place in which to browse and search for antique bargains.

FLOWERS

DECORENT SILK FLOWERS 6 B2   tram 1, 2, 5
Lijnbaansgracht 308-309 (1017 WZ); tel. 6246931. Tuesday to Friday 10 a.m.-6 p.m., Saturday 10 a.m.-5 p.m.
Silk flower decorations are sold and rented-out from these premises.

INTRATUIN WIELINGA   18 B2   tram 9
K. Onneslaan 5 (1097 DE); tel. 6653797. Monday 1-5.30 p.m., Tuesday, Wednesday, Friday 9 a.m.-6 p.m., Thursday 9 a.m.-9 p.m., Saturday 9 a.m.-5 p.m.
Amsterdam's largest garden centre, supplying garden tools and furniture, bulbs, flowers and pot plants.

SHOPPING

BOOKSHOPS

Antiquarian and Second-Hand Bookshops

Since the earliest days of printing, Amsterdam has been a major publishing centre. The fall of Antwerp sent Calvinist printers north to Amsterdam and the 17th-century city was a capital of international publishing. Relative freedom from the censorship prevalent in other European capitals allowed Amsterdam printers to churn out an extraordinary variety of books in Dutch, English, German, French, Italian, Greek, Latin and Hebrew.

Not surprisingly, Amsterdam's antiquarian booksellers have inherited a treasure trove. There are more than 120 antiquarian and second-hand booksellers in the city. Most of them are located in the centre, with a particularly dense cluster in an area bounded by Raadhuisstraat on the North, the Spui to the South, the Singel on the West and the Nieuwezijds Voorburgwal to the East.

There are regular book-fairs and a weekly book market on the Spui every Friday in which 23 booksellers take part. The Booksellers Association publishes a map of all antiquarian and second-hand bookshops. You can obtain a copy for ƒ 2 at most second-hand bookshops.

ANTIQUA   **8** A1   tram 1, 2, 4, 5, 9, 13, 16, 17, 24, 25
Herengracht 159 (1015 BH); tel. 6245998. By appointment only.
Music, literature, philosophy and sciences.

BOOK TRAFFIC   **8** A2   tram 13, 14, 17
Leliegracht 50 (1015 DH); tel. 6204690. Monday to Friday 10 a.m.-6 p.m., Saturday 10 a.m.-5 p.m.
There are 25,000 titles in Book Traffic's stock, covering any subject from cookery to philosophy, from Asimov to Zola. Books are both bought and sold by the firm.

S. EMMERING   **8** A2   tram 1, 2, 5
Nieuwezijds Voorburgwal 304 (1012 RV); tel. 6231476. Monday to Friday 10 a.m.-5 p.m.
Emmering's stocks include antiquarian and old prints, Old-Master engravings and Judaic and West Indian writings.

VAN GENNEP   **8** A2   tram 1, 2, 5
Nieuwezijds Voorburgwal 330 (1012 RW); tel. 6264448. Monday to Friday 10 a.m.-6 p.m., Thursday 10 a.m.-9 p.m., Saturday 10 a.m.-5 p.m.
Remainders in literature, politics, social studies and philosophy.

BOOKSHOPS

NICO ISRAEL **6** B2   tram 1, 2, 5,
Keizersgracht 489 (1017 DM); tel. 6222255, Fax 6382666. Monday to Friday 9 a.m.-5.30 p.m.
Old and rare books, old maps, atlases, travel books and natural history.

DE KLOOF **11** C1   tram 4, 9, 14, 16, 25, 25
Kloveniersburgwal 44 (1012 CW); tel. 6223828. Monday to Saturday 9 a.m.-6 p.m., Sunday 11 a.m.-5 p.m.
Stockists of 200,000 books, on four floors. Subjects include foreign languages such as French, German, Russian, Swedish and Japanese; law and criminology; medicine; philology; political science; technology; and travel.

A. KOK & ZOON **11** C1   tram 4, 9, 14, 16, 24, 25
Oude Hoogstraat 14-6 (1012 CE); tel. 6231191. Monday to Friday 9.30 a.m.-6 p.m., Saturday 9.30 a.m.-5 p.m.
Architecture, art, typography, archaeology and natural history.

DE LACH **6** B2   tram 13, 14, 17
1e Bloemdwarsstraat 6 (1016 LD); tel. 6202600. Monday to Saturday 11 a.m.-6 p.m.
Film and photography are De Lach's forte. It sells posters, photos, videos and film memorabilia.

DE SLEGTE **10** A1   tram 1, 2, 4, 5, 9, 14, 16, 24, 25
Kalverstraat 48-52 (1012 PE); tel. 6225933. Monday 11 a.m.-6 p.m., Tuesday, Wednesday, Friday 9.30 a.m.-6 p.m., Thursday 9.30 a.m.-9 p.m., Saturday 9.30 a.m.-5 p.m.
A vast depository of aging books, gathered together on four floors.

SPINOZA ANTIQUARIAAT **17** C1   tram 6, 7, 10
Den Texstraat 26 (1017 ZB); tel. 6242373. By appointment only.
A godsend for students of Judaic writings, philosophy, religion and theology.

WESTMANS WINKEL **8** B1   tram 1, 2, 5, 13, 17
Korte Lijnbaanssteeg 1 (1012 SL); Tuesday to Saturday 1-5 p.m.
All together there are about 50,000 titles stored here. Genres include children's literature, science fiction, detective thrillers and classic crime, illustrated books and photography, fantasy and horror, New Yorkers and cartoons.

SHOPPING

New Bookshops

A LA CARTE **11** C2 — tram 4
Utrechtsestraat 110-112 (1017 VS); tel. 6250679. Tuesday to Friday 9 a.m.-6 p.m., Saturday 9.30 a.m.-5 p.m.
As well as an extensive collection of travel guides and maps, A La Carte has a selection of globes.

ALLERT DE LANGE **9** C1 — tram 4, 9, 14, 16, 24, 25
Damrak 60 (1012 LM); tel. 6246744. Monday 1- 5 p.m., Tuesday to Friday 9 a.m.-6 p.m., Saturday 9 a.m.-5 p.m.
An internationally-oriented bookshop, specializing in maps, travel guides, art and culture.

AMERICAN DISCOUNT BOOK CENTER **10** A1 — tram 1, 2, 5, 4, 9, 14, 16, 24
Kalverstraat 185 (1012 XC); tel. 6255537. Monday to Saturday 10 a.m.-10 p.m., Sunday 11 a.m.-7 p.m.
An American bookstore with a wide assortment of titles, especially New Age books and comics.

ATHENEUM BOEKHANDEL **10** A1 — tram 1, 2, 5
Spui 14-16 (1012 XA); tel. 6226248. Monday 1-6 p.m., Tuesday to Friday 9 a.m.-6 p.m., Thursday 9 a.m.-9 p.m., Saturday 9 a.m.-5 p.m.
Amsterdam's best-known bookshop. The non-fiction section is particularly good and titles are stocked in many languages. Atheneum also has an international news centre, next door (open till late).

CENTRO JOSE MARTI **7** C2 — tram 13, 14, 17
Herengracht 259 (1016 BJ); tel. 6269590. Monday 1-6 p.m., Tuesday to Friday 10 a.m.-6 p.m., Saturday 11 a.m.-5 p.m.
Portuguese and Spanish books fill the shelves and the premises also house a Latin-American cultural centre.

THE ENGLISH BOOKSHOP **6** B2 — tram 13, 14, 17
Lauriergracht 71 (1016 RH); tel. 6264230. Monday to Friday 11 a.m.-6 p.m., Saturday 11 a.m.-5 p.m.
This haven for lovers of English-language books is hidden away in the corner of Hazenstraat. There's a fine selection of literature, children's books, travel guides and discounted stock.

BOOKSHOPS

INTERNATIONAL THEATRE 6 B2
AND FILM BOOKSHOP
tram 1, 2, 5, 6, 7, 10
Leidseplein 26 (1017 PT); tel. 6226489. Monday to Saturday 10 a.m.-6 p.m.
Situated in the Stadsschouwburg, this bookshop has supplies of magazines, books and videos about theatre, film and dance.

DE KOOKBOEK HANDEL 6 B2
tram 1, 2, 5
Runstraat 26 (1016 GK); tel. 6224768. Tuesday, Wednesday, Friday 11 a.m.-6 p.m., Thursday 11 a.m.-9 p.m., Saturday 11 a.m.-5 p.m.
Formerly Titia Bodon, this shop is now a good source for books on cooking and wine. The subjects are covered in great detail and titles are available in many languages.

MILIEU WINKEL 12 A2
tram 9, 14
Henri Polaklaan 42 (1018 CT); tel. 6244989. Monday 1-6 p.m., Tuesday to Friday 10 a.m.-6 p.m.
Stockists of books and documentation about environmental issues in The Netherlands and abroad.

PIED A TERRE 10 A1
tram 1, 2, 5
Singel 393 (1012 WN); tel. 6274455. Monday to Saturday 11 a.m.-5 p.m.
Maps and guides for mountaineering, walking and cycling.

ROBERT PEMSELA 16 B2
tram 2, 3, 5, 12
Van Baerlestraat 78 (1071 BB); tel. 6624266. Monday 1-6 p.m., Tuesday to Friday 9 a.m.-6 p.m., Saturday 9.30 a.m.-5 p.m.
Art books are the prime concern of Robert Premsela. This fine bookshop is adjacent to a language book centre and near a sheet-music shop, by the Concertgebouw.

HET SIENJAAL 17 C1
tram 6, 10, 7
Weteringschans 177 (1017 XD); tel. 6230961. Monday 12.30-6 p.m., Tuesday, Thursday 10 a.m.-6 p.m., Wednesday, Friday 9 a.m.-6 p.m., Saturday 10 a.m.-5 p.m.
An old-fashioned bookshop containing Dutch and foreign literature and poetry, English books, children's books and books about architecture.

VROLIJK 8 A2
tram 1, 2, 4, 5, 9, 14, 16, 24, 25
Paleisstraat 135 (1012 ZL); tel. 6235142. Monday to Wednesday, Friday 10 a.m.-6 p.m., Thursday 10 a.m.-9 p.m., Saturday 11 a.m.-5 p.m.
Gay and lesbian fiction and non-fiction. Half of the stock is in English. Posters and postcards are among the merchandise, which is kept on two floors.

SHOPPING

VROUWENBOEKHANDEL XANTIPPE 6 B1   tram 1, 2, 5
Prinsengracht 290 (1016 HJ); tel. 6235854. Monday 1-6 p.m., Tuesday to Friday 10 a.m.-6 p.m.
A women's bookshop near the English Bookshop (see above) and the women's café, Saarein (see NIGHTLIFE: GAY). A huge selection of feminist literature is stored.

DIE WEISSE ROSE 6 B2   tram 13, 14, 17
Rozengracht 166 (1016 NK); tel. 6383959. Tuesday to Friday 10 a.m.-6 p.m., Saturday 11 a.m.-5 p.m.
German-language books. "Alle Bücher zum deutschen Preis" (all books are sold at the same price as they are in Germany) is the boast.

MUSIC

BACKBEAT 6 B1   tram 13, 14, 17
Egelantiersstraat 19 (1015 PT); tel. 6271657. Monday to Saturday 11 a.m.-6 p.m.
Black music specialists: soul, blues, R&B and jazz. In addition, there's a fair supply of world music and a second-hand section. Staff are very knowledgeable.

BOUDISQUE/BLACKBEAT 9 C1   tram 4, 9, 16, 24, 25
Haringpakkersteeg 10-6/Nieuwendijk 114 (1012 MS); tel. 6232603. Monday to Wednesday, Friday 10 a.m.-6 p.m., Thursday 10 a.m.-9 p.m., Saturday 10 a.m.-5 p.m.
A legendary record shop which includes a dance department (Blackbeat) for club and MTV hits. Practically every genre can be found here.

CONCERTO 11 C2   tram 4
Utrechtsestraat 54-60 (1017 VP); tel. 6266577. Monday to Wednesday, Friday 10 a.m.-6 p.m., Thursday 10 a.m.-9 p.m., Saturday 10 a.m.-5 p.m.
An old-fashioned record shop with a large selection of second-hand CDs, both classical and pop.

CRISTOFORI 6 B2   tram 1, 2, 5
Prinsengracht 579 (1016 HT); tel. 6268485. Monday to Saturday 10 a.m.-6 p.m.
A very exclusive store where pianos are sold, rented out and repaired. Cristofori also arranges concerts in its 400-seat hall on the premises.

MUSIC

FAME MUSIC   **10** A1   tram 1, 2, 4, 9, 14, 16, 24, 25
Kalverstraat 2-4 (1012 PC); tel. 6382525. Monday 11 a.m.-6 p.m. Tuesday, Wednesday, Friday 9.30 a.m.-6 p.m., Thursday 9.30 a.m.-9 p.m., Saturday 9.30 a.m.-5 p.m.
One of the biggest and most modern CD megastores in Amsterdam, but it is not always the cheapest.

FOREVER CHANGES   **6** A2   tram 3, 12, 17
Bilderdijkstraat 148 (1053 LB); tel. 6126378.
A rather idiosyncratic selection of new sounds and music from the 1960s is kept at Forever Changes (named after an album from hippy band Love). There's also a wide range of second-hand CDs.

SAUL GROEN   **17** C2   tram 16, 24, 25
Ferdinand Bol 6-8 (1072 LJ); tel. 6794634. Monday to Wednesday, Friday 10 a.m.-6 p.m., Thursday 10 a.m.-9 p.m., Saturday 10 a.m.-5 p.m.
Despite its unlikely location opposite the Heineken Brewery, this is one of Amsterdam's most highly-respected CD shops for classical music.

HAMPE MUSICAL INSTRUMENTS   **10** A1   tram 1, 2, 5
Spui 11-13 (1012 WX); tel. 6242323. Monday 1-6 p.m., Tuesday to Friday 9 a.m.-6 p.m., Saturday 9 a.m.-5 p.m.
A narrow Amsterdam house with three floors crammed with musical instruments, mainly acoustic.

JAZZ INN   **17** C1   tram 16, 24, 25
Vijzelgracht 9 (1017 HM); tel. 6235662. Monday to Wednesday, Friday 10 a.m.-6 p.m., Thursday 10 a.m.-9 p.m., Saturday 10 a.m.-5 p.m.
A feast for the collector of jazz and blues.

SOUND OF THE FIFTIES   **6** B2   tram 1, 2, 5
Prinsengracht 669 (1017 JT); tel. 6239745. Monday to Friday 10 a.m.-6 p.m., Saturday 10 a.m.-5 p.m.
Recordings from the 1950s and 1960s, including many new pressings and collector's items.

DIRK WITTE   **10** B2   tram 16, 24, 25
Vijzelstraat 53 (1017 HE); tel. 6264655. Tuesday, Wednesday, Friday 10 a.m.-6 p.m., Thursday 9 a.m.-9 p.m., Saturday 10 a.m.-5 p.m.
Musical instruments and repairs. Dirk Witte is a major name in the Amsterdam pop world.

SHOPPING

GOURMET FOODS

BANKETBAKKERIJ LANSKROON 10 A1   tram 1, 2, 5, 17, 13
Singel 385 (1012 WL); tel. 6237743. Tuesday to Friday 7.30 a.m.-5 .30 p.m., Saturday 7.30 a.m.-5 p.m.
Get your early morning croissants here. The speciality is Stollen at Easter and Christmas.

DE BIERKONING 8 A2   tram 1, 2, 5, 17
Paleisstraat 125 (1012 RB); tel. 6252336. Monday 1-6 p.m., Tuesday to Friday 11 a.m.-6 p.m., Thursday 11 a.m.-9 p.m., Saturday 11 a.m.-5 p.m.
About 750 beers from all corners of the world are stocked at Bierkoning, as well as the glasses in which to drink them.

CHATEAU P.C. HOOFT 16 B1
Honthorststraat 1 (1071 DC); tel. 6649371. Monday 11 a.m.-6 p.m., Tuesday to Friday 9 a.m.-6 p.m., Saturday 9 a.m.-5 p.m.
An exclusive wine merchants.

DE EERSTE AMSTERDAMSE WATERWINKEL   tram 3, 12, 24
R Hartstraat 10 (1071 VH); tel. 6755932. Monday 1-6 p.m., Tuesday, Wednesday, Friday 9 a.m.-6 p.m., Saturday 9 a.m.-5 p.m.
A range of no less than 200 varieties of mineral water is sold from these premises, including melted North Pole ice.

EICHHOLTZ 10 A2   tram 1, 2, 5
Leidsestraat 48 (1017 PC); tel. 6797151. Monday 10 a.m.-6 p.m., Tuesday to Friday 9 a.m.-6 p.m., Thursday 9 a.m.-9 p.m., Saturday 9 a.m.-5 p.m.
Eichholtz is famed for its Dutch and international cheeses, but it also sells chocolates.

FEDUZZI   tram 16, 24, 25
Nieuwe Weteringstraat 47 (1017 ZX); tel. 6259562. Tuesday to Friday 9 a.m.-6 p.m., Saturday 9 a.m.-5 p.m.
Home-made pasta and Italian delicacies.

HERMAN KWEKKEBOOM 10 B2   tram 4, 9, 14
Reguliersbreestraat 36 (1017 CN); tel. 6231205. Monday to Friday 9 a.m.-5.45 p.m., Saturday 9 a.m.-5 p.m.
Delicious gateaux and world-famous croquettes. These savoury ragoût-filled delicacies are wonderful with a cup of coffee.

GOURMET FOODS

LEONIDAS 8 B2 tram 4, 9, 14, 16, 24, 25
Damstraat 11 (1012 JL); tel 6253497. Monday 10 a.m.-6 p.m., Tuesday to Friday 10 a.m.-6 p.m., Saturday 10 a.m.-5 p.m. Also at Ceintuurbaan 81 (1072 EW); tel. 6790243.
Crafted Belgian chocolates, for the addict who can't make it to Antwerp.

POMPADOUR 6 B2 tram 13, 14, 17
Huidenstraat 12 (1016 ES); tel. 6239554. Monday 9 a.m.-5 p.m., Tuesday to Friday 9 a.m.-6 p.m., Sunday 9 a.m.-5 p.m.
A delicatessen with tearoom. Home-made gateaux and 40 kinds of chocolates are among the mouth-watering goods sold.

YAMA FOOD PRODUKT 17 C2 tram 24, 25
Ferd. Bolstraat 333 (1072 LH); tel. 6787111. Monday to Saturday 10 a.m.-6 p.m.
Japanese ingredients and cookbooks. Located inside the Okura Hotel.

Coffee and Tea

Amsterdam has trade, largely with the Far East, to thank for its international name in tea and coffee (Anne Frank's father was in the business). The city still has old-fashioned shops selling exclusive blends. The interiors are a joy to the eye, providing a glimpse into the past. The staff are invariably so friendly you feel nostalgic for the good old days.

KEIJZER KOFFIE EN THEEHANDEL 6 B1 tram 7, 13, 14
Prinsengracht 180 (1016 HB); tel. 6240823. Monday to Saturday 9 a.m.-5.30 p.m.
Many varieties of coffee and tea are sold here, alongside all kinds of accessories to make the perfect cuppa.

SIMON LEVELT 9 C1 tram 1, 2, 4, 5, 9, 13, 16, 17, 24, 25
Prins Hendrikkade 26 (1012 TM); tel. 6248014. Monday to Saturday 8.30 a.m.-5.30 p.m.
An incredible assortment of tea and coffee is available here, including a wide range for the lover of organically-grown beverages.

NEDERLANDSE STOOMKOFFIEBRANDERIJ 8 B2
GEELS & CO tram 4, 9, 16, 24, 25
Warmoesstraat 67 (1012 HX); tel. 6240683. Monday to Friday 9 a.m.-5.30 p.m., Saturday 9 a.m.-5 p.m.
Lovely, old-fashioned shop selling own-brand tea and coffee.

SHOPPING

EVENING SHOPPING

Amsterdam's shops have very restricted and strictly-applied opening hours. The only places to buy food and drink in the evenings are at special night shops, open from 5 p.m. or 6 p.m. to 1 am.

AVONDMARKT **6** B1 tram 10
De Wittenkade 90-96 (1051 AK); tel. 6864919. Daily 6 p.m.-1 a.m.
The biggest selection of goods is available here, in Amsterdam's best late-night shop. But unfortunately, it's off the beaten track in the Stadsliedenbuurt.

BALTUS-STERK **10** B2 tram 16, 24, 25
Vijzelstraat 127 (1017 HJ); tel. 6269069. Daily 6 p.m.-1 a.m.
Groceries and delicatessen.

VAN DOORNEVELD **6** A2 tram 13, 17
De Clercqstraat 1-7 (1053 AA); tel. 6181727. Daily 6 p.m.-1 a.m.
A large evening shop with a wide variety of groceries, meats and take-away food. It even has a special champagne section.

HEUFT'S FIRST CLASS NIGHTSHOP **18** A2 tram 12, 25
Rijnstraat 60 (1079 HJ); tel. 6424048. Daily 5 p.m.-1 a.m., Sunday 4 p.m.-1 a.m.
Heuft's also has a branch on Constantijn Huigenstraat.

HEALTHCARE

See PRACTICAL INFORMATION for a list of pharmacies.

CONDOMERIE **8** B2
"HET GULDEN VLIES" tram 4, 9, 16, 24, 25
Warmoesstraat 141 (1012 JB); tel. 6274174. Monday to Friday 1-6 p.m., Saturday noon-5 p.m.
The Golden Fleece is a splendid name for Amsterdam's first specialist shop for condoms. You'll find them in all shapes and sizes.

JACOB HOOIJ **11** C1 Ⓜ Nieuwmarkt
Kloveniersburgwal 12 (1012 CT); tel. 6243041. Monday 12.30-6 p.m., Tuesday to Friday 8.15 a.m.-6 p.m., Saturday 8.15 a.m.-5 p.m.
This wonderful herbalist's business was founded in 1743. It stocks a range of chemist's goods alongside more than 400 herbs and spices for cooking and medicinal use.

STATIONERY

DE WITTE TANDENWINKEL 6 B2   tram 1, 2, 5
Runstraat 5 (1016 GJ); tel. 6233443. Monday 1-6 p.m., Tuesday to Friday 10 a.m.-6 p.m., Saturday 10 a.m.-5 p.m.
The White Toothbrush Shop has everything you might need for dental care, including brushes in all shapes and sizes and toothpaste to suit all palates.

TATTOO ARTIST

HANKY PANKY 9 C2   tram 4, 9, 16, 24, 25
Oudezijds Voorburgwal 141 (1012 ES); tel. 6274848. Monday to Friday 1-7 p.m., Saturday noon-8 p.m.
One of Holland's best-known tattoo artists operates from here. Prices start at ƒ 50. But be warned, tattooing can cause medical complications. The shop also has a small museum.

STATIONERY

FIRMA J. VLIEGER 10 B1   tram 4, 9, 14
Amstel 52 (1017 AB); tel. 6235834. Monday noon-5 p.m., Tuesday to Friday 9 a.m.-5.30 p.m., Saturday 9 a.m.-5 p.m.
Suppliers of paper, artists' materials, wrappings and stationery.

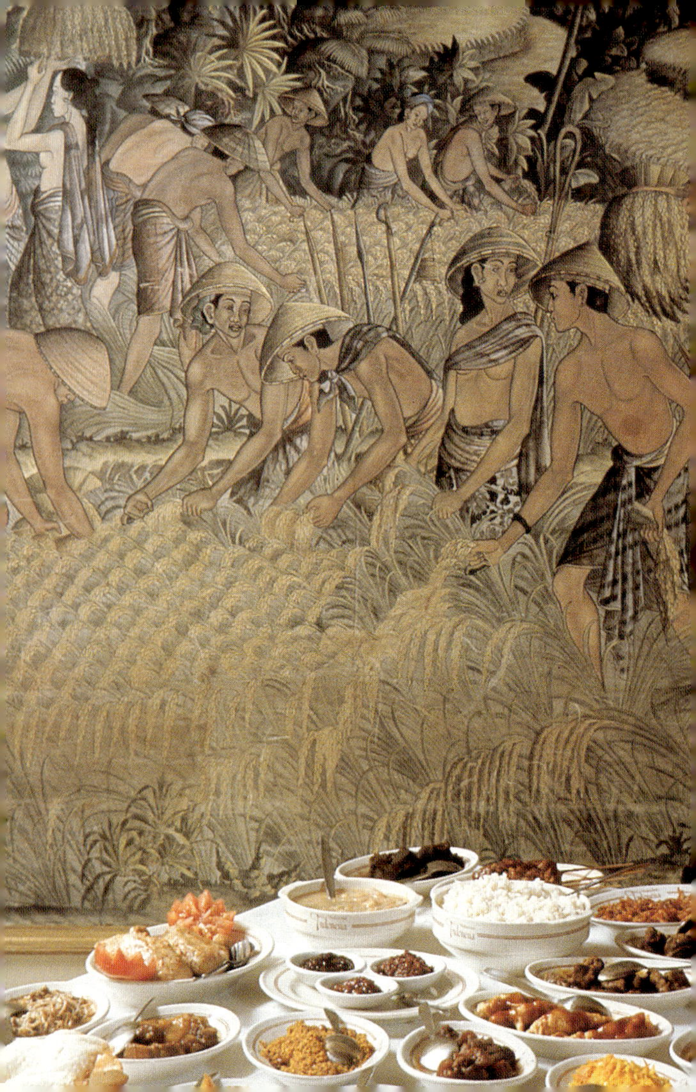

RESTAURANTS

The Dutch do not have a great reputation for their cuisine. But in addition to a few idiosyncratic dishes of their own (usually with a touch of cinnamon or cloves), they have developed a taste for food from almost anywhere. This gives Amsterdam a bewildering collection of restaurants from all parts of the world. It is difficult to give any accurate indications of price, because of the range of meals available. While you may take three or four courses in a French restaurant, one would suffice in a Surinamese restaurant. The prices included are for an average meal, but excluding drink.

At home, the Dutch tend to eat meat and two veg, with the accent on the veg. Ask a Dutchman what he is going to eat for dinner and he's quite likely to name only the vegetables. While The Netherlands may not be famous for its food (apart from cheese), it probably has the heartiest winter fare in Europe. Dutch pea soup and a variety of variations similar to the English bubble-and-squeak, with smoked sausage, stewed meat and lashings of gravy, are essential for refuelling on any winter day out.

EXTRAVAGANT

Here are some of Amsterdam's most sophisticated, creative (and inevitably expensive) restaurants.

BALI 10 A2 tram 1, 2, 5
Leidsestraat 89 (1017 NZ); tel. 6227878. Monday to Saturday noon-10.30 p.m., Sunday 5-10.30 p.m. (ƒ 70).
One of the best-known names in Indonesian food and an unusually smart venue in which to sample this cuisine.

BEDDINGTONS tram 3, 12, 16, 24, 25
Roelof Hartstraat 6 (1071 VH); tel. 6765201. Monday to Saturday: lunch noon-2 p.m., dinner 6-10 p.m. (ƒ 60).
Haute cuisine in an elegant modern interior. The (English) owner wields the baton in her own kitchen. Very French with a hint of Japan. Pricey.

The Indonesian rijsttafel is a succulent, spicy and vast experience. Indonesian restaurants are commonplace in Holland, a legacy from colonial days.

RESTAURANTS

BOLS TAVERNE 6 B1 — tram 13, 14, 17
Rozengracht 106 (1016 NH); tel. 6245752. Monday to Saturday 5 p.m.-midnight. (f 50).
Once one of the best fish restaurants in town, Bols Taverne is still pretty exclusive. It features a chauffeur-driven service to pick you up from your hotel.

CARTOUCHE 6 B1 — tram 13, 14, 17
Anjeliersstraat 177 (1015 NG); tel. 6227438. Daily: lunch noon-3 p.m., dinner 5.30-10.30 p.m. (f 60).
Cartouche serves French cuisine the way it should be. Expensive, but well worth it.

CHRISTOPHE 8 A2 — tram 13, 14, 17
Leliegracht 46 (1015 DH); tel. 6250807. Monday to Saturday 7-11 p.m. (From f 60).
A very exclusive French restaurant that has been awarded one cherished Michelin star. Wonderful interior, but pretentious staff.

LE CIEL BLEU (OKURA HOTEL) 17 C2 — tram 12, 25
Ferdinand Bolstraat 333 (1072 LH); tel. 6787111. Daily 6-11 p.m. (f 70).
A top-class French restaurant in the Japanese Okura Hotel. It has a good reputation among Amsterdammers.

L'ENTRECÔTE 16 B1 — tram 2, 3, 5, 12
P.C. Hooftstraat 70 (1071 CB); tel. 6737776. Tuesday to Sunday 5-11 p.m. (f 50).
L'Entrecôte specializes in classical French cuisine. Years of experience have gone into preparing the finest entrecôtes. A classy joint in a very classy street.

LE GARAGE 16 B2 — tram 16, 24, 25
Ruysdaelstraat 54 (1071 XE); tel. 6797176. Daily 6 p.m.-midnight. (f 60).
Despite the name, this restaurant is a meeting place for the Dutch jet set. It is run by the former owner of the Kersentuin. The cuisine is international in origin.

DE GRAAF — tram 2
Emmalaan 25 (1075 AT); tel. 6624884. Monday to Friday noon-2 p.m., 6-9.30 p.m., Saturday 6-9.30 p.m. (f 50).
Many business wizards meet here to enjoy the great (international) menu. You can eat in the kitchen, by special arrangement.

EXTRAVAGANT

HALVEMAAN tram 5
Van Leijenberglaan 20 (1082 GM) Amsterdam-Buitenveldert; tel. 6440348. Monday to Friday: lunch noon-2 p.m., dinner 7-10 p.m. Saturday: dinner only. (f 50).
The culinary art of top-chef John Halvemaan justifies a trip out of town to this suburban restaurant. In the summer, you can eat outside by the water.

DE KERSENTUIN 16 B2 tram 16
Dijsselhofplantsoen 7 (1077 BS); tel. 6642121. Monday to Saturday: lunch noon-3 p.m., dinner 6-10.30 p.m. (f 60).
High-class French food at a hefty price. Very exclusive.

LES QUATRE CANETONS 17 C1 tram 16, 24, 25
Prinsengracht 1111 (1017 JJ); tel. 6246307. Monday to Saturday: lunch noon-2 p.m., dinner 6-10.30 p.m. (f 60).
One of the very top restaurants in the Netherlands. French, expensive, but worth it.

TOUT COURT 6 B2 tram 13, 14, 17
Runstraat 13 (1016 GJ); tel. 6258637. Daily noon-11.30 p.m. (f 50).
Hidden away inconspicuously in the Jordaan, Tout Court is one of The Netherlands' best French restaurants.

TREASURE RESTAURANT 8 B1 tram 1, 2, 5, 13, 17
Nieuwezijds Voorburgwal 115 (1012 RH); tel. 6260915. Daily noon-2 p.m., 5-11 p.m. (f 50).
An exclusive venue and possibly the best Chinese restaurant in Amsterdam. Specialities: Peking duck and friendly service.

HET TUINHUYS 10 A2 tram 16, 24, 25
Reguliersdwarsstraat 28 (1017 BM); tel. 6276603. Monday to Friday: lunch noon-2 p.m., dinner 6 -11 p.m., Saturday, Sunday: dinner only. (f 50).
A new restaurant where you can eat quietly in the heart of the city. Both meat and fish dishes are of a high quality and the cooking is international in style.

D'VIJFF VLIEGHEN 8 A2 tram 1, 2, 5
Spuistraat 294 (1012 VX); tel. 6248369. 5.30 p.m.-midnight. (f 50).
Amsterdam's best-known eating house. Enjoy a top-class meal (international cuisine) in one of the nooks and crannies of this famous restaurant, restored to its original glory.

RESTAURANTS

YAMAZOTO (OKURA HOTEL) 17 C2   tram 12, 24
Ferdinand Bolstraat 333 (1072 LH); tel. 6787111. Daily: lunch noon-2 p.m., dinner 6-10 p.m. (f 70).
The Okura is a Japanese Hotel and hence has a reputation to maintain. It succeeds, but the price is high. Book in advance.

YOICHI 17 C1   tram 6, 7, 10
Weteringschans 128 (1017 XV); tel. 6226827. Thursday to Tuesday 6 p.m.-midnight. (f 60).
One of the best Japanese restaurants, with traditional service.

ECONOMICAL

See also: EETCAFÉS, LUNCH/SNACKS and SURINAMESE.

DE EENHOORN 6 B1   tram 13, 14, 17
2nd Egelantiersdwarsstraat 6 (1015 SC); tel. 6238352. Dinner 5-11 p.m. (f 20).
Real Jordaan service, impressive helpings of Dutch food and fine steaks. You may have to wait a while, but it's worth it.

DE KEUKEN VAN 1870 8 B1   tram 1, 2, 5, 13, 17
Spuistraat 4 (1012 TS); tel. 6248965. Daily 11.30 a.m.-8 p.m. (f 10).
Tramps and businessmen rub shoulders, while eating hearty Dutch meals at bargain prices in this simple and old-fashioned soup kitchen.

DE LELIE 8 A2   tram 1, 2, 5, 13, 17
Oude Leliestraat 7 (1016 BD); tel. 6201414. Monday to Friday noon-10 p.m., Saturday, Sunday 4-10 p.m. (f 15).
An inconspicuous snackbar near the Royal Palace that serves excellent Surinamese food.

MOEDERS 6 B2   tram 13, 14, 17
Rozengracht 251 (1016 SX); tel. 6267957. Friday to Wednesday 5 p.m.-midnight. (f 20).
Excellent and original Dutch cuisine in simple yet elegant surroundings.

MOY KONG 8 C2   Ⓜ Nieuwmarkt
Zeedijk 87 (1012 AT); tel. 6241906. Tuesday to Sunday 1-10.30 p.m. (f 15).
An authentic Chinese restaurant. The food is on the table before you finish your order.

DUTCH

PANCAKE CORNER tram 6, 7, 10
Kleine-Gartmanplantsoen 51 (1017 RP); tel. 6276303. Daily noon-10 p.m. (f 15).
Though a tourist venue, this is still a great place to try pancakes at their best.

DEL PONTE 6 B2 tram 13, 14, 17
Hartenstraat 3 (1016 BZ); tel. 6222471. Daily 6-11 p.m. (f 20).
Come here for unpretentious pizzas and a nice chat with the owner. You can even watch TV.

THEEHUIS VONDEL 16 B1 tram 6
Vondelpark 7 (1075 VR); tel. 6796791. Daily 11 a.m.-6 p.m. (f 10).
A pancake house at the end of Vondelpark. Ideal for the kids.

DUTCH

DE BLAUWE HOLLANDER tram 1, 2, 5
Leidsekruisstraat 28 (1017 RJ); tel. 6233014. Daily 5-10 p.m. (f 30).
A typical Dutch restaurant, with good helpings at bargain prices.

'T FORNUIS 11 C2 tram 4
Utrechtsestraat 33 (1017 VH); tel. 6269139. Tuesday to Sunday 5.30-11 p.m. (f 30).
First-class food straight from a (Dutch) mother's kitchen.

HAESJE CLAES 8 B1 tram 1, 2, 5
Nieuwezijds Voorburgwal 320 (1012 RV); tel. 6249998. Monday to Saturday noon-10 p.m., Sunday 5-10 p.m. (f 30).
Old Dutch food in an Old Dutch interior. You'll be served with a nice piece of meat and a generous helping of Dutch potatoes and vegetables.

OUD HOLLAND 8 B1 tram 1, 2, 5, 13, 17
Nieuwezijds Voorburgwal 105 (1012 RG); tel. 6246848. Monday to Saturday noon-9.30 p.m. (f 40).
Hearty Dutch food for cold evenings, near the Royal Palace.

RESTAURANTS

PIET DE LEEUW　**17** C1　　　　　　　　　　　　　tram 16, 24, 25
Noorderstraat 11 (1017 TR); tel. 6237181. Monday to Saturday noon-11.30 p.m., Sunday 5-11.30 p.m. (f 40).
Known by Amsterdammers to have the best steaks and the largest sole in town. The Old-Dutch interior is nice and cosy.

DIE PORT VAN CLEVE　**8** B1　　　　　　　　　tram 1, 2, 5, 13, 17
Nieuwezijds Voorburgwal 178-180 (1012 SJ); tel. 6244860. Noon-9 .30 p.m. (f 40).
Renowned for its pea soup, this fine old hotel also has a wonderful dining room with a historic tiled frieze.

WITTEVEEN　**17** D1　　　　　　　　　　　　　　　　tram 3
Ceintuurbaan 256 (1073 SH); tel. 6624368. Daily 5-11 p.m. (f 30).
A large and old-fashioned grand café in the Pijp district, with excellent food at a reasonable price. Book in advance on Sundays and holidays.

Eetcafés

Many bars and cafés in Amsterdam also serve excellent meals, but beware: the Dutch tend to eat early and you could find yourself hungry after 8 p.m., when some stop serving food.

CAFECOX　**6** B2　　　　　　　　　　　　　　　　tram 1, 2, 5, 10
Marnixstraat 247 (1017 PT); tel. 6207222. Sunday to Thursday 10 a.m.-1 a.m. Friday to Saturday 10 a.m.-2 a.m.. Dinner 5.30-11.30 p.m. (f 30).
Located in the Stadsschouwburg and named after its director (Cox Habbema), this is an ideal spot for a bite to eat before or after the show.

DE DOFFER　**6** B2　　　　　　　　　　　　　　　　tram 1, 2, 5
Runstraat 12 (1016 GK); tel. 6226686. Monday to Thursday 11 a.m.-2 a.m., Friday, Saturday 11 a.m.-3 a.m., Sunday noon-2 a.m. Dinner 6-10 p.m. (f 20).
One of many eating establishments, of varied plumage, in this street. De Doffer is simple and cosy.

DE EETTUIN　**6** B1　　　　　　　　　　　　　　　tram 13, 14, 17
Tweede Tuindwarsstraat 10 (1015 RZ); tel. 6237706, 5-11 p.m. (f 20).
One of the first restaurants in Amsterdam with a salad bar. Good food on a tight budget. Excellent cordon bleu and steaks. The service is always amazingly friendly.

DUTCH

FRASCATI 10 B1   tram 4, 14, 16, 19, 24, 25
Nes 59 (1012 KD); tel. 6241324. Sunday to Thursday 4 p.m.-1 a.m., Friday, Saturday 4 p.m.-2 a.m. Dinner 5.30-10.30 p.m. (f 20).
The oldest of the theatre-bars in Nes. The spare ribs and apple pie are recommended.

VAN HALE 17 C1   tram 16, 24, 25
Saenredamstraat 39 (1072 CC); tel. 6762495. Thursday to Saturday 6-10 p.m. (f 25).
The cuisine encompasses a different theme every month. Cosy relaxed atmosphere.

KAPITEIN ZEPPOS 10 B1   tram 4, 14, 16, 19, 24, 25
Gebed zonder end 5 (1012 HS); tel. 6242057. Monday to Thursday 11 a.m.-1 a.m., Friday 11 a.m.-2 a.m., Saturday 1.30 p.m.-2 a.m., Sunday 1.30 p.m.-1 a.m. Dinner 6-10 p.m. (f 30).
The owner is an ex-GP who abandoned his surgery in favour of running a bar. Homely atmosphere and live music on Sunday afternoons and Wednesday evenings.

LUCULLUS 17 C2   tram 3
Tweede van der Helststraat 7 (1073 AE); tel. 6793138. 6-9.30 p.m. (f 20).
Bargain prices for excellent and original cuisine in the heart of the Pijp.

HET MOLENPAD 6 B2   tram 1, 2, 5
Prinsengracht 653 (1016 HV); tel. 6259680. Sunday to Thursday noon-1 a.m., Friday, Saturday till 2 a.m. Dinner 6-10 p.m. (f 20).
A favourite of business people and lawyers from the courts opposite. Fine food in a modest setting.

MUCHO MAS 17 A1   Ⓜ Wibautstraat
Andreas Bonnstraat 44 (1091 BA); tel. 6928674. Tuesday to Thursday 12.30 p.m.-1 a.m., Friday, Saturday 4 p.m.-2 a.m. Dinner 6-9.30 p.m. (f 20).
An eetcafé with a Spanish twist. Enjoy the tapas outside on a sunny afternoon. Great food for a good price.

'T ORKESTJE 16 B2   tram 2, 3, 5, 12
Van Baerlestraat 51 (1071 AP); tel. 6736222. Monday to Friday 11 a.m.-1 a.m., Saturday, Sunday 4 p.m.-1 a.m. Lunch noon-2 .30 p.m.; dinner 5-11 p.m. (f 35).
Another jolly haunt, near the Concertgebouw. Old 78s are played on request.

RESTAURANTS

DE PRINS 6 B1   tram 13, 14, 17
Prinsengracht 124 (1015 EB); tel. 6249382. Sunday to Thursday 10 a.m.-1 a.m., Friday, Saturday 10 a.m.-2 a.m. Service 10 a.m.-10 p.m. (f 20).
A great place for lunch, though the kitchen is open all day. The high frontage gives you a fascinating view of this picturesque corner of Amsterdam. Very busy in the evening.

VAN PUFFELEN 6 B2   tram 13, 14, 17
Prinsengracht 377 (1016 HL); tel. 6246270. Sunday to Thursday 2 p.m.-1 a.m. Friday, Saturday till 2 a.m. Dinner 6-11 p.m. (f 30).
A brown café that prides itself on its food.

DE REIGER 6 B1   tram 13, 14, 17
Nieuwe Leliestraat 34 (1015 ST); tel. 6247426. Sunday to Thursday 11 a.m.-1 a.m., Friday, Saturday 11 a.m.-2 a.m. Dinner 6-10.30 p.m (f 20).
This popular brown café in the Jordaan is frequented by students and the younger generation. Simple menu with reasonable table d'hôte.

SPANJER EN VAN TWIST 8 B2   tram 4, 14, 16, 19, 24, 25
Nes 41 (1012 KC); tel. 6203316. Sunday to Thursday 11 a.m.-1 a.m., Friday, Saturday 11 a.m.-2 a.m. Dinner 5 p.m.-midnight (f 15).
Situated in a narrow street of theatres. Pleasant surroundings for dinner on a tight budget.

TRAMLIJN BEGEERTE 6 B1   tram 10
Van Limburg-Stirumsplein 4 (1051 BE); tel. 6865027. Monday to Friday 9 p.m.-1 a.m., Saturday, Sunday noon-1 a.m. Dinner Monday to Friday 6-8 p.m. (f 15).
The name of this cosmopolitan café translates as "A Streetcar Named Desire". Hans and Jenny serve exquisite food at ridiculously low prices.

LATE-NIGHT PLACES

BARK 16 B2   tram 3,12
Van Baerlestraat 120 (1071 BD); tel. 6750210. Lunch noon-3 p.m., dinner 5.30 p.m.-1.30 a.m. (f 40).
Speciality: a variety of fish dishes including two kinds of oysters.

ETHNIC

BOJO 6 B2 — tram 1, 2, 5
Lange Leidsedwarsstraat 51 (1017 NG); tel. 6227434. Sunday to Thursday 5 p.m.-2 a.m, Friday, Saturday 5 p.m.-5.30 a.m. (f 20).
Renowned among Amsterdam's nightlife. Good Indonesian food for the late eater.

DE KNIJP 16 B2 — tram 3, 12
Van Baerlestraat 134 (1071 BD); tel. 6714248. Daily: lunch noon-3 p.m., dinner 5.30 p.m-1.30 a.m. (f 40).
An intimate place for a late-night bite after the show. Anything from a salad to a brochette: la Knijp.

RUM RUNNERS 6 B1 — tram 13, 14, 17
Prinsengracht 277 (1016 GW); tel. 6274079. Monday to Thursday 4 p.m.-1 a.m., Friday 4 p.m.-2 a.m., Saturday 2 p.m.-2 a.m., Sunday 2 p.m.-1 a.m. (f 30).
A genuine Caribbean atmosphere is created in this former gymnasium, sited between Westerkerk and Anne Frank House. The interior is dominated by a cage full of twittering birds. The food is not always as good as the atmosphere.

ETHNIC

British

O'HENRY'S 8 B2 — tram 14, 16, 24, 25
Rokin 89 (1012 KL); tel. 6251498. Sunday to Thursday noon-1 a.m., Friday, Saturday noon-2 a.m. (f 40).
An international restaurant, with a hint of the English in spite of its name.

Chinese

CHINA CORNER 8 B2 — tram 4, 9, 14, 16, 24, 25
Damstraat 1 (1012 JL); tel. 6228816. Daily noon-11 p.m. (f 25).
Downstairs is the traditional Chinese menu, but go upstairs if you want to try the dim sum.

RESTAURANTS

HOI TIN   9 C2   Ⓜ Nieuwmarkt
Zeedijk 122 (1012 BB); tel. 6256451. Daily 11 a.m.-11 p.m. (f 15).
The Zeedijk, once the haunt of sailors, later of prostitutes and junkies, is also at the heart of the Chinese quarter. Its restaurants are not the smartest, but they do provide the best food.

MANCHURIAN   6 B2   tram 1, 2, 5, 10
Korte Leidsedwarsstraat 51 (1017 PW); tel. 6231330. Daily: lunch noon-3 p.m., dinner 5.30-10.45 p.m. (f 40).
A candidate for the best Chinese restaurant in the entertainment district.

SEA PALACE   9 D1   tram 1, 2, 4, 5, 9, 13, 16, 17, 24, 25
Oosterdokskade 8 (1011 AE); tel. 6264777. Daily noon-11 p.m. (f 40).
The Sea Palace occupies a floating Chinese pagoda and has room to seat and feed 900 people. Arrive by watertaxi and eat in one of the many specialist sections with a view of the harbour.

Egyptian

SCARABEE   tram 6, 7, 10
Amsteldijk 125 (1078 RS); tel. 6752870. Tuesday to Sunday 4-11 p.m. (f 25).
An Egyptian oasis in a good location by the River Amstel.

Filipino

AT MANGO BAY   6 B1   tram 10
Westerstraat 91 (1015 LX); tel. 6381039. Friday to Wednesday 6-10 p.m. (f 35).
Grilled Filipino specialities and fish, with plenty of fruit garnish. Live music at the weekend.

Flemish

DE BRAKKE GROND   10 B1   tram 4, 9, 14, 16, 24, 25
Nes 43 (1012 KD); tel. 6260044. Tuesday to Saturday 5.30-10 p.m. (f 30).
A Belgian corner of Amsterdam and part of the Flemish Cultural Centre. The cinnamon ice cream is recommended.

ETHNIC

CHEZ GEORGE 8 A1   tram 1, 2, 5, 13, 17
Herenstraat 3 (1015 BX); tel. 6263332. Thursday to Tuesday 6-10.30 p.m. (f 45).
An excellent and intimate restaurant. Very suitable for a romantic meal.

LIEVE 8 A1   🚌 18, 22
Herengracht 88 (1015 BS); tel. 6249635. Monday, Tuesday, Thursday 6-10 p.m., Friday, Saturday 6-10.30 p.m. (f 25).
Waterzooi and *paling in 't groen* (stewed eel) is served in these spacious Belgian surroundings. There's an impressive selection of beer.

French

BORDEWIJK 6 B1   🚌 22
Noordermarkt 8 (1015 MV); tel. 6243899. Daily noon-11 p.m. (f 40).
Great attention to detail, excellent service.

LE CRIGNON 8 A2   tram 1, 2, 5, 13, 17
Gravenstraat 28 (1012 NM); tel. 6246428. Monday to Saturday 6-10 p.m. (f 30).
Be sure to book, but even then you are not guaranteed a table of your own. This small two-storey restaurant is recommended for its cheese fondue and other specialities.

DE IMPRESSIONIST 6 B2   tram 13, 14, 17
Keizersgracht 312 (1016 EX); tel. 6276666. Sunday to Thursday 6-10.30 p.m., Friday, Saturday 6-11 p.m. (f 50).
An excellent, but small restaurant. There's a varied menu for a fixed price.

SZMULEWICZ 10 B2   tram 4, 9, 14
Bakkerstraat 12 (1017 CW); tel. 6202822. Daily 5.30-10 p.m. (f 25).
Good creative cuisine and not expensive. A trendy establishment with young staff.

Greek

DELPHI 16 B1   tram 1, 2, 5, 6
Stadhouderskade 61 (1072 AC); tel. 6646487. Daily 4.30-10 .30 p.m. (f 25).
The right address for a delicious peasant salad (*choriatiki*) or grilled kebab (*souvlaki*). The fish stew (*saganaki-psari*) is also highly recommended.

RESTAURANTS

MYKONOS 6 A2   tram 1, 3, 12
1e Constantijn Huygenstraat 86 (1054 BX); tel. 6852626. Daily 4-11 p.m. (f 25).
Mykonos has a simple yet refined menu. An open kitchen and Greek scenes on the walls complete the décor. It is one of those restaurants where the maître always offers you another drink when you ask for the bill.

POSEIDON 6 A2   tram 13, 14
De Clercqstraat 105 (1053 AH); tel. 6124027. Tuesday to Sunday 5-11 p.m. (f 25).
A very popular restaurant. Book in advance or try the snacks in the Ouzeria opposite.

Indian

MAYUR 6 B2   tram 1, 2, 5, 10
Korte Leidsedwarsstraat 203 (1017 RB); tel. 6232142. Wednesday to Monday: lunch 12.30-2.30 p.m., dinner 5-11 p.m. Tuesday: dinner only (f 30).
It's a toss-up as to whether Mayur or Pakistan serves the best Indian food in Amsterdam. But the breads from the clay oven are better here.

PAKISTAN 6 A2   tram 13, 17
De Clercqstraat 65 (1053 AD); tel. 6181120. Daily 5-11 p.m. (f 25).
A gem in the suburbs. Pakistan serves one of the best curries in town, certainly the most elegant.

THE TANDOOR 6 B2   tram 1, 2, 5, 6, 7, 10
Leidseplein 19 (1017 PS); tel. 6234415. Daily 5-11 p.m. (f 30).
There's a fine view over Leidseplein and the curries are good, but the speciality here is obviously Tandoori.

Indonesian

No visit to The Netherlands is complete without an Indonesian meal. The Dutch were quick to recognize the culinary wealth of their oriental colony and the Malay dishes for which it is rightly famous. It is no exaggeration to say that Indonesian food has been adopted by the Dutch as their own.

ETHNIC

The easiest way to get a taste of the variety of Indonesian food is to try a *rijsttafel* (rice table). If you do you will certainly have no need to order anything else, but pay special attention when a waiter tells you which of the dishes are especially spicy.

DJANOKO   **16** B2   tram 2, 3, 5, 12
Van Baerlestraat 61 (1071 AR); tel. 6629665. Tuesday to Sunday noon-9.30 p.m. (f 50).
Convenient for the Concertgebouw and the museums.

DJAWA   **6** B2   tram 1, 2, 5, 10
Korte Leidsedwarsstraat 18 (1017 RC); tel. 6246016. Daily 5-11 p.m. (f 50).
Good food, by the Bios disco on Leidseplein.

INDONESIA   **10** A1   tram 16, 24, 25
Singel 550 (1017 AZ); tel. 6232035. Summer: daily noon-10.30 p.m. Winter: daily noon-10 p.m. (f 60).
Authentic Indonesian food, with several different *rijsttafel* on the menu. The restaurant boasts a splendid view over Muntplein.

KANTJIL & DE TIJGER   **8** A2   tram 1, 2, 5
Spuistraat 291 (1012 VS); tel. 6022994. Monday to Thursday 3.30-11 p.m., Friday, Saturday 5 p.m.-midnight. (f 40).
Budget Indonesian food is served here in simple yet stylish surroundings. This is one of the few establishments in Amsterdam with a no-smoking area.

PADI MAS   **16** B1   tram 2, 5
P.C. Hoofdstraat 87 (1017 BP); tel. 6646421. Daily 5-10 p.m. (f 60).
An intimate, small restaurant in Amsterdam's most exclusive shopping street.

SAMA SEBO   **16** B1   tram 2, 5
P.C. Hoofdstraat 27 (1017 BL); tel. 6628146. Monday to Saturday: lunch noon-2 p.m., dinner 6-10 p.m. (f 60).
A favourite with the business community.

SPECIAAL   **6** B1   tram 13, 14, 17
Nieuwe Leliestraat 142 (1015 SX); tel. 6249706. Daily 5.30-11 p.m. (f 50).
Great Indonesian food in the heart of the Jordaan. It's Prince Philip's favourite too (to judge by his photo on the wall).

RESTAURANTS

SUKASARI 8 B2   tram 4, 9, 14, 16, 24, 25
Damstraat 26-28 (1012 JM); tel. 6240092. Monday to Saturday noon-9 p.m. (f 40).
Cheap, fast food. Great spring rolls.

TEMPOE DOELOE 11 C2   tram 4
Utrechtsestraat 75 (1017 VJ); tel. 6256718. Monday to Saturday 6-11.30 p.m., Sunday 5-11 p.m. (f 60).
Good food and a nice garden in which to eat it, weather permitting.

International

Amsterdam is the most cosmopolitan city in Europe. It has a reputation as a place where émigrés and tourists alike can feel at home. This is reflected in the spectrum of food available to suit all palates and pockets. The following restaurants have a wide-ranging international cuisine, with French being the major influence.

DE GEPARKEERDE MOSSEL 8 A2   tram 1, 2, 5, 13, 17
Nieuwezijds Voorburgwal 306 sous (1012 RV); tel. 6249425. Monday to Saturday 6-10 p.m. (f 35).
Luc Hermans is patron and chef in this diminutive living room. He provides a fine evening out at a reasonable price.

GRAND CAFÉ 1E KLAS 9 C1   tram 1, 2, 4, 5, 9, 13, 16, 17, 24, 25
Platform 2b, Central Station (1012 AB); tel. 6250131. Monday to Wednesday 9.30 a.m.-11 p.m., Thursday to Saturday 9.30 a.m.-midnight, Sunday 10.30 a.m.-11 p.m. (f 35).
Once the first-class waiting room at Central Station, now a first-class restaurant and meeting place. The interior has been painstakingly restored and is well worth a visit even if you don't fancy a bite or a drink.

HEMELSE MODDER 9 D2   tram 4
Oude Waal 9 (1011 BZ); tel. 6243203. Tuesday to Sunday 5.30 p.m.-midnight. Dinner 6-10 p.m. (f 35).
"Heavenly Mud" started as a semi-illegal and unlicensed squatters' haunt. The owners have now acquired a reputation for good food.

DE LUWTE 8 A2   tram 13, 14, 17
Leliegracht 26 (1015 DG); tel. 6258548. Tuesday to Sunday 6-10 p.m. (f 35).
A superb and romantic restaurant with a canalside location and a Tuscan interior. The surprise salads are marvellous.

ETHNIC

PIER 10 9 D1 tram 1, 2, 4, 5, 9, 13, 16, 17, 24, 25
De Ruyterkade, pier 10 (1011 AA); tel. 6248276. Daily 6.30 -10 .30 p.m. (f 40).
Located behind Central Station on a pier jutting out into the River IJ. You'll need to book in advance to enjoy a fine meal in this historic monument to the New Realist architecture of the 1930s. There's a spectacular view across the water.

VERBUNT 8 A2 tram 1, 2, 5, 13, 17
Paleisstraat 105 (1012 ZL); tel. 6385470. Daily 11 a.m.-1 a.m. (f 40).
Located in the cellars of what was once a newspaper printing works, near the Royal Palace. French food with a few Indonesian, Japanese and Italian influences.

VERTIGO 16 B1 tram 1, 2, 3, 5, 6, 12
Vondelpark 3 (1071 AA); tel. 6123021. Daily 11 a.m.-1 a.m., Friday, Saturday till 2 a.m. Dinner: daily 5.30-11.30 p.m. (f 25).
Good food and drink in the basement of the Film Museum.

Italian

LA BOTTE 6 B2 tram 10, 13, 14, 17
Lijnbaansgracht 120 (1016 VV); tel. 6235539. Daily 4-11 p.m. (f 20).
Pizzas and pastas delivered to your doorstep, anywhere in Amsterdam.

CAFFÉ PANINI 17 C1 tram 16, 24, 25
Vijzelgracht 5 (1017 HM); tel. 6264939. Monday to Saturday 9.30 a.m.-9 .30 p.m., Sunday 10.30 a.m.-9 .30 p.m. (f 25).
Home-made Italian bread. Great for lunch or a light dinner.

CAPRI 6 B1 🚌 18, 22
Lindengracht 63 (1015 KC); tel. 6244940. Sunday to Friday 3-10 p.m., Saturday 9 a.m.-9 p.m. (f 15).
An ice-cream parlour and pizzeria with wonderful warm Italian bread rolls and mozzarella.

CASA DI DAVID 10 A1 tram 1, 2, 5
Singel 426 (1017 AV); tel. 6245093. Daily 5-11.30 p.m. (f 40).
Mediterranean haute cuisine. Pricey but certainly worth it. An excellent Italian restaurant.

RESTAURANTS

CIRELLI 9 C1   tram 1, 2, 4, 5, 9, 13, 16, 17, 24, 25
Oudezijds Kolk 69 (1011 AL); tel. 6243512. Sunday to Thursday 5.30-10 p.m., Friday, Saturday 5.30-11 p.m. (f 35).
After an enervating afternoon traipsing around the Red-Light District, CiRelli provides a welcome relief and surprising décor. The owner Dok Wintzen designed the interior, his wife is in the kitchen and his children serve at table. Highly recommended.

DA NOI 7 C1   tram 3 18, 22
Haarlemmerdijk 128 (1013 JJ); tel. 6201409. Tuesday to Sunday 5.30-11 p.m. (f 30).
This unassuming little paninoteca is easy to overlook, but it serves some of the best Sardinian food in town. The staff also make all their own pasta and bread, not to forget the amazing gateaux.

LA TORRE DI PISA 10 B2   tram 4, 7, 10
Reguliersgracht 95 (1017 LN); tel. 6250512. Daily 5-10 p.m. (f 40).
A first-class and tiny Italian restaurant by the waterside. The Italian owner is also the chef. His Dutch wife serves the customers.

TOSCANINI 6 B1   18, 22
Lindengracht 75 (1015 KD); tel. 6232813. Wednesday to Monday 6-10.30 p.m. (f 40).
The exquisite food at Toscanini is not to be hurried. And the service can be eccentric, but it's all worth it. Book before you arrive in The Netherlands! Half-portion pastas are available for those who want to leave room for a main course.

VASSO 10 A1   tram 4, 9, 14, 16, 24
Rozenboomsteeg 12-14 (1012 PR); tel. 6260158. Daily 6.30-10 .30 p.m. (f 35).
Highlights are the home-made pasta and the delicious prima piati which can also be ordered as a main meal. Take-away next door.

Japanese

See also: EXTRAVAGANT.

AKITSU 6 B1   tram 13, 14, 17
Rozengracht 228 (1016 SZ); tel. 6253254. Tuesday to Sunday 6-10 p.m. (f 50).
For those who want to eat good Japanese food in a relaxed atmosphere at a reasonable price.

ETHNIC

KAIKO **17** C2 tram 12, 25
Jekerstraat 114 (1078 MJ); tel. 6625641. Monday to Friday 6-10.30 p.m. (ƒ 60).
The best sushis in Amsterdam. Even fresh uni (sea-urchin) is almost always on the menu. You can phone and order take-away sushis.

Louisiana

CAJUN **17** C2 tram 3
Ceintuurbaan 260 (1072 GH); tel. 6644729. Daily 5-11 p.m. (ƒ 40).
The French-American touch, with Louisiana cajun cuisine served in a tropical interior. Eat "blackened fish" or oysters gratin. Expensive, new-wave cooking.

Mexican

CAFÉ PACIFICO **9** C1 tram 1, 2, 4, 5, 9, 13, 16, 17, 24, 25
Warmoesstraat 31 (1012 HV); tel. 6242911. Monday to Thursday 5.30-10 p.m., Friday to Sunday 5.30-11 p.m. (ƒ 30).
One of the first Mexican restaurants in Europe, Café Pacifico still has an atmosphere all of its own.

CARAMBA **6** B1 tram 10
Lindengracht 342 (1015 KN); tel. 6271188. Daily 5.30-10 .30 p.m. (ƒ 30).
A Dutch Mexican restaurant that is reputedly the hang-out of foreign rock stars. Good food.

ROSE'S CANTINA **10** A1 tram 4, 16, 24, 25
Reguliersdwarsstraat 38-40 (1017 BM); tel. 6259797. Daily 5-11.30 p.m. (ƒ 30).
So successful that the owners keep adding extensions to cope with the crowds.

Moroccan

MARRAKESCH **8** B1 tram 1, 2, 5
Nieuwezijds Voorburgwal 134 (1012 SH); tel. 6235003. Daily 5-10 p.m. (ƒ 30).
It is a sad fact that one of Amsterdam's largest immigrant communities is so under-represented in its restaurant life. Marrakesch offers excellent couscous and a tea corner.

RESTAURANTS

Portuguese

LISBOA 10 A2   tram 1, 2, 5
Kerkstraat 35 (1017 GB); tel. 6256490. Daily 5 p.m.-midnight. (f 30).
Portuguese food at its best. Accompany it with a full-blooded Dão or a sparkling vinho verde.

Russian

DATSCHA ALEXANDER 17 C2   tram 3
Rustenburgerstraat 160 (1073 GJ); tel. 6735420. Monday to Saturday 7.30 p.m.-midnight (f 40).
A legendary Russian experience in the least likely of places. Anonymously situated in a narrow suburban street. You have to book and arrive on time for an evening to remember.

Spanish

EL BARCO 17 C1   tram 16, 24, 25
Daniel Stalpertstraat 93 (1072 XD); tel. 6795092. Daily 3 -11 p.m. (f 30).
El Barco (the boat) has even added the nautical touch to its bar. The Spanish food is of a high quality and there's an outdoor area in the summer.

CENTRA 9 C1   tram 1, 2, 4, 5, 9, 13, 16, 17, 24, 25
Lange Niezel 29 (1012 GS); tel. 6223050. Daily 1-11 p.m. (f 25).
A small, basic and very busy Spanish restaurant in the heart of the Red-Light District. Book in advance with a large group.

EL NARANJO 6 B1   18, 22
Boomstraat 41a (1015 LB); tel. 6222402. Tuesday, Wednesday, Friday to Sunday, 4 p.m.-1 a.m. (f 30).
A nice Spanish restaurant in the heart of the Jordaan. Highest garlic rating in town.

ETHNIC

Surinamese

The Dutch colony on the northern coast of South America has been home to a wide variety of peoples, from American Indians to Indonesians, Indians, Africans and Dutch. The blend of cultures has resulted in a fascinating Indo-Caribbean cuisine that is, unfortunately, seriously underrated. There are no high-class Surinamese restaurants, but plenty of take-aways and snack bars where you can try *rotis*, *bakkeljauw*, *baka bana* and *moksi meti*.

ASIAN CARIBBEAN RESTAURANT 8 B2   tram 4, 9, 14, 16, 24, 25
Warmoesstraat 170 (1012 JK); tel. 6271545. Daily 4-11 p.m., for dancing at the weekend till 5 a.m. (f 20).
Hidden away behind the Bijenkorf is one of the few places you can eat Surinamese food in a real restaurant. The Asian Caribbean is also a venue for (very) late-night dancing every weekend, in a Caribbean atmosphere.

MAROWIJNE 17 C1   tram 16, 24, 25
A. Cuypstraat 70 (1072 CW); tel. 6624845. Tuesday to Sunday noon-10 p.m. (f 6).
This take-away was named after the famous river in Surinam. Try the rotis.

WARUNG SWIETIE 6 A2   tram 7, 17
Ten Katestraat 18 (1053 CE); tel. 6833568. 11 a.m.-9 p.m. (f 6).
A Surinamese take-away/restaurant on the Ten Kate market. The rotis are among the best in town.

Thai

DYNASTY 10 A2   tram 16, 24, 25
Reguliersdwarsstraat 30 (1017 BJ); tel. 6268400. Wednesday to Monday 6-11 p.m. (f 50).
Excellent Chinese-Thai cuisine.

KLAAS COMPAEN 11 C1   tram 7, 10
Raamgracht 9 (1011 KH); tel. 6238708. Daily 5-9.45 p.m. (f 30).
This must rate as the most unusual and is certainly the oldest, Oriental restaurant in Europe. The food may no longer be strictly Thai, but this place has been serving Oriental food since 1563!

RESTAURANTS

KOONING VAN SIAM 9 C2   tram 1, 2, 4, 5, 9, 13, 16, 17, 24, 25
Oudezijds Voorburgwal 42 (1012 GE); tel. 6237293. Daily 6-10 p.m. (f 50).
High-class Thai food on the edge of the Red-Light District.

TOM YAM 11 C1   Ⓜ Waterlooplein
Staalstraat 22 (1011 JM); tel. 6229533. Daily 6-10 p.m. (f 50).
A cosy restaurant, very popular with the artistic in-crowd. There's usually a choice of four menus, but you are obliged to take a complete set meal. The owner tends to get very upset if you just want one main dish. Don't fail to try the soup (*Tom Ka Kay*).

Turkish

ANKARA 8 B1   tram 1, 2, 5
Spuistraat 3a (1012 SP); tel. 6236110. Daily 5-11.30 p.m. (f 30).
A modest Turkish restaurant near Central Station.

TURKIYE 8 A2   tram 1, 2, 5
Nieuwezijds Voorburgwal 169 (1012 RK); tel. 6229919. Daily 5-11.30 p.m. (f 30).
Many Turks live in Amsterdam, but their cuisine is sorely under-represented. Turkiye is an agreeable restaurant behind the Royal Palace. It comes complete with live music and belly dancer.

FISH

LUCIUS 8 A2   tram 2, 5
Spuistraat 247 (1012 VP); tel. 6241831. Daily noon-midnight. (f 60).
The excellent and bewildering range of fish dishes is the main attraction at Lucius. Great oysters. The Dutch interior is sober, but the service is friendly.

DE OESTERBAR 6 B2   tram 1, 2, 5
Leidseplein 10 (1017 PT); tel. 6263463. Daily noon-midnight. (f 60).
The place for oysters, but of course only when there's an R in the month. Also a broad selection of other (fish) dishes.

LUNCH/SNACKS

LE PECHEUR 10 A2   tram 1, 2, 5
Reguliersdwarsstraat 32 (1017 BH); tel. 6243112. Monday to Friday noon-midnight., Saturday, Sunday 5 p.m.-midnight. (f 60).
Sited in the midst of the entertainment district, this is one of the better fish restaurants.

SLUIZER 11 C2   tram 4
Utrechtsestraat 45 (1017 VH); tel. 6263557. Daily noon-midnight. (f 30).
In the simple wooden interior you can eat good fish dishes. Sluizer has become a well-known meeting place.

LUNCH/SNACKS

Everything is not what it seems in the Dutch world of snacks and take-away food. Middle Eastern kebabs are a favourite late-night snack, sold under the name *Shawarma* (and spelt in a myriad ways). These claim to be Israeli, but are usually made and sold by Egyptians or Turks. (The best can be had from Ben Cohen, Rozengracht 239.) The Turks also run many of Amsterdam's "Italian" pizzerias, so try some of the more exotic Turkish varieties (with minced lamb and garlic). The city is also dotted with Chinese restaurants claiming to sell Indonesian food. Some have even been taking advantage of the recent interest in Surinamese food. A typical Dutch lunchtime snack is fried or raw fish, bought from a fish shop (which do not serve chips). For the best herrings, try the stall on the corner of Raadhuisstraat and Singel. Chips (with mayonnaise or peanut satay sauce) are sold at snackbars (which do not serve fish), where you can also obtain a variety of weird and wonderful sausages and meatballs. But most Dutch have a cold lunch of bread or rolls with an amazing variety of fillings: cheese, cold meats and salads. Drop into Broodje van Kootje on Spui or Leidseplein for a late-night bread roll with tartare. Expect to pay between f 5 and f 20 for a modest lunch.

CASA MOLERO 17 C1   tram 16, 24, 25
Gerard Doustraat 66 (1072 VR); tel. 6761707. Tuesday to Saturday 9a.m.-6 p.m.
Spanish sausages are the speciality.

DELICIOUS TRAITEUR 10 A1   tram 1, 2, 5
Heisteeg 8 (1012 WC); tel. 6224850. Sunday to Friday 4-9 p.m., Saturday noon-9 p.m.
For Italian take-away snacks.

RESTAURANTS

EETSALON VAN DOBBEN   10 B2   tram 4
Korte Reguliersdwarsstraat 5 (1017 BH); tel. 6244200. Monday to Thursday 9.30 a.m.-1 p.m., Friday, Saturday 9.30 a.m.-2 p.m., Sunday 11.30 a.m.-8 p.m
The finest lunch-room in Amsterdam, with an incredible range of filled rolls. This is the only snackbar to put lobster in the lobster salad (most use ocean sticks).

FLEMISH FRITES   10 A1   tram 1, 5
Voetboogstraat 33 (1012 XK). Monday to Friday 11 a.m.-6 p.m., Saturday, Sunday 11 a.m.-5 p.m.
Most shopkeepers in Kalverstraat are willing to make a detour for these fine chips, served in the best Belgian tradition.

PUCCINI   10 B1   Ⓜ Waterlooplein
Staalstraat 21 (1054 ES); tel. 6265474. Tea-room: daily 9 a.m-6 p.m. Take-away: Tuesday to Saturday 9 a.m.-6 p.m.
A tearoom with a shop next door supplying take-away desserts.

SANDWICHSHOP SAL MEIJER   17 C2   tram 12, 25
Scheldestraat 45 (1078 GG); tel. 6731313. Monday to Saturday 10 a.m.-7 p.m., Sunday 10 a.m.-8.30 p.m.
The best place in town for Kosher bread rolls. Famous for its *broodjes halfom* (liver and salt meat) and pastrami.

TIS FRIS   9 C2
St Anthoniebreestraat 142 (1011 HB); tel. 6220472. Daily 10 a.m.-1 p.m.
Great gateaux and cheap tacos near Rembrandt's House.

TOKO SARI   10 A2   tram 16, 24, 25
Kerkstraat 161 (1017 GG); tel. 6232364. Tuesday to Friday 11 a.m.-6 p.m., Monday noon-6 p.m.
For quick Indonesian snacks.

B. WOUDA   10 A1   tram 1, 2, 5
Rozenboomsteeg 8 (1012 PR); tel. 6223072. Monday to Friday 8.30 a.m.-5 p.m., Saturday 10 a.m.-4 p.m.
Among the favourite fillings for rolls served at this tiny snack-bar are warm roast pork, followed by chocolate hundreds and thousands (*hagelslag*). Wash them down with a glass of fresh orange.

VEGETARIAN

VEGETARIAN

DE BOLHOED 6 B1 🚌 18, 22
Prinsengracht 60 (1015 DX); tel. 6261803. Daily 11 a.m.-10 p.m. (f 20).
There's an intriguing fluorescent interior in this Jordaan post-modern (or PoMo as the locals say) restaurant.

GOLDEN TEMPLE 11 C2 tram 4
Utrechtsestraat 126 (1017 VL); tel. 6268560. Daily 5-9 p.m. (f 20).
White garb and turbans are in evidence to remind you of Amsterdam's balmy days of yore as a trading nation.

SISTERS 10 B1 tram 14, 16, 24, 25
Nes 102 (1012 KE); tel. 6263970. Monday to Thursday noon-9.30 p.m., Friday, Saturday 2 -9.30 p.m. (f 20).
For good yet inexpensive vegetarian fare in an alcohol and smoke-free environment.

DE VLIEGENDE SCHOTEL 6 B1 tram 13, 14, 17
Nieuwe Leliestraat 162 (1015 HE); tel. 6252041. Daily 5.30-10.15 p.m. (f 20).
The "Flying Saucer" has a good reputation with vegetarians who want a cheap but wholesome meal. The menu also includes fish.

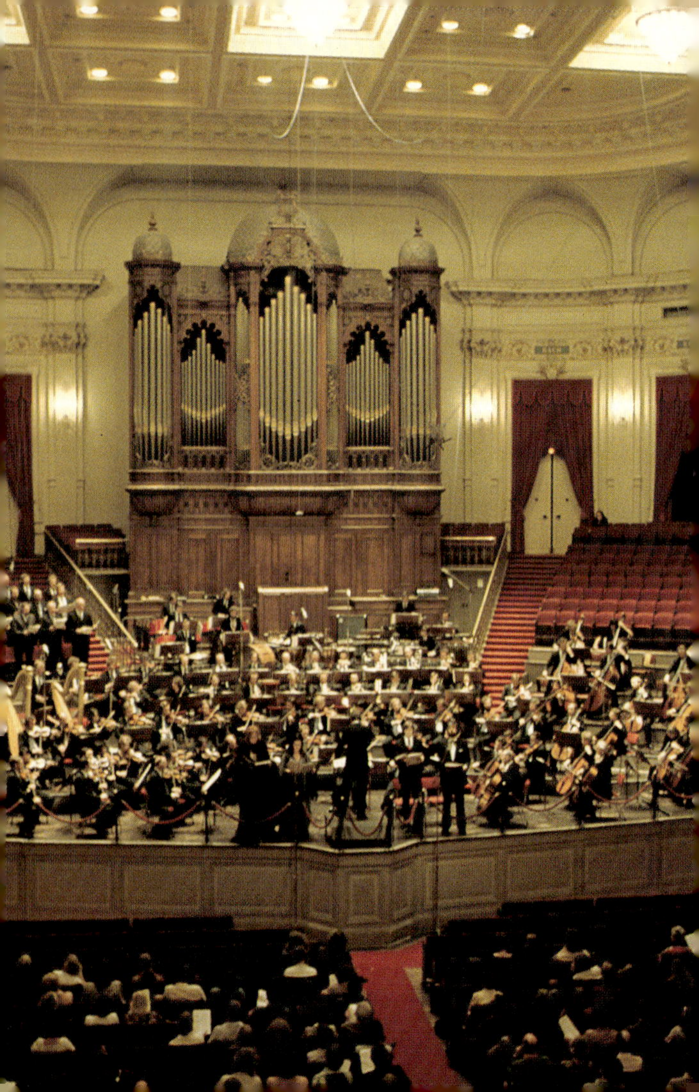

Amsterdam has plenty to offer for a good night out. The city has a startling variety of bars, the best known of course being the "brown cafés", which have a thick layer of nicotine on their walls and ceilings to thank for the name. *Proeflokalen* are the bars in which to try the famous Dutch liqueurs and gins: the name means "tasting centre". In addition, Amsterdam has bars to suit all tastes and pockets, from post-modern hang-outs to sing-along pubs.

Some of Amsterdam's cinemas are worth visiting just to see the spectacular Art Deco interiors (all films are shown in their original language with Dutch subtitles); and the city boasts plenty of live-music venues, from bars to an opera house. There is also a wealth of small theatres providing drama, dance and even English-language theatre. Amsterdammers don't get much sleep. Many pubs open in the morning, and, though the first bars start to close at 1 a.m., others may stay open as late as 4 a.m. By then even the Red-Light District is starting to wilt.

BARS

Proeflokalen (Tasting Centres)

The Dutch are world famous for their liqueurs and gins. These can be drunk anywhere, but you can pretend a level of academic interest by visiting a proeflokaal (tasting centre)—another name for a pub.

DE ADMIRAAL 7 C2   tram 1, 2, 5
Herengracht 319 (1016 AV); tel. 6254334. Monday to Saturday 4 p.m.-midnight.
De Admiraal has a large and comfortable interior and provides an opportunity to taste the liqueurs still produced in a corner of the Jordaan.

DE DRIE FLESCHJES 8 A2   tram 1, 2, 4, 5, 9, 24, 25
Gravenstraat 18 (1012 NM); tel. 6248443. Monday to Saturday noon-8.30 p.m.
Behind the Nieuwe Kerk near Dam Square. Usually crowded.

Opened in 1888, the Royal Concertgebouw is home to the world-famous orchestra of the same name.

NIGHTLIFE

IN DE OLOFSPOORT 9 C1   Ⓜ Nieuwmarkt
Nieuwebrugsteeg 13 (1012 AG); tel. 6243918. Monday to Friday 4 p.m.-1 a.m., Saturday, Sunday 4 p.m.-2 a.m.
Hidden away behind the Zeedijk and St Olof's Chapel is one of the oldest and quaintest places to try traditional Dutch distilled.

IN DE WILDEMAN 8 B1   tram 1, 2, 5, 13, 14, 17
Kolksteeg 3 (1012 PT); tel. 6382348. Sunday to Thursday 11 a.m.-1 a.m., Friday, Saturday 11 a.m.-2 a.m.
Beer is the speciality of this cosy proeflokaal. The ales (and there are many) come either on draught or from the bottle. This is one of Amsterdam's very few venues with a non-smokers' section.

Brown Cafés

BOLLE JAN 10 B1   tram 4, 9, 14
Korte Reguliersdwarsstraat 3 (1017 BH); tel. 6259376. Sunday, Thursday 10.30 a.m.-1 a.m., Friday, Saturday 10.30 a.m.-2 a.m.
A well-known old-Amsterdam bar where tear-jerkers are sung at the weekend. This is where local stars are born.

DE DRUIF 11 D1   tram 4
Rapenburgplein 83 (1011 VK); tel. 6244530. Sunday to Thursday 11 a.m.-1 a.m., Friday, Saturday 11 a.m.-2 a.m.
Five bar stools, three tables and 12 chairs: De Druif is one of Amsterdam's oldest and friendliest establishments.

EIJLDERS 6 B2   tram 1, 2, 5, 6, 7, 10
Korte Leidsedwarsstraat 47 (1017 PW); tel. 6242704. Sunday to Thursday noon-1 a.m., Friday, Saturday noon-2 a.m.
One of the meeting places on Leidseplein for artists and writers.

DE GIETER 6 B2   tram 1, 2, 5, 6, 7
Korte Leidsedwarsstraat 174 (1017 RD); tel. 6252731. Sunday to Thursday 7 p.m.-2 a.m., Friday, Saturday 7 p.m.-3 a.m.
Students and squatters make up most of the clientele here. It is friendlier than most cafés in the area and has a jukebox.

GOLLEM 10 A1   tram 7, 10
Raamsteeg 4 (1012 WZ); tel. 6266645. Daily 4 p.m.-1 a.m.
Renowned for its wide range of beers. Tiny, but that's how a good Amsterdam bar should be.

BARS

HOPPE **10** A1   tram 1, 2, 5
Spui 18 (1012 XA); tel. 6237849. Sunday to Thursday 8 a.m.-1 a.m., Friday, Saturday 8 a.m.-2 a.m.
Every weekday afternoon at 5 p.m. Hoppe is overcrowded with the smarter set, who look down their noses at the Bohemians to be found next door at Zwart.

SCHELTEMA **8** A2   tram 1, 2, 5, 14, 13, 17
Nieuwezijds Voorburgwal 242 (1012 RR); tel. 6232323. Monday to Friday 8 a.m.-11 p.m., Saturday 8 a.m.-9 p.m.
A brown café journalists' hang-out, with a wide selection of reading material.

SCHUTTER **10** A1   tram 1, 2, 4, 5, 16, 24, 25, 4
Voetboogstraat 13-15 (1012 XK); tel. 6224608. Sunday to Thursday 11 a.m.-1 a.m., Friday, Saturday 11 a.m.-2 a.m.
Hearty meals at a reasonable price are served and there's sometimes live entertainment upstairs.

'T SMALLE **6** B1   tram 13, 14, 17
Egelantiersgracht 12 (1015 RL); tel. 6239617. Sunday to Thursday 10 a.m.-1 a.m., Friday, Saturday 10 a.m.-2 a.m.
A homely living room atmosphere survives in what was once Pieter Hoppe's distillery. Benches on the bank of the canal provide a grandstand position to watch boat-owning Amsterdammers on parade.

DE TWEE ZWAANTJES **6** B1   tram 13, 14, 17
Prinsengracht 114 (1018 VX); tel. 6252729. Monday to Thursday 4 p.m.-midnight, Friday to Sunday 4 p.m.-1.30 a.m.
A real Jordaan bar. On Sunday nights you can join in the sing-song.

Grand Cafés

AMERICAN HOTEL **6** B2   tram 1, 2, 5, 6, 7 10
Leidseplein 28 (1017 PN); tel. 6245322. Daily 11 a.m.-11 p.m.
The wonderful art deco interior alone is enough to justify a visit. This has for years been one of Amsterdam's prime literary meeting places.

NIGHTLIFE

DANTZIG **11** D1 tram 4, 9, 14 Ⓜ Waterlooplein
Waterlooplein 1 (1011 JB); tel. 6209039. Sunday to Thursday 10 a.m.-1 a.m., Friday, Saturday 10 a.m.-2 a.m.
Named after the ex-director of the Dutch National Ballet, Rudi van Dantzig, this grand and post-modern establishment could do with having more atmosphere, but it is a convenient and stunning place for a quick drink and ideally located for the market or a show at Het Muziektheater. It has a huge pavement café in the summer with spectacular views across the River Amstel.

EAST OF EDEN **18** B1 tram 6, 9, 10
Linnaeusstraat 11a (1092 CR); tel. 6650743. Sunday to Thursday 11 a.m.-1 a.m., Friday, Saturday 11 a.m.-2 a.m.
An exotic haven in the eastern suburbs, opposite the Tropical Museum. The finest pavement café in the east.

GRAND CAFÉ BERLAGE **18** B2 tram 9, 14, 16, 24, 25
Beursplein 1 (1012 JW); tel. 6384639. Tuesday to Saturday 10 a.m.-11 p.m., Sunday 11 a.m.-6 p.m.
A fine Grand Café in Hendrik Berlage's famous exchange building.

DE HEEREN VAN AEMSTEL **10** B2 tram 4, 9, 14
Thorbeckeplein 5 (1017 CS); tel. 6202173. Monday to Thursday 4 p.m.-1 a.m., Friday, Saturday noon-2 a.m.
Live music is staged here six days a week. There's a large pavement café in the summer and modest, but delicious, food.

DE HEINEKEN HOEK **6** B2 tram 1, 2, 5, 6, 7, 10
Kleine-Gartmanplantsoen (1017 RP); tel. 6230700. Sunday to Thursday 10 a.m.-1 a.m., Friday, Saturday 10 a.m.-2 a.m.
The best-known location on Leidseplein. This was the prototype grand café; it sells the beer that does much to boost Dutch export income.

DE JAREN **10** B1 tram 4, 9, 14, 16, 24, 25
Nieuwe Doelenstraat 20-22 (1012 CP); tel. 6255771. Sunday to Thursday 10 a.m.-1 a.m., Friday, Saturday 10 a.m.-2 a.m.
Important attractions are the terrace by the waterside, the reading table with plenty of Dutch and foreign newspapers and the fine restaurant upstairs (one of the few in Amsterdam with a non-smoking area). To top it all, Rembrandt once lived on the site.

BARS

DE KROON 10 B2   tram 4, 9, 14
Rembrandtplein 15 (1017 CT); tel. 6384006. Sunday to Thursday 10 a.m.-1 a.m., Friday, Saturday 10 a.m.-2 a.m.
A huge and very popular place for a drink with the in-crowd. Sitting in the conservatory above the square can give you a good view of social relations in Amsterdam, outdoors and in.

DU LAC 7 C1   tram 2, 3, 5, 17
Haarlemmerstraat 118 (1013 EX); tel. 6244265. Sunday to Thursday 11 a.m.-1 a.m., Friday, Saturday 11 a.m.-2 a.m.
A spacious and unusual venue, decorated in fine colours and what is becoming known as nouveau kitsch. It was once a bank and the safe is now used to store the beer.

LIDO   tram 1, 2, 5, 6, 7, 10
Max Euweplein 62 (1017 MB); tel. 6201006. Casino: daily 2 p.m.-3 a.m., closed May 4 and New Year's Eve.
The new Lido houses one of the largest casinos in Europe. In the traditional gaming room you can find French, American and Twin Roulette, Punto Banco and Black Jack. Holland Casino also introduces two new games: Sic Bo and Big Wheel. The jackpot club has more than 300 machines which pay out cash (not like most machines in The Netherlands which have to pay out tokens). You can raise the stakes in peace in the Cerle Prive, which is stylishly located in the old restored Lido building, once one of Holland's top nightspots. The same old villa houses the Holland Casino Bingo Room with 52 bingo units. The Lido also comprises a Café Brasserie, a French-Asian restaurant, a theatre-restaurant and a nightclub.

LUXEMBOURG 10 A1   tram 1, 2, 5
Spui 22-24 (1012 XA); tel. 6206264. Sunday to Thursday 10 a.m.-1 a.m., Friday, Saturday 10 a.m.-2 a.m.
The Luxembourg's art deco interior is an excellent place to eat lunch.

L'OPERA 10 B2   tram 4, 9, 14
Rembrandtplein 27-31 (1017 CT); tel. 6275232. 11 a.m.-1 a.m., Friday, Saturday 11 a.m.-2 a.m.
L'Opera's chic interior has plenty of marble and glass. Outside, there's a huge pavement café, covered in the winter. Pricey.

NIGHTLIFE

SCHILLER 10 B2   tram 4, 9, 14
Rembrandtplein 26 (1017 CV); tel. 6249846. Sunday to Thursday 4 p.m.-1 a.m., Friday, Saturday 4 p.m.-2 a.m.
Back in the 1930s, the café was adjacent to the Schiller Theatre and was a meeting place for cabaret artists, many refugees from Nazi Germany. Their photos still hang in the bar.

WILDSCHUT   tram 3, 5, 12, 24
Roelof Hartplein 1 (1071 TR); tel. 6738622. Sunday to Thursday 9 a.m.-2 a.m., Friday, Saturday 9 a.m.-3 a.m.
A nicely decorated Jugendstil Grand Café for the young in-crowd of the Concertgebouw area. Dinner costs from about ƒ 20.

Other Cafés

THE BAMBOO BAR 6 B2   tram 1, 2, 5, 6, 7, 10
Lange Leidsedwarsstraat 64 (1017 NM); tel. 6243993. Sunday to Thursday 9 p.m.-2 a.m., Friday, Saturday 9 a.m.-3 a.m.
A busy bar with live music every night. The beer is expensive, but the service is good.

LA BASTILLE 6 B2   tram 6, 7, 10
Lijnbaansgracht 245 (1017 RK); tel. 6235604. Daily 4 p.m.-1 a.m.
Every year on 14 July, the assault on La Bastille is celebrated here with a festival of live music (also on the Queen's official birthday, 30 April).

DE BERRY 6 B2   tram 1, 2, 5, 6, 7, 10
Leidseplein 8 (1017 PT); tel. 6232156. Sunday to Thursday 10 a.m.-1 a.m., Friday, Saturday 10 a.m.-2 a.m.
Often busy and very noisy, a real Leidseplein bar for 18 to 48 year-olds.

BLACK AND WHITE 6 B2   tram 1, 2, 5, 6, 7, 10
Leidseplein 18 (1017 PT); tel. 6264966. Summer: 9 a.m.-1 a.m., Saturday till 2 a.m. Winter: 10 a.m.-1 a.m., Friday, Saturday till 2 a.m.
One of the famous Leidseplein bars, with a regular crowd of mostly hardrock and rock 'n' roll lovers.

DE BLAFFENDE VIS 6 B1   tram 3, 10
Westerstraat 118 (1015 MN); tel. 6251721. Monday 7 a.m.-1 a.m., Tuesday to Friday 9 a.m.-1 a.m., Saturday 11 a.m.-2 a.m., Sunday 11 a.m.-1 a.m.
From Monday to Friday, a good plain meal is served here for only ƒ 10.

BARS

'T BLAUWE THEEHUIS   16 A1   tram 1, 2, 6
Vondelpark (1071 AA). Open in the Summer: daily 9 a.m.-7.30 p.m.
The largest pavement café in the Vondelpark (closed in the winter). It has become a meeting place for Amsterdam's young people.

DE BRIT   6 B2   tram 1, 2, 5, 6, 7, 10
Korte Leidsedwarsstraat 24 (1017 RC); tel. 6263739. Sunday to Thursday 5 p.m.-1 a.m., Friday, Saturday 5 p.m.-2 a.m.
A long and narrow bar with a darts board at the back. Great atmosphere, if you can cope with the decibels.

CARELS'S CAFÉ 1   17 C1   tram 3
Frans Halsstraat 76 (1072 BV); tel. 6794836. Sunday to Thursday 11 a.m.-1 a.m., Friday, Saturday 11 a.m.-2 a.m.
One of a small chain of bars on adjacent corners in the Pijp. Large wooden tables are always crowded with locals. Dinner will cost you about *f* 15.

DE ENGELBEWAARDER   11 C1   tram 1, 2, 5, 17
Kloveniersburgwal 59 (1011 JZ); tel. 6253772. Monday to Thursday noon-1 a.m., Friday, Saturday noon-2 a.m., Sunday 2 p.m.-1 a.m.
A literary haunt with live jazz every Sunday afternoon and good cheap pub food.

ESPRIT CAFÉ   10 A1   tram 1, 2, 5
Spui 10a (1012 WZ); tel. 6221967. Daily 10 a.m.-midnight.
This trendy clothing shop also incorporates a pub which does an excellent lunch and coffee.

GAFFA   10 B1   tram 9, 14, 16, 24, 25
St. Pieterspoortsteeg 3 (1012 HM); tel. 6200523. Sunday to Thursday 10 a.m.-3 a.m., Friday, Saturday 10 a.m.-4 a.m.
A late-night haunt for the pub-crawler. The place only hots-up after 1 a.m. It isn't very large, but it gets busy and the music is loud.

DE GELAGHKAMER   10 B1   tram 6, 7, 10, 16, 24, 25
Nieuwe Vijzelstraat 1 (1012 HT); tel. 6206075. Sunday to Thursday 6 p.m.-1 a.m., Friday, Saturday 6 p.m.-2 a.m.
A meeting place for local celebrities in the arts and theatre.

KABUL   8 B2   tram 1, 2, 4, 5, 9, 16, 24, 25
Warmoesstraat 42 (1012 JE); tel. 6237158. Sunday to Thursday 2 p.m.-1.30 a.m., Friday, Saturday 2 p.m.-2 a.m.
Kabul is in the heart of the city and attracts an international crowd of young people. Live music at the weekend. Busy and cheap.

NIGHTLIFE

A meeting place for local celebrities in the arts and theatre.

KABUL 8 B2   tram 1, 2, 4, 5, 9, 16, 24, 25
Warmoesstraat 42 (1012 JE); tel. 6237158. Sunday to Thursday 2 p.m.-1.30 a.m., Friday, Saturday 2 p.m.-2 a.m.
Kabul is in the heart of the city and attracts an international crowd of young people. Live music at the weekend. Busy and cheap.

'T KALFJE 8 A1   B 22
Prinsenstraat 5 (1015 DA); tel. 6263370. Daily 7 p.m.-2.30 a.m.
You can get a drink here when the locals close.

LAND VAN WALEM 6 B2   tram 1, 2, 5
Keizersgracht 449 (1017 DK); tel. 6253544. Sunday to Thursday 11 a.m.-1 a.m., Friday, Saturday 11 a.m.-2 a.m.
Trendy bar with trendy clientele, fine sandwiches and excellent meals.

THE MINDS 10 A1   tram 1, 2, 5
Spui 245 (1012 VP); tel. 6236784. Sunday to Thursday 10 a.m.-2 a.m., Friday, Saturday 10 a.m.-3 a.m.
Alternative young people's bar. Noisy and crammed with drunken youth. The last call on a pub crawl.

MORLANG 6 B2   tram 1, 2, 5
Keizersgracht 451 (1017 DK); tel. 6252681. Sunday to Thursday 10 a.m.-1 a.m., Friday, Saturday 10 a.m.-2 a.m.
Like its next-door neighbour, Land van Walem (see above), but slightly quieter and with better service.

SHORTS OF LONDON 10 B2   tram 4, 9, 14
Rembrandtplein 18 (1017 CV); tel. 6225656. Monday, Wednesday, Thursday 8 a.m.-2 a.m., Friday, Saturday 8 a.m.-3 a.m., Sunday 4 p.m.-1 a.m. Closed on Tuesday.
Shorts used to be an English-style pub, but the music is now true Amsterdam.

SJAALMAN 6 B2   tram 13, 14, 17
Prinsengracht 178 (1016 HB); tel. 6202440. Daily noon-midnight.
A café-restaurant where Thai/Surinamese cuisine is served in Dutch surroundings. A pool table is available.

TRAMLIJN BEGEERTE 6 B1   tram 10
Van Limburg Stirumplein 4 (1051 BE); tel. 6865027. Sunday to Thursday 10 a.m.-1 a.m., Friday, Saturday 10 a.m.-2.30 a.m.

A cosmopolitan bar in the Staaslieden neighbourhood. It includes a pavement café and excellent food on weekdays from 6-9 p.m.

DE TWEE PRINSEN **8** A1 tram 13, 14, 17
Prinsenstraat 27 (1015 DB); tel. 6249722. Sunday to Thursday 11 a.m.-1 a.m., Friday, Saturday 11 a.m.-2 a.m.
A very popular bar in the Jordaan. The heated pavement café means you can sit outside well into autumn.

WEBER **6** B1 tram 7, 10
Marnixstraat 397 (1017 PJ); tel. 6229910. Sunday to Thursday 1 p.m.-1 a.m., Friday, Saturday 2 p.m.-3 a.m.
The bar of Café Weber is usually busy, noisy and full. The lower ground floor is however quietly furnished with ratan chairs and pastel colours.

WELLING **16** B1 tram 2, 3, 5, 12, 16
J.W. Brouwerstraat 32 (1017 NC); tel. 6620155. Daily 3 p.m.-1 a.m.
A rather eccentric musical haunt behind the Concertgebouw. Popular with the Bohemians.

CINEMA

Amsterdam, like most places, has seen the number and size of its cinemas decline in recent years. In a city with 20 channels of television on cable (including BBC1, BBC2, CNN, Super Channel, MTV, Lifestyle, TV Cinq, RAI Uno, Germany 1, 2 and 3), it is no surprise that cinemas are losing out. But Amsterdam still has a couple of the finest Art Deco cinemas in Europe, plus a wide range of screens and film theatres (albeit not enough of the latter) to suit all tastes.

With the exception of some children's features (e.g Disney cartoons), all films are shown in the original language with subtitles. The daily newspapers include brief lists of screenings every day and a full listing in the Wednesday evening/Thursday morning editions. Many bars also hang

NIGHTLIFE

DESMET **12** A2   tram 7, 9, 14
Plantage Middenlaan 4a (1018 DD); tel. 6273434.
A cinema where art films are screened in wonderful Art Deco surroundings. It often has thematic festivals providing a welcome chance to see documentaries and minority films.

KRITERION **12** A2   tram 6, 7, 10
Roetersstraat 170 (1018 WE); tel. 6231708. Wednesday, Saturday, Sunday afternoon.
Art house which calls itself a children's film house three days a week.

THE MOVIES **7** C1   tram 3 🚃 18, 22, 44
Haarlemmerdijk 161 (1013 KH); tel. 6386016. Children: Wednesday, Saturday afternoon.
An Art Deco cinema showing a high class of film. This is how a cinema should be: snug, small, with a fine bar and even a restaurant .

RIALTO FILMHUIS **17** C2   tram 3, 12, 24, 25
Ceintuurbaan 338 (1072 GN); tel. 6623488. Sunday to Wednesday afternoon.
An old-fashioned cinema, once threatened with destruction, now an art house in the Pijp.

TUSCHINSKI **10** B2   tram 4, 9, 14, 16, 24, 25
Reguliersbreestraat 26 (1017 CN); tel. 6231510.
A six-screen cinema contained in a magnificent monument to Art Deco. The building dates from 1921 and has been painstakingly maintained in its original condition with hand-made Persian carpeting and massive chandeliers. Guided tours are run in the summer on Sunday and Monday mornings from 10.30 a.m. and cost ƒ 5. The interior is a must for anyone visiting Amsterdam. Mainstream films are shown.

THEATRE

The language barrier makes Dutch theatre rather inaccessible to English-language speakers, but this is not a great loss. Dutch theatre often seems rather stilted and artificial. Much of it is certainly experimental, which is about all that can be said for it.

The ratio of theatres to the population in Amsterdam means that productions in smaller theatres seldom run for longer than two weeks and in larger theatres seldom for longer than a few performances. All

THEATRE

performing arts companies in The Netherlands are required to go on tour. The programmes are continually changing and the visitor is therefore advised to consult *What's On*, or the daily papers (especially on Thursday morning, when they include the week's listings). The ticket agency, AUB Uitlijn (tel. 6211211; open Monday to Saturday from 10 a.m.-6 p.m.), sells tickets for most theatres, etc. in Amsterdam, but you must phone at least five days in advance and the tickets will be mailed to your address. This service also costs a surcharge of ƒ 5 a ticket. You can call the theatres direct to book seats, but will usually have to be there at least 30 mintutes in advance of the show. Most theatres are closed on Mondays.

AMSTERDAMSE BOS
OPEN-AIR THEATRE
65, 125, 146, 147

Nw Kalfjeslaan 4 (1182 BA) Amstelveen; tel. 6431414. Tuesday to Saturday in July and August.

Every year in July and August, a major open-air production is mounted in the Amsterdamse Bos. Performances begin at 9 p.m. Admission is free, but you can make a donation if you want to. There is seating for 1,750 people. Blankets are handed out if the evening is chilly. Details of performances can be found in *What's On*.

BALIE
tram 1, 2, 5, 6, 7, 10

Kleine-Gartmanplantsoen 10 (1017 RR); tel. 6232904. Closed on Monday. Bookings: Tuesday to Saturday 4.30-8.30 p.m., Sunday matinée 1-5 p.m.

Calls itself a political-cultural centre and regularly presents plays on political themes, occasionally in English or other European languages. Literary evenings and political discussions are also programmed. These activities are often thematically linked to the plays. There are three small theatres, two of which are in regular use. Small productions are sometimes staged in the foyer. The building also houses a bar and a modest restaurant.

BELLEVUE THEATRE
tram 1, 2, 5, 6, 7, 10

Leidsekade 90 (1017 PN); tel. 6247248. Bookings: Monday 11 a.m.-4 p.m., Tuesday to Friday 11 a.m.-12.30 p.m., Saturday 1-8.30 p.m., Sunday 11 a.m.-4 p.m. and 7-8.30 p.m.

The Bellevue presents plays (often by Toneelgroep Amsterdam) and modern dance by renowned companies, both local and international. Plays and lunchtime performances are produced in the smaller theatre. The Smoeshaan restaurant serves food before a show (your tickets are placed on your table). The theatre bar is a popular haunt of actors.

NIGHTLIFE

BRAKKE GROND   10 B1   tram 4, 9, 16, 24, 25
Nes 45 (1012 KD); tel. 6266866. Bookings: Monday to Saturday 10 a.m.-4 p.m. Evenings from 7 p.m.
A number of years ago this complex was acquired by the Belgian Government and it is now an outpost of Flemish culture in The Netherlands. However it also presents Dutch productions and some co-productions. There are three auditoriums; the oldest has fixed seating and balconies. There is also a studio for small-scale productions. The bar sells Belgian beer and rolls with Belgian cheese. The restaurant has an international menu with a number of Belgian specialities.

FELIX MERITIS (See below: CLASSICAL MUSIC, DANCE AND OPERA)

FRASCATI   10 B1   tram 4, 9, 16, 24, 25
Nes 63 (1012 KD); tel. 6266866. Bookings: Monday to Saturday 10 a.m.-4 p.m. Evenings: tel. 6235723 after 7 p.m.
Frascati was originally a cigar factory, then a dance hall and now has two theatres and a rehearsal room in which performances are occasionally given. The programme consists predominantly of plays and music-theatre productions, but dance productions are also presented. Performances are occasionally presented in English.

KLEINE KOMEDIE   10 B2   tram 4, 9, 16, 24, 25
Amstel 56 (1017 AC); tel. 6240534. Bookings: Monday to Saturday 11 a.m.-3 p.m. and from 6 p.m.
Amsterdam's oldest theatre. The outside looks rather unprepossessing and the foyer doesn't seem very promising either, but the auditorium is intimate and beautifully ornate. Although it is primarily a revue and cabaret theatre, occasionally dance productions and plays are staged. English-language productions are rare. Tickets cost from ƒ 16 to ƒ 23.50.

MEERVAART   tram 1, 17 🚌 19, 23
Osdorpplein 205 (1069 SW); tel. 6107393. Bookings: Monday to Saturday 11 a.m.-4 p.m. and 1 hour before the show.
Programmes at this cultural centre consist of films, music, dance and plays. It is a receiving theatre, visited by many touring companies. The fact that it is suburban makes it no less interesting. It is possible to see productions here that you missed during their central Amsterdam run.

NIEUWE DE LA MAR   6 B1   tram 1, 2, 5, 6, 7, 10
Marnixstraat 404 (1017 PL); tel. 6233462. Bookings: see Bellevue (above).

THEATRE

Situated close to Leidseplein, this theatre presents musicals, cabaret and plays. It is not affiliated to any particular theatre company and functions as a receiving theatre for touring productions. English-language productions are presented fairly regularly.

OPEN-AIR THEATRE IN VONDELPARK 6 B1   tram 1, 2, 3, 5, 6, 12
Marnixstraat 427 (1017 PK); tel. 6731499/6250435 ext. 31. Wednesday afternoon, Friday evening, Saturday afternoon, Sunday afternoon.
Situated in the middle of Vondelpark, this theatre stages performances from June until August. On Wednesday afternoons there is children's theatre. Music, dance or cabaret is performed on Sunday afternoons. Sometimes there are string quartets, choirs or orchestras, admission is free. The theatre has 900 seats and there is standing room for 400 more. For details of performances see *What's On*.

ROB VAN REIJN THEATRE   7 C1   tram 3   18, 22, 44
Haarlemmerdijk 31hs (1013 KA); tel. 6279988. Wednesday to Sunday.
The mime artist Rob van Reijn started this as a pantomime theatre, but he now presents a wider programme, including one-act plays and shows in all shapes and sizes. American and English companies perform here regularly. This small, friendly theatre seats 100 people.

ROYAL CARRÉ   10 B2   tram 3, 6, 7, 10
THEATRE   Ⓜ   Waterlooplein or Weesperstraat
Amstel 115-125 (1018 EM); tel. 6225225. Daily Sunday to Saturday.
The Carré was originally built as a circus theatre and it still presents international circuses at least once a year. On the guided tour of the building (Wednesday and Saturday at 3 p.m. for ƒ 2.50) you are also shown the animal stalls. This is one of the largest theatres in Amsterdam (2,000 seats) and it is often used for staging musicals such as Cats and Les Miserables. Tickets cost from ƒ 25 to ƒ 90. On its centenary it received the designation "Royal".

SOETERIJN (See below: CLASSICAL MUSIC, DANCE AND OPERA)

STADSSCHOUWBURG   6 B2   tram 1, 2, 5, 6, 7, 10
Leidseplein 26 (1017 PT); tel. 5237700. Bookings: Monday to Saturday 10 a.m. to curtain-up, Sunday and public holidays to half an hour before curtain-up.
At present this 19th-century theatre provides a home for Toneelgroep Amsterdam, the largest repertory company in Holland. There is a main stage, a theatre upstairs and sometimes performances are given in the

NIGHTLIFE

foyer. On the main stage, dance productions are presented as well as plays. Major touring productions in English are also presented. The theatre upstairs stages small-cast plays by less well-known companies. Lunchtime plays are often well worth the visit; they begin at 12.30 p.m. (except Sunday and Monday). During July and August, guided tours are given on Wednesday and Friday at noon.

DE STALHOUDERIJ 6 B2   tram 13, 14, 17
1e Bloemdwarsstraat 4 (1016 KS); tel. 6262282. Opening times depend on the production.
The smallest theatre in Amsterdam, seating between 30 and 44 people, depending on the amount of space required by the play. All productions are in English. Tickets cost between ƒ 12.50 and ƒ 15.

TRUST THEATER 10 A1   tram 4, 9, 16, 14, 24, 25
Heiligeweg 19 (1012 XN); tel. 6383990.
The Trust Theater Company has converted this unused swimming pool into a theatre. The company presents a regular repertoire, but is also often on tour. Worth a visit, if only to see the venue.

CLASSICAL MUSIC, DANCE AND OPERA

For its size, Amsterdam has a great deal to offer anyone interested in the performing arts. Perhaps most famous is the Concertgebouw Orchestra, whose former conductor, Bernard Haitink, is now conducting at Covent Garden in London.

Dutch dance companies, such as the Netherlands Dance Theatre and the Dutch National Ballet, have also achieved international fame. Names such as Rudi van Dantzig and Hans van Manen are well known to lovers of dance. Opera fans are treated to the work of the Netherlands Opera under its new director Pierre Audi, formerly of the Almeida Theatre in London.

BEURS VAN BERLAGE 8 B2   tram 4, 9, 16, 24, 25
Damrak 243 (1012 LK); tel. 6270466. Bookings: Tuesday to Friday 12.30-6 p.m., Saturday 12.30-5 p.m.
The old Stock Exchange building designed by Berlage now has two auditoriums: the Wang, which seats 600 and the AGA, which seats 180.

CLASSICAL MUSIC, DANCE AND OPERA

It is the home of the Netherlands Philharmonic Orchestra and the Netherlands Chamber Orchestra. They give between 10 and 20 performances at the Beurs every month. Other orchestras also play here.

FELIX MERITIS 6 B1 tram 1, 2, 5, 13, 17
Keizersgracht 324 (1016 EZ); tel. 6231311. Bookings: Tuesday to Saturday 7-9 p.m. Telephone reservations: Monday to Friday 3-5 p.m.
There are three theatres in this complex, formerly called the Shaffy Theater. The repertoire is mostly avant-garde and experimental and includes music, dance and plays. Felix Meritis is a beautiful, old building with a modern interior. The bar and restaurant are recommended.

IJSBREKER 18 A2 tram 3
Weesperzijde 23 (1091 ER); tel. 6681805. Sunday to Thursday 11 a.m.-1 a.m., Friday, Saturday 11 a.m.-2 a.m.
A small auditorium situated by the River Amstel. Its programme consists almost exclusively of music, particularly modern and experimental. The bar spills out onto the pavement and is pleasant on summer evenings.

MEERVAART (See above: Theatre)

HET MUZIEKTHEATER 11 C1 tram 4, 9, 14 Ⓜ Waterlooplein
Waterlooplein 22 (1011 PG); tel. 6255455. Bookings: Monday to Saturday 10 a.m. to curtain-up, Sunday and public holidays 11.30 a.m. to curtain-up.
Het Muziektheater, which seats 1,600 people, was completed in 1986. It provides a home for the Netherlands Opera and the Dutch National Ballet, but also presents dance and operatic productions from around the world.

The stage is vast and equipped with the most modern technical innovations. All the seats in the auditorium have an excellent view, so you will never find yourself sitting behind the proverbial pillar. The building was designed by Wilhelm Holzbauer and Cees Dam and was extremely controversial at the time. Building costs went over the budget by more than the total costs of the new dance theatre in The Hague. Amsterdammers nicknamed it *het kunstgebit* meaning "false teeth", which is what it looks like when viewed from across the River Amstel. There are guided tours of the building, but not on days when there are matinée performances.

NIGHTLIFE

ROYAL CONCERTGEBOUW tram 2, 3, 5, 12, 16
Concertgebouwplein 2-6 (1071 LN); tel. 6718345. Bookings: daily 10 a.m.-7 p.m. After 7 p.m. bookings are only taken for that evening's performance.
The Concertgebouw is world renowned, partly due to the Concertgebouw Orchestra. It is a beautiful building with excellent acoustics. The main auditorium has a particularly intimate feel to it. The repertoire is predominantly classical, but occasional jazz and pop concerts are given.

SOETERIJN **18** B1 tram 9
Linnaeusstraat 2 (1092 CK); tel. 5688500. Bookings: Monday to Friday 10 a.m.-4 p.m.
This theatre is housed in the Royal Tropical Institute. It describes itself as a platform for non-western culture and presents a programme of films, music, dance and plays from Africa, Asia, the Middle East and Latin America. The theatre restaurant serves specialities from around the world.

POP AND ROCK CONCERTS

DE MELKWEG **6** B2 tram 1, 2, 5, 6, 7, 10
Lijnsbaangracht 234a (1017 PH); tel. 6241777. Sunday to Thursday 10 a.m.-2 a.m., Friday, Saturday 10 a.m.-3 p.m. Box office: Monday to Friday noon-5 p.m., Wednesday to Friday from 7.30 p.m., Saturday, Sunday from 4 p.m.
A former milk factory, hence the name (known as the Milky Way in English). It has been converted to a cultural centre for the city's youth. De Melkweg became widely renowned in the 1960s and it is still one of Amsterdam's major rock venues. Food, theatre, film, photography and art are also on the menu.

PARADISO **17** C1 tram 2, 6, 7
Weteringschans 6-8 (1017 SG); tel. 6264521. Opening times vary, depending on the show. Membership for a month: f 3.
Formerly a Protestant church, now Amsterdam's premier rock temple. All the major names in rock have performed in this legendary venue, although it is much too small to accommodate bands once they have made it into the big time. Paradiso also organizes congresses, lectures and chamber concerts in an attempt to reach a larger audience (and to continue to serve its greying old faithfuls).

DISCOS AND NIGHTCLUBS

JAZZ CAFÉS

ALTO 6 B2 tram 1, 2, 5, 6, 7, 10
Korte Leidsedwarsstraat 115 (1017 PX); tel. 6263249. Daily 9 p.m.-3 a.m.
A late-night drinking haunt where live music, from rap to folk, from heavy metal to jazz, is played seven nights a week.

BIMHUIS 11 D1 Ⓜ Nieuwmarkt
Oude Schans 73-77 (1011 KW); tel. 6233373. Monday to Thursday 8 p.m.-2 a.m., Friday, Saturday 8 p.m.-3 a.m.
Amsterdam's major jazz venue and home of the Union of Improvising Musicians (the BIM, in Dutch). It is the centre of The Netherlands' quirky and fascinating jazz tradition, which ranges from brass band to Latin funk.

JOSEPH LAM tram 3 🚌 28
Van Diemenstraat 8 (1013 NH); tel. 6228086. Saturday 9 p.m.-3 a.m. Admission f 6.
A modest jazz club, sited way out in the western docks. The club can be hired for parties the rest of the week.

DISCOS AND NIGHTCLUBS

DANSEN BIJ JANSEN 10 A1 tram 1, 2, 5
Handboogstraat 11 (1012 XN); tel. 6201779. Sunday to Thursday 10 p.m.-2 a.m., Friday, Saturday 10 p.m.-5 a.m.
Far too well known and hence often far too busy. Dansen bij Jansen's is small enough to give you a free sauna on crowded nights.

ESCAPE 10 B2 tram 4, 9, 14
Rembrandtsplein 11-15 (1017 CT); tel. 6223542. Thursday 10 p.m.-3 a.m., Friday to Sunday 10 p.m.-4 a.m.
The biggest disco in Amsterdam. Laser lights, video clips and the most popular of pop.

HOMOLULU 10 A2 tram 1, 2, 5
Kerkstraat 23 (1017 GA); tel. 6246387. Sunday to Thursday 10 a.m.-4 a.m., Friday, Saturday 10 p.m.-5 a.m.
A gay disco for a mixed clientele. Sunday is karaoke night.

NIGHTLIFE

IT 11 C2 tram 4, 9, 14
Amstelstraat 24 (1017 DA); tel. 6240111. Sunday, Wednesday, Thursday 10 p.m.-4 a.m., Friday, Saturday 10 p.m.-5 a.m.
The largest acid-house disco in Amsterdam. Largely gay.

KORSAKOFF 6 B2 tram 7, 10
Lijnbaansgracht 161 (1016 VX); tel. 6257854. Sunday to Thursday 10 p.m.-2 a.m., Friday, Saturday 11 p.m.-3 a.m.
An alternative disco, next door to Miles (see below). Live bands play every Wednesday, when admission is just ƒ 2.50. The rest of the week, admission is free. The musical bent changes nightly, with industrial, hard-core punk and techno on Sundays.

MAZZO 6 B2 tram 14, 17
Rozengracht 114 (1016 NH); tel. 6267500. Sunday to Thursday 11 p.m.-4 a.m., Friday, Saturday 11 p.m.-5 a.m.
Remember the street number, because the front of Mazzo changes monthly. Hard and progressive music, as opposed to head-banging disco, is on the turntable.

MILES 6 B2 tram 7, 10
Lijnbaansgracht 163 (1016 VX); tel. 6270495. Sunday to Thursday 10 p.m.-3 a.m., Friday, Saturday 10 p.m.-4 a.m.
Salsa and funk, with regular live bands from Amsterdam's Caribbean and Latin community. Admission is free, but the cloakroom is compulsory.

ODEON 10 A1 tram 1, 2, 5
Singel 460 (1017 AW); tel. 6249711. Sunday to Thursday 10 p.m.-4 a.m., Friday, Saturday 10 p.m.-5 a.m.
A mainly student disco in a beautiful venue. A puny sound system in the cellar pumps out music from the 1950s to the 1970s.

ROXY 10 A1 tram 1, 2, 5
Singel 489 (1012 WD); tel. 6200354. Wednesday, Thursday 11 p.m.-4 a.m., Friday, Saturday 11 p.m.-5 a.m.
Located in the former Roxy cinema. The original Art Deco interior has been restored and is now home to an acid-house disco. Dress trendily and you might just get in.

THE SOUL KITCHEN 11 C2 tram 4, 9, 14
Amstelstraat 32 (1017 DA); tel. 6202333. Wednesday, Thursday, Sunday 10 p.m.-4 a.m., Friday, Saturday 10 p.m.-5 a.m.

RED-LIGHT DISTRICT

A new disco for old timers. Soul and Motown is on the menu; house is off. The Kitchen takes half a teacup of bass, a pound of fatback drums, places them on the burner and beats well.

ZORBA THE BUDDHA 8 B2   tram 4, 9, 14, 16, 24, 25
Oudezijds Voorburgwal 216 (1012 GJ); tel. 6259642. Thursday, Sunday 10 p.m.-3 a.m., Friday, Saturday 10 p.m.-4 a.m.
Although it started as a Baghwan disco (as the name suggests), Zorba is now more mainstream-trendy for the young crowd.

RED-LIGHT DISTRICT

The Red-Light District, to the east of Dam Square, has been a centre for prostitution for centuries. Yet the sight of women of many shapes, sizes, ages and nationalities displaying their wares for all to see, from the dubious comfort of red-velvet, wickerwork or black-leather chairs can still surprise the foreign visitor. The women have grown accustomed to being a major tourist attraction, but they still don't like cameras. So unless you feel like a cooling swim in a canal, take your memories home in your mind and not on film.

CASA ROSSO EROTIC THEATRE 9 C2   Ⓜ Nieuwmarkt
Oudezijds Achterburgwal 106-108 (1012 DS); tel. 6278954. Daily 8 p.m.-2 a.m.
The Netherlands' most famous live sex show. No holds are barred, but all is bared. Predictably, men make up most of the audience, but women do not need to feel (unduly) embarrassed about attending.

CUL-DE-SAC 9 C2   Ⓜ Nieuwmarkt
Oudezijds Achterburgwal 99 (1012 DD); tel. 6254548. Sunday to Thursday 2 p.m.-1 a.m., Friday, Saturday 2 p.m.-2 a.m.
A quiet bar in the heart of the Red-Light District (it calls itself an oasis in a sea of madness). It has a regular local following and you might also bump into a performer from one of the local sex clubs.

YAB YUM 10 A1   tram 1, 2, 5
Singel 295 (1012 WH); tel. 6249503. Daily 8 p.m.-4 a.m.
The most exclusive and chic sex club in Amsterdam. It even boasts its own limousine service. Not in the Red-Light District, but discreetly located among the banks, offices and embassies on Singel.

NIGHTLIFE

GAY

Amsterdam has a name as a major gay centre: the San Francisco of Europe. The city has a large and vocal gay population and its social/night life is concentrated in three main areas of the centre: Warmoesstraat, Reguliersdwarsstraat and Amstelstraat/Amstel. The city also has a monument (Homomonument) to the gay and lesbian victims of World War II. It is located by the Westerkerk in the form of a huge triangle extending into the Keizersgracht.

AMSTEL TAVEERNE 10 B2   tram 4, 9, 14
Amstel 54 (1017 AB); tel. 6234254. Daily 3 p.m.-1 a.m.
One of many brown cafés for mustachioed gays along the River Amstel. In quite a few of them, female guests are not made to feel at home.

APRIL 10 B2   tram 1, 2, 4, 5, 9, 14, 16, 24, 25
Reguliersdwarsstraat 37 (1017 BK); tel. 6259572. Sunday to Thursday 2 p.m.-1 a.m., Friday, Saturday 2 p.m.-2 a.m.
A modern and trendy café; a favourite with the up-market gay scene.

ARGOS 8 B2   tram 4, 9, 16, 24, 25
Warmoesstraat 37 (1012 HV); tel. 6226595. Daily 8 p.m.-4 a.m., Sunday earlier closing.
Leather bar on the edge of the Red-Light District.

COC 6 B2   tram 13, 14, 17
Rozenstraat 14 (1016 NX); tel. 6263087/6234079. Dancing: Friday 10 p.m.-3 a.m., women only on Saturday 10 p.m.-3 a.m.
The home of the Dutch gay pressure group, COC. A café, bar and disco are run for gay men and women.

COCK-RING 8 B2   tram 4, 9, 16, 24, 25
Warmoesstraat 96 (1012 JH); tel. 6239604. Sunday to Thursday 10 p.m.-5 a.m., Friday, Saturday 10 p.m.-7 a.m.
A gay disco for all types: there are no dress restrictions. Spectacular lights, great sound and lasers. Women are only admitted on Sundays.

DESMET GAY CINEMA 12 A2   tram 7, 9, 14
Plantage Middenlaan 4a (1018 DD); tel. 6273434.
This straight film house also programmes gay films at midnight on Saturday and 4 p.m. on Sunday.

GAY

GAY AND LESBIAN SWITCHBOARD
Tel. 6236565. Daily 10 a.m.-10 p.m.
Information and advice.

HAVANA 10 B2   tram 1, 2, 4, 5, 9, 14, 16, 24, 25
Reguliersdwarsstraat 17 (1017 BJ); tel. 6206788. Monday to Friday 4 p.m.-1 a.m., Saturday, Sunday 2 p.m.-2 a.m.
A modern café with a disco upstairs.

SAAREIN 6 B2   tram 7, 10, 17
Elandstraat 119 (1016 RX); tel. 6234901. Monday 8 p.m.-1 a.m., Sunday, Tuesday to Thursday 3 p.m.-1 a.m., Friday, Saturday 3 p.m.-2 a.m.
One of the few women's bars in Amsterdam. A brown café with no men.

LA STRADA 8 B1   tram 1, 2, 5, 13, 17
Nieuwezijds Voorburgwal 94-96 (1012 NK); tel. 6250276. Daily 4 p.m.-1 a.m., kitchen 6 -10 p.m.
A meeting place for gay and mixed couples. Reasonable cuisine is served and monthly art exhibitions are held.

THERMOS DAY 6 B2   tram 7, 10
Raamstraat 33 (1016 XL); Monday to Friday noon-11 p.m., Saturday, Sunday noon-6 p.m.
Gay sauna (admission ƒ 22.50) for the daytime sauna lover. Thermos Night is located on Kerkstraat 58-60 and is open from 11 p.m. to 8 a.m.

VROLIJK 8 A2   tram 1, 2, 4, 5, 9, 14, 16, 24, 25
Paleisstraat 135 (1012 ZL); tel. 6235142. Monday to Friday 10 a.m.-6 p.m., Thursday 10 a.m.-9 p.m, Saturday 11 a.m.-5 p.m.
Gay and lesbian fiction and non-fiction. Half of the stock is in English. Posters and postcards are among the other wares sold on the two floors.

VROUWENBOEKHANDEL XANTIPPE 6 B2   tram 1, 2, 5
Prinsengracht 290 (1016 HJ); tel. 6235854. Monday 1-6 p.m., Tuesday to Friday 10 a.m.-6 p.m.
A women's bookshop near the English Bookshop and the women's café, Saarein. It stocks a huge selection of feminist literature.

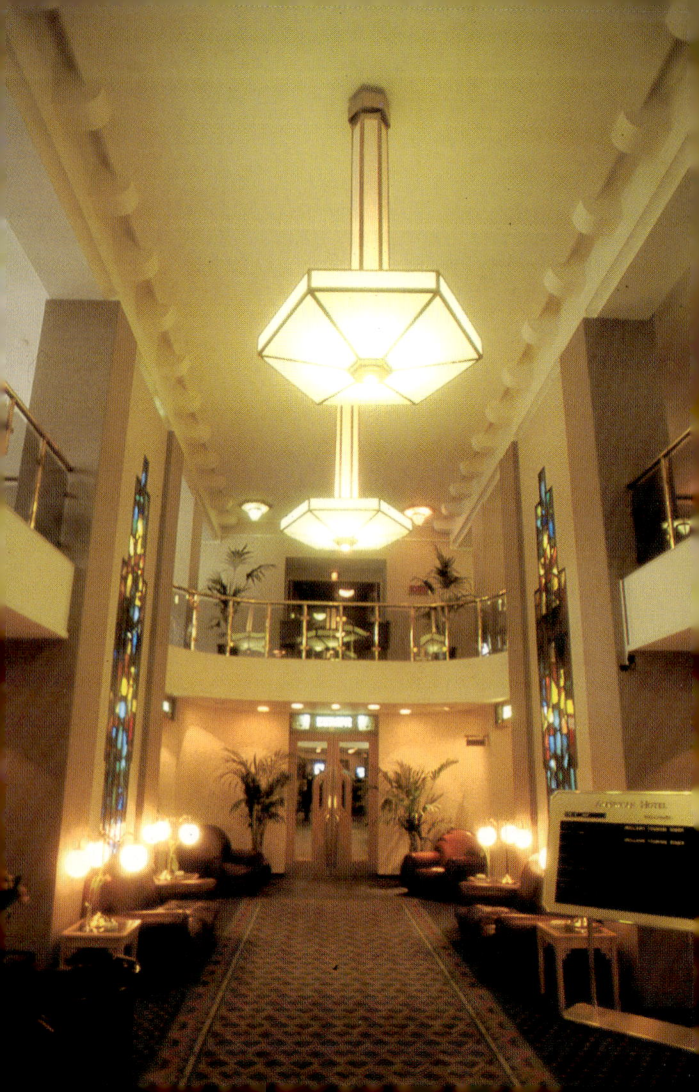

HOTELS

Amsterdam is a small town with big city aspirations. For its size, it has a relatively large amount of hotel accommodation to suit all pockets. This has developed and is maintained largely thanks to the congress trade and of course the tourists. Yet for a city as interesting to the visitor as Amsterdam, there always seems to be a shortage of reasonably priced accommodation and in peak seasons it is always advisable to book well in advance.

The VVV tourist office has its own hotel booking service for late-comers: join the queue at the tourist office facing Central Station or call 6266444.

The following selections are from the various categories on offer. The VVV tourist office operates a star system, but this is based on a listing of facilities which may not always be relevant to those seeking a good night's rest between the exertions of getting to know the city. The following list has been compiled by price and comprises recommended hotels offering good value for money, irrespective of whether there is a lift or all mod cons. All prices include breakfast, which ranges from Continental to international, and can include bread and jam along with eggs, bacon, cornflakes, muesli and the Dutch additions of ham and cheese as well as a variety of ginger bread called breakfast cake (*ontbijtkoek*).

Following the campsites and youth accommodation, hotels have been divided into the categories Budget (under *f* 100), Medium-price (*f* 100-*f*200), Deluxe (*f* 200-*f*400) and Top-price (over *f* 400).

CAMPSITES

GAASPER CAMPING
Ⓜ Gaasperplas
Loosdrechtdreef 7 (1108 AZ); tel. 6967326.
An excellent family campsite with all the advantages of a rural location, yet conveniently situated at the end of the metro line.

The American Hotel on Leidseplein is something of a city tradition, established in 1880 and full of character. Its Jugendstil Restaurant is protected as an architectural monument.

HOTELS

VLIEGENBOS 12 B1 🚌 32, 39
Meeuwenlaan 138 (1022 AM); tel. 6368855.
A campsite for young travellers, just across the River IJ in the north of the city.

ZEEBURG 🚌 22
Zuider IJdijk 44 (1095 KN); tel. 6944430.
A youth campsite looking out over the IJsselmeer to the east of Amsterdam.

YOUTH HOSTELS

ADAM & EVA 12 B2 tram 6, 7, 10
Sarphatistraat 105 (1018 GA); tel. 6246206. 78 beds in dormitories, f 17 per night. No credit cards.
A fine place to stay for those travelling rough.

HANS BRINKER 10 A2 tram 1, 2, 5, 6, 7, 10
Kerkstraat 136 (1017 GR); tel. 6220687, fax 6382060. 255 beds, singles f 67–f 86, doubles f 103–f 139, dormitory f 29.
An excellent student and youth hostel in a central location near Leidseplein.

EBEN HAEZER 6 B2 tram 13, 14
Bloemstraat 179 (1016 LA); tel. 6244717. 114 beds, dormitory f 14. No credit cards.
A Christian youth hostel in the heart of the Jordaan. Don't get back too late after a night out: there's a curfew.

THE SHELTER 9 C2 Ⓜ Nieuwmarkt
Barndesteeg 21 (1012 BV); tel. 6253230, fax 6232282. 166 beds, dormitory f 14. No credit cards.
Van Gogh once taught at the Sunday School on this site in the heart of the Red-Light District. Now it houses a Christian youth hostel with a midnight curfew (1 a.m. at weekends). Not recommended for single women, who may find the neighbours somewhat daunting.

BUDGET HOTELS (UP TO ƒ 100)

SLEEP-IN MAURITSKADE **18** A1 tram 6, 9, 10, 14
's Gravesandestraat 51 (1092 AA); tel. 6947444. 550 beds, dormitory ƒ 13. No credit cards.
Once a nunnery, this large building in Oosterpark now houses a hostel and rehearsal spaces for bands and theatre groups. It opens to admit new guests at 4 p.m.

STADSDOELEN (IYHF) **11** C1 Ⓜ Nieuwmarkt
Kloveniersburgwal 97 (1011 KB); tel. 6246832. 184 beds, dormitory ƒ 20. No credit cards.
A youth hostel near the Red-Light District. Those wanting a quiet stay in Amsterdam would be better off at the Vondelpark hostel (see below).

VONDELPARK (IYHF) **16** A1 tram 1, 2, 5, 6
Zandpad 5 (1054 GA); tel. 6831744, fax 6166591. 300 beds, dormitory ƒ 20, doubles ƒ 45. No credit cards.
Many a luxury hotel would be jealous of this youth hostel's prime location, overlooking the Vondelpark behind the new Byzantium complex.

ZEEZICHT **12** B1 🚋 28
Piet Heinkade 15 (1019 BR); tel. 6278706. 30 beds, dormitory ƒ 40.
Four young visitors can have a room to themselves for a bargain price. Not for the faint-hearted: Zeezicht also provides a home for problem kids.

BUDGET HOTELS (UP TO ƒ 100)

ACACIA **6** B1 tram 3
Lindengracht 251 (1015 KH); tel. 6221460, fax 6380748. 33 beds, singles ƒ 90, doubles ƒ 110.
On a quiet corner in the heart of the Jordaan, facing the Lijnbaansgracht and adjacent to the Saturday street market. Don't park outside the front on Friday night.

ASTERISK **17** C1 tram 6, 7, 10
Den Texstraat 16 (1017 ZA); tel. 6262396, fax 6382790. 43 beds, singles ƒ 60–ƒ 85, doubles ƒ 75–ƒ 149.
A modest hotel near the Weteringscircuit (by the Heineken Brewery). The kind of place to use as a base.

HOTELS

BELGA 6 B2   tram 13, 14, 17
Hartenstraat 8 (1016 CB); tel. 6249080, fax 6236862. 22 beds, singles f 65, doubles f 100–f 115.
A small yet very popular hotel among the exquisite shops and restaurants that cram the narrow streets between the canals. Excellent value.

ENGELAND 16 B1   tram 1, 2, 3, 5, 6, 12
Roemer Visscherstraat 30a (1054 EZ); tel. 6129691, fax 6184575. 75 beds, singles f 60–f 115, doubles f 105–f 155.
Located between Vondelpark and Leidseplein, this hotel is a bargain in an expensive area.

L'ESPÉRANCE 16 B1   tram 6, 7, 10
Stadhouderskade 49 (1072 AA); tel. 6714049. 13 beds, singles f 65–f 70, doubles f 100–f 125.
A tiny hotel providing a secluded setting for elderly visitors. Very close to the Rijksmuseum.

FANTASIA 11 D2   Ⓜ Waterlooplein, Weesperplein
Nieuwe Keizersgracht 16 (1018 DR); tel. 6238259, fax 6223913. 38 beds, singles f 70–f 95, doubles f 105–f 140.
Good value, close to the River Amstel and the Royal Carré Theatre.

DE FILOSOOF 16 A1   tram 1, 6
Anna v.d. Vondelstraat 4-6 (1054 GZ); tel. 6833013, fax 6853750. 54 beds, singles f 90–f 165, doubles f 110–f 175.
An old-style Dutch hotel in a quiet street near Vondelpark. Thoroughly recommended.

FOX 17 C1   tram 6, 7, 10
Weteringschans 67 (1017 RX); tel. 6228338, fax 6243805. 40 beds, singles f 45–f 60, doubles f 75–f 90.
A great place to stay for the young. The staircases are too steep and narrow for more portly or mature visitors.

DE GERSTEKORREL 8 B2   tram 16, 24, 25
Damstraat 22-24 (1012 JM); tel. 6249771, fax 6232640. 55 beds, singles f 70–f 150, doubles f 100–f 180.
An old-fashioned hotel in a very central location. Revellers in the Damstraat may keep you awake.

GROENHOF 16 A1   tram 1, 6
Vondelstraat 74 (1054 GN); tel. 6168221. 60 beds, singles f 75–f 105, doubles f 110–f 145.
Excellent value in a prime location.

BUDGET HOTELS (UP TO ƒ 100)

VAN HAALEN 6 B2   tram 1, 2, 5, 6, 7, 10
Prinsengracht 520 (1017 KJ); tel. 6264334. 40 beds, singles ƒ 75–ƒ 100, doubles ƒ 105–ƒ 160. No credit cards.
A fine place to stay, on Prinsengracht near Leidseplein.

KING 6 B2   tram 1, 2, 5, 6, 7, 10
Leidsekade 85-86 (1017 PN); tel. 6249603, fax 6207277. 65 beds, singles ƒ 55–ƒ 80, doubles ƒ 75–ƒ 125.
Young visitors are well-catered for at this hotel, situated next to Bellevue Theatre and close to the nightlife around Leidseplein.

DE MUNCK 17 D1   tram 4, 6, 7, 10
Achtergracht 3 (1017 WL); tel. 6236283, fax 6206647. 24 beds, singles ƒ 80–ƒ 90, doubles ƒ 110–ƒ 160. No credit cards.
A high-quality hotel at a budget price. Situated on a quiet canal near the River Amstel.

PARK LANE 7 D2   tram 9, 14
Plantage Parklaan 16 (1018 ST); tel. 6224804. 22 beds, singles ƒ 65–ƒ 115, doubles ƒ 135–ƒ 155.
The Park Lane Hotel is indeed on Parklaan between the Jewish Historical Museum and Artis Zoo.

PARKZICHT 16 B1   tram 1, 2, 3, 5, 6, 12
Roemer Visscherstraat 33 (1054 EW); tel. 6181954, fax 6180897. 27 beds, singles ƒ 55–ƒ 85, doubles ƒ 125–ƒ 145.
With a little effort you can see Vondelpark from this establishment, which is a stone's throw from Leidseplein.

PIET HEIN 16 B1   tram 1, 2, 5, 6, 7, 10
Vossiusstraat 53 (1071 AK); tel. 6628375, fax 6621526. 55 beds, singles ƒ 80–ƒ 110, doubles ƒ 115–ƒ 155.
A pleasant hotel, looking out over Vondelpark near Leidseplein.

REMBRANDT 12 A2   tram 1
Plantage Middenlaan 17 (1018 DA); tel. 6272714, fax 6380293. 25 beds, singles ƒ 70–ƒ 95, doubles ƒ 95–ƒ 135.
Facing Artis and not far from Rembrandt's own home, this small hotel has an excellent reputation.

ROKIN 8 B2   tram 4, 16, 24, 25, 89
Rokin 73 (1012 KL); tel. 6267456, fax 6256453. 80 beds, singles ƒ 55–ƒ 115, doubles ƒ 75–ƒ 130.
A remarkable bargain in the heart of the city. But Rokin is not the quietest of areas and parking might be a problem.

HOTELS

RONNIE 8 A2   tram 13, 14
Raadhuisstraat 41 (1016 DD); tel. 6242821, fax 6269448. 21 beds, singles ƒ 45, doubles ƒ 90.
A centrally-located hotel with plenty of trams and cars nearby, should you need an alarm call.

SEVEN BRIDGES 10 B2   tram 16, 24, 25
Reguliersgracht 31 (1017 LK); tel. 6231329. 22 beds, singles ƒ 75–ƒ 120, doubles ƒ 100–ƒ 155. No credit cards.
The seven bridges over the Reguliersgracht are renowned and can be seen in all their glory by everyone who takes a boat trip on the canals. The hotel is close to the Rembrandtplein.

DE STERN 11 C2   tram 4
Utrechtsestraat 18 (1017 VN); tel. 6265619. 15 beds, singles ƒ 50–ƒ 75, doubles ƒ 95–ƒ 110. No credit cards.
An excellent choice for those wanting a reliable hotel without the frills.

THORBECKE 10 B2   tram 4, 16 , 24, 25
Thorbeckeplein 3 (1017 CS); tel. 6232601, fax 6382559. 22 beds, singles ƒ 50–ƒ 65, doubles ƒ 80–ƒ 150.
On Rembrandtplein in the heart of the entertainment area.

TITUS 6 B2   tram 1, 2, 5, 6, 7, 10
Leidsekade 74 (1017 PM); tel. 6265758, fax 6385870. 50 beds, singles ƒ 65–ƒ 75, doubles ƒ 100–ƒ 120.
One of several bargain hotels on a quiet canalside near Leidseplein.

VICTORIE 18 A2   tram 12, 25
Victorieplein 40-42 (1078 PH); tel. 6623233, fax 6766398. 52 beds, singles ƒ 85, doubles ƒ 120–ƒ 135.
Near the RAI congress and exhibition centre to the south of the city.

MEDIUM-PRICE HOTELS (ƒ 100-ƒ 200)

AMS HOTEL HOLLAND 16 B1   tram 1, 2, 3, 5, 6, 12
P.C. Hooftstraat 162 (1071 CH); tel. 6764253, fax 6765956. 126 beds, singles ƒ 110–ƒ 160, doubles ƒ 160–ƒ 230.
Reasonably priced, considering its position on The Netherlands' most exclusive and expensive shopping street.

MEDIUM-PRICE HOTELS (ƒ 100-ƒ 200)

AGORA   **10** A1   tram 1, 2, 5
Singel 462 (1017 AW); tel. 6272200, fax 6272202. 27 beds, singles ƒ 98–ƒ 150, doubles ƒ 105–ƒ 180.
A fine hotel near the flower market and Spui.

ALTEA AMSTERDAM   60
Joan Muyskenweg 10 (1096 CJ); tel. 6658181, fax 6948735. 356 beds, singles ƒ 185–ƒ 205, doubles ƒ 215–ƒ 240.
An excellent motel on the outskirts by the motorway to Utrecht.

AMBASSADE   **7** C2   tram 13, 14
Herengracht 341 (1016 AZ); tel. 6262333, fax 6245321. 103 beds, singles ƒ 190–ƒ 210, doubles ƒ 240–ƒ 250.
Modest yet exclusive, a favourite of seasoned travellers who want peace and quiet in their hotel.

AMSTERDAM WIECHMANN   **6** B2   tram 7, 10
Prinsengracht 328-332 (1016 HX); tel. 6263321, fax 6268962. 77 beds, singles ƒ 135–ƒ 150, doubles ƒ 175–ƒ 200. No credit cards.
Once the haunt of rock bands playing in Amsterdam, Wiechmann is now a tranquil and comfortable family hotel on a quiet section of Prinsengracht.

BORGMANN   **16** A1   tram 2
Koningslaan 48 (1075 AE); tel. 6735252. 31 beds, singles ƒ 125–ƒ 135, doubles ƒ 195–ƒ 205.
A fine hotel in one of Amsterdam's quietest and most exclusive areas, by Vondelpark.

CANAL HOUSE   **6** B1   tram 7, 10
Keizersgracht 148 (1015 CX); tel. 6225182, fax 6241317. 36 beds, singles ƒ 170, doubles ƒ 190–ƒ 235.
This old-fashioned, family hotel is a favourite with many regular visitors to the city.

DELTA   **9** C1   tram 4, 9, 16, 24, 25
Damrak 42 (1012 LK); tel. 6202626, fax 6203513. 80 beds, singles ƒ 80–ƒ 115, doubles ƒ 95–ƒ 150.
Excellent service, all mod cons and a great restaurant are features of this worthwhile hotel, on Amsterdam's main street, near Central Station.

HOTELS

FLIPPER **18** A2   tram 4, 12, 25
Borssenburgstraat 5 (1078 VA); tel. 6761932, fax 6712053. 31 beds, singles f 75–f 120, doubles f 95–f 140.
A friendly hotel with cheerful staff. Make jokes about dolphins at your own risk.

MAAS **6** B2   tram 1, 2, 5, 6, 7, 10
Leidsekade 91 (1017 PN); tel. 6233868, fax 6222613. 40 beds, singles f 85–f 175, doubles f 110–f 300.
Suitably named after the river that runs through Rotterdam, this is Amsterdam's only hotel with waterbeds.

DE MOLEN **17** C1   tram 4
Prinsengracht 1015 (1017 KN); tel. 6231666, fax 6274946. 59 beds, singles f 145–f 165, doubles f 180–f 225.
Excellent value on Prinsengracht near the River Amstel. Within walking distance of the Muziektheater and the Carré.

NOVA **8** A2   tram 1, 2, 5, 13, 17
N.Z. Voorburgwal 276 (1012 RS); tel. 6230066, fax 6272026. 134 beds, singles f 115–f 153, doubles f 145–f 198.
A modern hotel near Dam Square and the Royal Palace.

OWL **16** B1   tram 1, 2, 3, 5, 6, 12
Roemer Visscherstraat 1 (1054 EV); tel. 6189484, fax 6189441. 63 beds, singles f 105–f 130, doubles f 135–f 175.
A comfy family hotel, in a secluded area near Vondelpark.

PRINS HENDRIK **9** C1   tram 4, 9, 16, 24, 25
Prins Hendrikkade 53 (1012 AC); tel. 6277931, fax 6274391. 40 beds, singles f 100–f 150, doubles f 160–f 200.
A modest hotel in an area where most are more expensive, or less salubrious.

TOREN **6** B1   22
Keizersgracht 164 (1015 CZ); tel. 6226352, fax 6269705. 90 beds, singles f 125–f 180, doubles f 160–f 235.
Toren boasts a fine, canal-side location near the Jordaan.

VONDEL **16** B1   tram 1, 6
Vondelstraat 28 (1054 GE); tel. 6120120, fax 6854321. 60 beds, singles f 120–f 125, doubles f 160–f 175.
An excellent hotel close to Leidseplein and Vondelpark.

DELUXE HOTELS (*f* 200-*f* 400)

DELUXE HOTELS (*f* 200-*f* 400)

AMERICAN 6 B2   tram 1, 2, 5, 6, 7, 10
Leidsekade 97 (1017 PN); tel. 6245322, fax 6253236. 332 beds, singles f 325–f 375, doubles f 400–f 450.
The American Hotel (Americain to the locals) is a legend. Its imposing architecture, marking the transition from Art Nouveau to Amsterdam School, houses a fine hotel and a bar which is still one of the city's prime meeting places. It is well worth a visit even if you are not planning to stay.

APOLLOFIRST 16 A2   tram 12, 25
Apollolaan 123 (1077 AP); tel. 6730333, fax 6750348. 72 beds, singles f 200–f 235, doubles f 210–f 275.
This suburban hotel with friendly service has recently opened an excellent French à la carte restaurant on the premises.

ATLAS 16 A1   tram 3, 12, 24
Van Eeghenstraat 64 (1071 GK); tel. 6766336, fax 6717633. 47 beds, singles f 150–f 170, doubles f 190–f 210.
Set in a quiet and dignified area near the Concertgebouw, the Atlas is a generally well-regarded hotel.

CARANSA KARENA 10 B2   tram 9, 14
Rembrandtplein 19 (1017 CT); tel. 6229455, fax 6222773. 132 beds, singles f 265, doubles f 335.
The central location and meeting facilities make this hotel perfect for a business-stay in the city.

DIKKER & THIJS 6 B2   tram 1, 2, 5, 6, 7, 10
Prinsengracht 444 (1017 KE); tel. 6267721, fax 6258986. 47 beds, singles f 240–f 265, doubles f 300–f 350.
A small and high-class hotel linked to one of Amsterdam's most exclusive restaurants and delicatessens.

DOELEN KARENA 10 B1   tram 9, 14
Nieuwe Doelenstraat 24 (1012 CP); tel. 6220722, fax 6221084. 160 beds, singles f 265–f 295, doubles f 335–f 375.
One of the oldest hotels in Amsterdam, this is reputed to be where Rembrandt painted his famous *Nightwatch*. The building has its own landing stage for boats and water taxis.

HOTELS

REMBRANDT KARENA   **7** C2   tram 13, 14
Herengracht 255 (1016 BJ); tel. 6221727, fax 6250630. 215 beds, singles f 230, doubles f 300.
The modest canalside location near the Royal Palace belies a fine hotel. One of the Karena chain.

SCANDIC CROWN VICTORIA   **9** C1   tram 4, 9, 16, 24, 25
Damrak 1-6 (1012 LG); tel. 6234255, fax 6274259. 622 beds, singles f 295–f 325, doubles f 370–f 395.
Some claim this is the city's best hotel. Its location could hardly be better, facing Central Station on the corner of Damrak.

SCHILLER KARENA   **10** B2   tram 9, 14
Rembrandtplein 26-36 (1017 CV); tel. 6231660, fax 6240098. 160 beds, singles f 225–f 375, doubles f 295–f 375.
Named after the Dutch painter Fritz Schiller, much of whose work is still on show in the hotel. It has a street café on Amsterdam's most entertaining square.

SWISSOTEL AMSTERDAM ASCOT   **8** B2   tram 4, 9, 16, 24, 25
Damrak 95-98 (1012 LP); tel. 6260066, fax 6270982. 210 beds, singles f 245–f 295, doubles f 310–f 360.
A good place to stay, if you don't mind the name.

TOP-PRICE HOTELS (OVER *f* 400)

AMSTERDAM HILTON   **16** A2   🚌 66
Apollolaan 138-140 (1077 BG); tel. 6780780, fax 6626688. 397 beds, singles f 390–f 480, doubles f 460–f 550.
You could—like John Lennon and Yoko Ono—spend the whole of your stay in Amsterdam in a Hilton bed. The hotel certainly has enough facilities to keep you busy. Juliana's Bar has a major reputation and the Japanese restaurant, Kei, is one of Amsterdam's best.

GARDEN HOTEL   **16** B2   🚌 66
Dijsselhofplantsoen 7 (1077 BJ); tel. 6642121, fax 6799356. 196 beds, singles f 340, doubles f 420.
Modern four-colour designs and jacuzzis are present in all of the Garden's rooms. The hotel's restaurant, De Kersentuin, is the holder of one of Amsterdam's two Michelin stars.

TOP-PRICE HOTELS (OVER ƒ 400)

**HILTON INTERNATIONAL,
SCHIPHOL** by train from Central Station.
Herbergierstraat (1118 ZK); tel. 6034567. 391 beds, singles ƒ 395–ƒ 425, doubles ƒ 460–ƒ 490.
The only hotel in the immediate vicinity of the airport.

HOTEL DE L'EUROPE   10 B1 tram 9, 14
Nieuwe Doelenstraat 2-8 (1012 CP); tel. 6234836, fax 6242962. 180 beds, singles ƒ 385–ƒ 485, doubles ƒ 485–ƒ 610.
Centrally located between Dam Square, the Muziektheater and Rembrandtplein, this classic hotel is part of the Heineken empire. One of Amsterdam's most luxurious hotels.

PULITZER   6 B2 tram 13, 14
Prinsengracht 315-331 (1016 GZ); tel. 5235235, fax 6276753. 440 beds, singles ƒ 355–ƒ 420, doubles ƒ 395–ƒ 470.
Occupying beautifully-preserved canal houses, the Pulitzer is a favourite haunt for the seasoned traveller.

RAMADA RENAISSANCE HOTEL   8 B1
AMSTERDAM tram 4, 9, 16, 24, 25
Kattengat 1 (1012 SZ); tel. 6212223, fax 6275245. 864 beds, singles ƒ 355–ƒ 465, doubles ƒ 415–ƒ 525.
Formerly the Sonesta, the Ramada is one of the friendliest of Amsterdam's luxury hotels. It even stages classical concerts in the adjacent Old Lutheran Church.

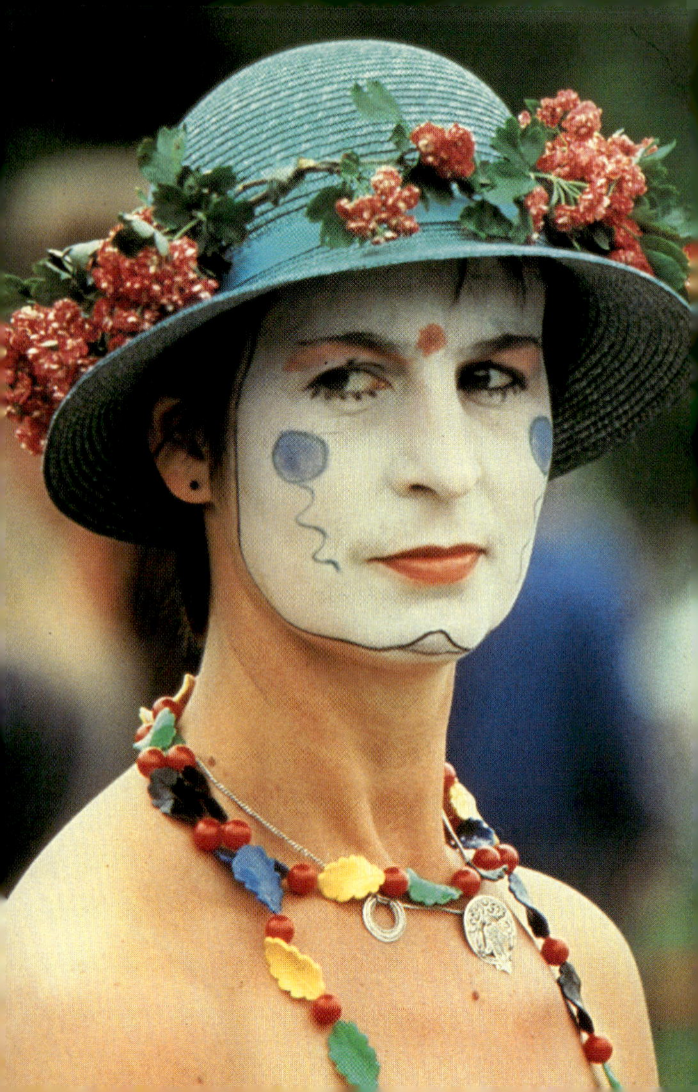

CHILDREN

Amsterdam may be a microcosmic world city for adults, but it is also a macrocosmic world city for children. The city has a wealth of places where children are in their element. These include Artis, one of the oldest zoos in the world (1838), and the Maritime Museum, with the fine East-India ship the *Amsterdam* (18th century). Amsterdam also has the bonus of being on a child-friendly scale, which puts everything in walking distance.

One warning: the car traffic and cyclists are less child friendly, which is why thousands of "little Amsterdammers" bollards have been sunk in the pavement by the roadside to provide as much protection as possible.

ATTRACTIONS

ARTIS ZOO   **12** A2   tram 7, 9, 14
Plantage Middenlaan 53 (1018 DC); tel. 5233400. Zoo: daily 9 a.m.-5 p.m., children's farm: daily 10 a.m.-1 p.m., 2-4.30 p.m. Admission: adults ƒ 16, under-10s ƒ 9.
Artis (the name is an abbreviation of Natura Artis Magistra) is the oldest zoo in Holland, dating from 1838. This friendly and diminutive zoo houses 600 animals. A ticket also admits you to the Zoological Museum, a unique aquarium (with 2,000 different fish), a spectacular planetarium and the children's farm. The seals can be fed at 11.30 a.m. and 3.30 p.m., the penguins at 3.30 p.m.

CIRCUS ELLEBOOG   **6** B2   tram 7, 10
Passeerdersgracht 32 (1016 XH); tel. 6269370. Saturday 1-5 p.m., Sunday 10.30 a.m.-4 p.m. (on alternate weekends). Admission: Saturday ƒ 5, Sunday ƒ 7.50.
Children from 6 to 16 can learn to juggle, walk the tight-rope, ride the unicycle and put on make-up. The staff speak English.

Street entertainment is part of life in Amsterdam, so there's plenty to keep the children amused.

CHILDREN

DIRIDAS PUPPET THEATRE 16 B1 tram 16
Hobbemakade 68 (1017 XM); tel. 6621588. Sunday 11 a.m. for under-5s. Saturday, Sunday 3 p.m. for over-5s. Book in advance.
Diridas puts on shows with marionettes and glove puppets. If warned in advance, performers can give a summary in English.

KINDERBOERDERIJ DE DIERENPIJP 17 D2 tram 4, 12
Lizzy Ansinghstraat 82 (1072 RD); tel. 6648303. Monday, Wednesday, Sunday 1-5 p.m. Admission free.
A traditional feature of the Dutch urban landscape: farm animals and pets in a small park for the benefit and edification of children. A visit to this children's farm in the Pijp can be combined nicely with a visit to the neighbouring NINT Museum of Technology.

KINDERBOERDERIJ DE UYLENBURG 15 C1 18, 19, 48, 64
Staalmeesterslaan 420 (1057 PH); tel. 6185235. May to August: daily 10 a.m.-5 p.m. September to April: daily 10 a.m.-4 p.m. Admission free.
This children's farm is in the expanse of the Rembrandtpark. There are free pony rides. Children can also build their own tree houses (under supervision).

DE KRAKELING 6 B2 tram 7, 10
Nieuwe Passeerdersstraat 1 (1016 XP); tel. 6253284. Wednesday, Saturday, Sunday 2 pm.
The Krakeling presents theatrical productions for a variety of age groups. Many are mime and puppet shows and hence also suitable for non-Dutch speakers. Check the monthly *Uitkrant* for programme details.

STEEPLE CLIMBING 9 C2
Oude Kerk: Monday, Thursday 2-5 p.m., Tuesday, Wednesday 11 a.m.-2 p.m. Westerkerk: Tuesday, Wednesday, Friday, Saturday: 2-5 p.m. Zuiderkerk: Wednesday: 2-5 p.m., Thursday, Friday 11 a.m.-2 p.m., Saturday 11 a.m.-4 p.m. Cost f 1. For addresses and further information, see Sights: Churches.
In the summer, the energetic can climb a number of 300-year-old church steeples, all under the supervision of a guide. The reward is some stunning views across the city.

TM-JUNIOR 18 B1 tram 3, 9, 10, 14
Linnaeusstraat 2 (1092 CK); tel. 5688300. Sunday noon-4 p.m. School holidays: Monday to Friday 11 a.m.-4 p.m. Admission: adults f 6, 6-12 f 3.
TM-Junior is a special young people's section of the Tropical Museum, providing children with a playful and direct impression of everyday life

EXCURSIONS OUTSIDE AMSTERDAM

in non-Western cultures. The museum re-opened in June 1992 after extensive renovations.

VOGELMARKT   **6** B1   tram 3, 10
Noordermarkt (1015 MV); Saturday 7-11 a.m.
Small and slowly being dwarfed by the adjacent crafts market, the Jordaan bird market is well worth a visit. Species range from canaries, to chickens and doves. There are also some rabbits: the Flemish Giant is an incredible sight, larger than the biggest tom cat.

EXCURSIONS OUTSIDE AMSTERDAM

CATTLE MARKET
By bus: No.100 from Central Station. By train to Purmerend from Central Station.
Purmerend Market, 26 kilometres (15 miles) north-east of Amsterdam. Cattle market: Tuesday. Cheese market: July to August, Thursday 11 a.m.-1 p.m.
Purmerend has seen explosive growth as a dormitory suburb, but the old village centre has remained intact, as has the cattle market held every Tuesday. Farmers from throughout the province of North Holland buy and sell using an age-old hand-clapping barter system. There is an old-fashioned Dutch cheese market on Thursdays in the summer (see also Walks, Tours and Day Trips).

DE EFTELING
By car: 120 kilometres (75 miles) south of Amsterdam. By train to Noord-Brabant from Central Station with an NS Day Excursion ticket (includes train, bus and admission).
Europaweg 1, Kaatsheuvel (5171 KW) Noord-Brabant; tel. 04167-88111. Easter to October: daily 10 a.m.-6 p.m. Admission f 21.
This Dutch Disneyland was designed by illustrator Anton Pieck and contains a fairytale forest with all the characters from Andersen and Grimm. Talking dustbins, a 19th-century carousel, a water organ and a spectacular roller-coaster complete this children's paradise.

LAND VAN OOIT
By car: 110 kilometres (69 miles) south. By train to Drunen NB from Central Station with an NS Day Excursion ticket (includes train, bus and admission).

CHILDREN

Parklaan 40, Drunen (5151 DG) Noord-Brabant; tel. 04163-77775. Easter to mid-October: 10 a.m.-6 p.m. daily. Admission f 14 adults, 4-11 f 12.
A fantasy park especially suitable for children under 12. All the fantasy vehicles (including water-bicycles shaped like a swan, cars like a shoe etc.) can be driven by the children. Fairy-tale figures are dotted around the site and there is also a puppet theatre.

LINNAEUSHOF

By car: 20 kilometres (12 miles) south-west of Amsterdam. By train to Bennebroek from Central Station with an NS Day Excursion ticket (includes train, bus and admission).
Rijksstraatweg 4, Bennebroek (2121 AE); tel. 02502-7624. April to October: daily 10 a.m.-6 p.m. Admission f 8.50.
A Wild West train, minigolf, water bikes and trampolines are among the 300 attractions for children on this former estate of the Swedish botanist Linnaeus. Woods, gardens and picnic sites are also on the site.

MADURODAM

By car: 57 kilometres (36 miles) south-west of Amsterdam. By train to The Hague from Central Station with an NS Day Excursion Ticket (includes train, bus, admission).
Haringkade 175, The Hague (2584 EE); tel. 070-3553900. March to May: daily 9 a.m.-10.30 p.m. June to August: daily 9 a.m.-11 p.m. October to January: daily 9 a.m.-6 p.m. Admission f 11 adults, f 6 2-12, under-2s free.
The important sights in The Netherlands can be found in miniature here. Exhibits include Schiphol, the Port of Rotterdam, the canals of Amsterdam and even modern architecture—all knee-high to Lilliput.

RESTAURANTS

COUNTRY HOUSE BOERDERIJ MEERZICHT 170, 171, 172
Koenenkade 56 (1081 KG) Amsterdamse Bos; tel. 6792744. March to October: daily noon-6 p.m. November to February: Sunday noon-6 p.m.
An ideal spot in which to eat pancakes after a visit to the surrounding parkland area. A special "Bos Bus" runs from Haarlemmermeer Station to the restaurant in the Amsterdamse Bos.

SHOPS

KINDERKOOKCAFE   **8** C2   Ⓜ Nieuwmarkt
Oudezijds Achterburgwal 193 (1012 DK); tel. 6253257. Saturday from 3 pm. (Monday to Friday: private parties only). Adults ƒ 13, children ƒ 10.
Roles are reversed in this restaurant: the children cook and the adults are the guests. The youthful chefs are brought along at 3 p.m. and at 6 p.m. the adults can come back to enjoy dinner. Book in advance, on Saturday from noon until 2 p.m.

THE PANCAKE BAKERY   **6** B2   tram 13, 14, 17
Prinsengracht 191 (1015 DS); tel. 6251333. Daily noon-9.30 p.m. From about ƒ 10.
The best assortment of pancakes in Amsterdam, with 55 varieties.

PAVILJOEN DE CAROUSSEL   **16** B1   tram 16, 24, 25
H.M. van Randwijkplantsoen (1017 SJ); tel. 6275880. Daily 9 a.m.-9 p.m. From about ƒ 10.
A spectacular range of pancakes are served here, only a few minutes' walk from the Rijksmuseum, opposite the Heineken Brewery. De Caroussel also has *poffertjes*, small fluffy pancakes doused in icing sugar, a traditional Dutch delicacy that children are mad about.

UPSTAIRS   **10** B1   tram 4, 9, 16, 24, 25
Grimburgwal 2 (1012 GA); tel. 6265603. Tuesday to Sunday 11 a.m. to 7 p.m. From ƒ 10.
A cosy, pancake restaurant in old-Dutch surroundings.

SHOPS

BELL TREE TOYS & GAMES   tram 6, 7, 10
Spiegelgracht 10 (1017 JR); tel. 6258830. Monday 1-4 p.m., Tuesday to Friday 9 a.m. to 6 p.m., Saturday 9 a.m.-5 p.m.
Specialists in antique dolls, mechanical toys and children's books. Adults might wince at the prices.

BEREND BOTJE   **15** D1   tram 1, 6
Zocherstraat 87 (1054 LW); tel. 6183349. Tuesday to Friday 10.30 a.m.-5 p.m.
A fine assortment of second-hand children's clothing is stocked in this shop.

CHILDREN

GOOCHEM WOODEN TOYS 16 B1 tram 3, 12
Constantijn Huygenstraat 29 (1054 BP); tel. 6124704. Tuesday to Friday 10 a.m.-6 p.m., Saturday 10 a.m.-5 p.m.
Some of Goochem's wooden toys are made in its own workshop.

KINDERBOEKWINKEL 8 A2 tram 1, 2, 5
Nieuwezijds Voorburgwal 344 (1012 RX); tel. 6227741. Tuesday to Friday 10 a.m.-6 p.m., Saturday 10 a.m.-5 p.m.
The Children's Bookshop has an enormous collection of books (some in English) for all ages. There is another branch at Rozengracht 44.

DE KINDERKLEDINGWINKEL 16 A2 tram 2
Valeriusstraat 35 (1071 MC); tel. 6640889. Tuesday to Friday 10 a.m.-4 p.m., Saturday 10 a.m.-5 p.m.
The Children's Clothes Shop makes and sells clothes for babies and children up to 10 years old.

LAMBIEK 10 A2 tram 1, 2, 5
Kerkstraat 78 (1017 GN); tel. 6267543. Monday to Friday 11 a.m.-6 p.m., Saturday 11 a.m.-5 p.m.
Lambiek opened its doors in 1968 as an eldorado for the cartoon-strip fan. The enormous and erudite range includes many collector's items. The gallery has a new exhibition every two months.

LANKAMP & BRINKMAN tram 7, 10
Spiegelgracht 19 (1017 JP); tel. 6234656. Monday 1-6 p.m., Tuesday to Friday 9 a.m-6 p.m., Saturday 10 a.m.-5 p.m.
The first floor of this bookshop has a large collection of prints and children's books from The Netherlands and abroad.

MECHANISCH SPEELGOED 6 B1 tram 3, 10
Westerstraat 67 (1015 LW); tel. 6381680. Monday, Wednesday to Saturday 11 a.m.-6 p.m. Closed on Tuesday.
A bizarre collection of old-fashioned toys in new versions finds shelf-space here. There are kaleidoscopes, puzzles, stickers and games, as well as an assortment of mechanical toys. Prices rise from 50 c to ƒ 200.

DE POPPENDOKTER 6 B2 tram 13, 14, 17
Reestraat 20 (1016 DN); tel. 6265274. Monday 1-6 p.m., Tuesday to Friday 10 a.m.-6 p.m., Saturday 10 a.m.-5 p.m.
Visit the doll's doctor to see the amazing collection of antique dolls, or to have a treasured doll repaired.

BABYSITTERS

STEMPELWINKEL POSTHUMUS   **10** A1   tram 1, 2, 5
St Luciensteeg 25 (1012 PM); tel. 6255812. Tuesday to Saturday 10 a.m.-4 p.m.
Rubber stamps are sold in all shapes and sizes here: from initials in gothic script, to animals and career icons. You'll also find a wide range of accessories.

'T SCHOOLTJE   **16** A1   tram 1, 2, 5
Overtoom 87 (1054 HC); tel. 6830444. Tuesday to Friday 10 a.m.-6 p.m., Saturday 10 a.m.-5 p.m.
An attractive, but pricey shop selling trendy baby's and children's clothing, along with children's shoes.

DE SPEELMUIS   **6** B2   tram 7, 10
Elandsgracht 58 (1016 TW); tel. 6385342. Tuesday to Friday 10 a.m.-6 p.m., Saturday 10 a.m.-5 p.m.
De Speelmuis is full of wooden toys of all shapes and sizes. Hand-made doll's houses, musical instruments and bears are also sold, as well as cooking utensils, wrapping paper and Victorian-style gifts.

WAMPIE   **6** B1   tram 3, 10
2e Anjeliersdwarsstraat 19 (1015 NS); tel. 6271675. Monday 10 a.m.-4 p.m., Tuesday to Saturday 10 a.m.-5 p.m.
A children's couturier, where brightly coloured garments are made for children up to the age of seven.

BABYSITTERS

BABYSIT CENTRALE BABYHOME   **5** D2   tram 12, 13, 14
Chassestraat 97 (1057 JB); tel. 6161119. Bookings: Monday and Thursday 3-5 p.m.
This service only employs women over 17 years of age. Booking in advance is advisable.

OPPASCENTRALE KRITERION   **6** B2   tram 13, 14, 17
2e Rozendwarsstraat 24 (1016 PE); tel. 6245848. Daily 24 hours.
Male and female students, all qualified for the job, are employed by Kriterion. It is advisable to book.

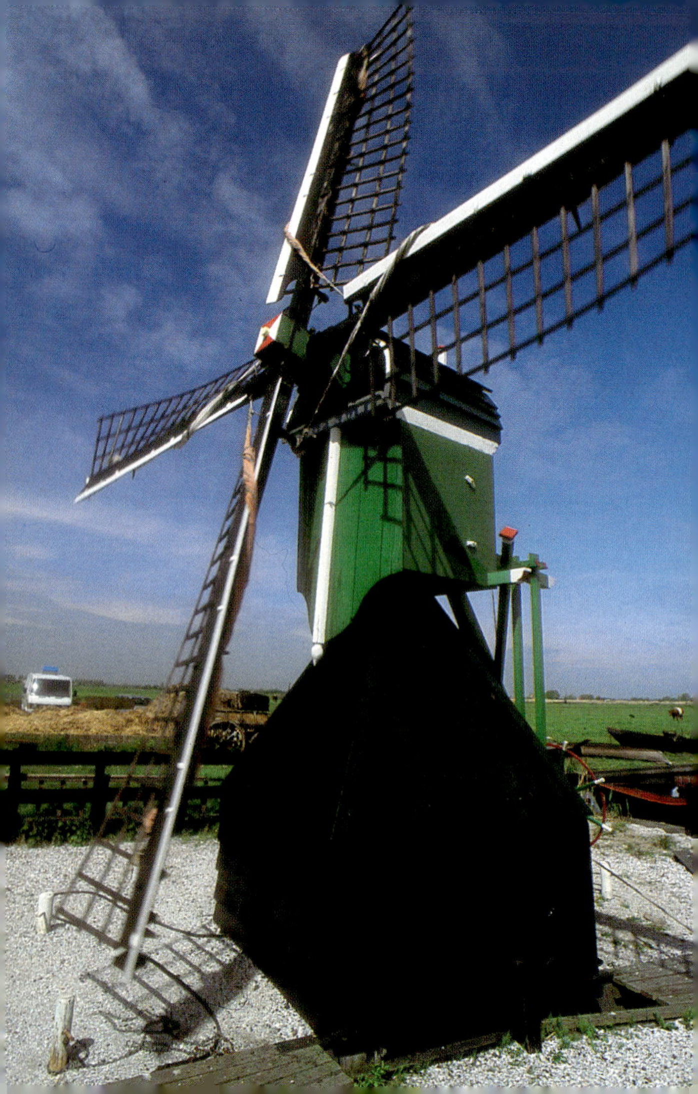

WALKS, TOURS AND DAY TRIPS

The last thing you need in Amsterdam is a car. The city is small enough to cross on foot within an hour and you can get around the centre faster by bike than on four wheels.

If you hire a bike, you can take the free passenger ferry from behind Central Station and within a few minutes find yourself enjoying an old Dutch village atmosphere of peace and tranquillity only a mile from the city centre.

Amsterdam is also an ideal base to see more of Holland. The VVV can provide a wealth of suggestions for a day out, be it by bus, train, bike or even car. Tulips, clogs and windmills are a common ingredient of many day trips, but Holland has more to offer. It has some of the most spectacular historic ports around the IJsselmeer and attractive beaches along the North Sea coast.

The Netherlands Railways organizes day trips to many destinations, among them the Port of Rotterdam, Het Loo Palace, the Zuiderzee Museum and the Zaanse Schans. It is possible to rent bicycles from most Dutch railway stations (for only ƒ 5 a day). You can also purchase Holland Rail Passes or Benelux TourRail Cards for unlimited rail travel on three or ten successive days (but you can only buy these tickets when outside Benelux). A Benelux TourRail Card costs £51 (£38 for a child). Further information can be obtained from the Netherlands Railways, 25/28 Buckingham Gate, London SW1E 6LD; phone 071 630 1735.

CITY SIGHTSEEING TOURS

There are various ways to get around the city and see the sights. Alongside the traditional bus and canal tours, bikes can be hired—either with two wheels or two hulls. Alternatively, you may prefer to use your feet to explore this compact city.

CANAL BIKE 10 B2
Amstel 57 (1018 EJ); tel. 6265574. April to October: daily 9 a.m.-6 p.m. High season (June to August):daily 9 a.m.-10 p.m. Cost: ƒ 29 for one hour for four (ƒ 19.50 for two).
Hire a canal bike to see the city at your own pace. A stiff peddle should get you half way round town in an hour. You can pick up the canal bike at any one of the following locations and drop it off at another:

There were once 700 working windmills at Zaanse Schans, now there are only five, left as reminders of foregone days.

WALKS, TOURS AND DAY TRIPS

Leidsebosje/Leidsekade, Keizersgracht/Leidsestraat, Rijksmuseum, Prinsengracht/Westermarkt (by Anne Frank House), Schreierstoren, Amstel.

HOLLAND INTERNATIONAL 8 B2
tram 1, 2, 4, 5, 9, 13, 16, 17, 24, 25
Dam 10 (1012 NP); tel. 6222550.
The main purveyor of bus tours, either of the city or of the surrounding countryside. The Grand Holland Tour (10 a.m. daily for 8 hours, cost: *f* 62, under-14s *f* 31) includes the Aalsmeer flower auction, the Pauw Delft Blue factory, a city tour of Rotterdam and The Hague, then via Scheveningen to Madurodam. In the weekend the flower auction is closed, so you can visit a clogmaker and the Mesdag Panorama. As well as the inevitable windmill tour, in the summer (June to September) there is a Zuiderzee tour, round the IJsselmeer visiting Urk, Hindeloopen (Museum), and the Makkum earthenware factory with a stop on the Dijk (*f* 62, under-14s *f* 31).

MEE IN MOKUM 6 B2
tram 13, 14, 17
Hartenstraat 18 (1016 CB); tel. 6251390. Monday to Friday 1-4 p.m.
The Historical Museum is the starting point for guided tours organized by "Mee in Mokum". These city walking tours are run under the expert guidance of elderly Amsterdammers, united in a 'guild' of pensioners. There are tours of the inner city, the Jordaan and a surprise tour. The tours start at 11 a.m. from the Historical Museum and cost *f* 4.

VVV AMSTERDAM 6 B2
tram 1, 2, 5
Leidsestraat 106 (1001 AS); tel. 6266444. Monday to Saturday 9 a.m.-5 p.m.
The Amsterdam Tourist Information Office has put together a number of walking guides, covering various areas and about different aspects of Amsterdam. They provide a good framework in which to explore the city, on foot or by bicycle. The pamphlets can be obtained from the VVV Office facing Central Station, or on Leidsestraat.

YELLOW BIKE 8 B1
tram 1, 2, 5, 13, 17
Nieuwezijds Voorburgwal 66 (1012 SC); tel. 6206940. 30 March to 31 October: daily.
Regular bike tours of the city are run by Yellow Bike. They start at 9 a.m. and 1 p.m., last 3½ hours, and cost *f* 25 including bike hire. Countryside bike tours depart at 8.30 a.m. and noon, last 6½ hours, and cost *f* 39. The company also runs walking tours of the city.

CANAL BOAT TRIPS

One of the best ways to get a first glimpse of Amsterdam is from a boat. Most companies cover more or less the same route around the city. The standard tour price is ƒ 10.

HOLLAND   **9** C1
INTERNATIONAL   tram 1, 2, 4, 5, 9, 13, 16, 17, 24, 25
Prins Hendrikkade 33a (1012 TM); tel. 6227788. Summer: daily 9 a.m.-6 p.m., departs every 15 min; 6-10pm departs every 45 min. Winter: daily 10 a.m.-4 p.m., departs every 45 min.
Holland International is the largest local-tour organizer, offering boat and bus tours of Amsterdam and day-trips to many sights throughout Holland.

As well as the traditional canal cruise, there are two-hour candlelight cruises (ƒ 42.50, under-14s ƒ 25) including wine, mixed nuts and a glass of genever in a bar. The dinner cruise costs ƒ 135 (under-14s ƒ 95) and is 3 hours long including a cocktail, four-course dinner and all drink. The lunch cruise (three hours for ƒ 52,50 (under-14s ƒ 42.50) also takes in a visit to the Rembrandthoeve cheese farm on the River Amstel.

REDERIJ D'AMSTEL   **17** C1   tram 16, 24, 25
Nicolaas Witsenkade 21 (1017 ZS); tel. 6265636. Summer: daily 9 a.m.-5 p.m. and 7-9 p.m., departs every half hour. Winter: departs every hour.

REDERIJ P. KOOIJ   **10** B1   tram 4, 9, 14, 16, 24, 25
Rokin opposite 125 (1012 KK); tel. 6234186. Summer: daily 9 a.m.-6 p.m., departs every 15 min; 6-10 p.m. departs every 30 min. Winter: daily 10 a.m.-5 p.m. departs every 30 min.

REDERIJ LOVERS   **9** C1   tram 1, 2, 4, 5, 9, 13, 16, 17, 24, 25
Prins Hendrikkade t/o 25-27 (1000 AV); tel. 6222181. Summer: daily 9 a.m.-6 p.m., departs every 15 min; 6-7.30 p.m. departs every 30 min.
Day tickets are available for the Museum Boat. The tour price includes discounts for several museums. The boat makes seven stops at convenient central locations.

REDERIJ PLAS   **9** C1   tram 1, 2, 4, 5, 9, 13, 16, 17, 24, 25
Damrak, Quay 3 (1012 JX); tel. 6245406. Summer: 9 a.m.-6 p.m., departs every 10 minutes; 6-9 p.m. departs every half hour. Winters: daily 10 a.m.-4 p.m., departs every half hour.

WALKS, TOURS AND DAY TRIPS

DAY TRIPS OUTSIDE AMSTERDAM

The Dutch Railways has a major programme of excursions to and from Amsterdam, including admission to events or attractions and even discounts on cycle hire (call 06-9292, cost: 50 c. per minute). Holland International and other operators also run bus trips and tours to many of these attractions.

AALSMEER FLOWER AUCTION

🚌 172 from Central Station to Aalsmeer, then 🚌 140

15 km (9 miles) south-west of Amsterdam. Legmeerdijk 313 Aalsmeer; tel. 02977-34567. Monday to Friday 7.30 a.m.-noon. Admission f 4, under-12s free.

The largest flower auction in the world sells 3.5 billion cut flowers and 400 million pot plants every year. The visitors' hall provides a view of the auction floor, which is as big as 100 soccer pitches.

ALKMAAR CHEESE MARKET

train, direct from Central Station

37 km (22 miles) north of Amsterdam. Waagplein, Alkmaar. Mid-April to mid-September: Friday 10 a.m.-noon. VVV Tourist Office, Waagplein 3, Alkmaar; tel. 072-114284.

The Cheese Market in Alkmaar is the most famous in The Netherlands, even though it no longer trades large quantities of cheese and two other towns gave their names to Holland's most famous cheeses. The market dates from 1300 and has been preserved with all its rituals and traditional dress. Alkmaar also has a Cheese Museum, a Beer Museum and the Hans Brinker Museum dedicated to the little boy who supposedly saved the country by sticking his finger in a dike.

AMSTERDAM WINDMILLS

Both tulips and windmills have their origins in the Middle East, but have become synonymous with Holland. Amsterdam only has six windmills left, dotted around the city. They are: D'Admiraal (Noord Hollandse Kanaaldijk, bus 34, 37, 39); De Bloem (Haarlemmerweg, bus 18); De Gooyer (Zeeburgerstraat, tram 10, bus 22, 28); De Rieker (Amsteldijk, bus 148); 1100 ROE (Herman Bonpad, bus 19, 68); and 120 ROE (Haarlemmerweg, bus 85).

BEACHES

Beach cafés are open from April to September.

Virtually the entire coast of Holland consists of sand dunes and there are many coastal resorts. Favourites among Amsterdammers are Zandvoort

DAY TRIPS OUTSIDE AMSTERDAM

(busy) and IJmuiden (quiet). Both are about 30 minutes by car, train or bus. Children will love the beautiful sandy beaches of Wijk aan Zee (35 minutes), Castricum (50 minutes.) and Bergen aan Zee (60 minutes). Within close reach of The Hague are Scheveningen (busy), Kijkduin (quiet), Wassenaar (quiet) and Noordwijk (busy).

BROEKER AUCTION train from Central Station to Alkmaar then 🚌 155
36 km (22.5 miles) north of Amsterdam. Voorburggracht 1, Broek-op-Langendijk; tel. 02903-13807. Easter to 30 September: Monday to Friday 10 a.m.-5 p.m. Admission f 7, under-12s f 4, for auction plus boat trip.
The oldest flower auction in the world has been preserved in its traditional state. Alongside the museum is a sales room where fruit and vegetables are auctioned along with the flowers. A boat trip completes this excursion.

DELFT train, direct from Central Station (two per hour)
60 km (37.5 miles) south-west of Amsterdam. VVV Tourist Office, Markt 85, Delft; tel. 015-126100.
Delft was made world famous by the painter Johannes Vermeer and by its Delft Blue pottery. In Dutch history, it is best known as the site of the murder of William I of Orange (1584). Today, Delft is a compact and photogenic city. The Old (1381) and New (16th century) churches and the Lambert van Meertens Museum are the main attractions.

EDAM CHEESE MARKET 🚌 110, 112, or 114 from Central Station
train from Central Station
10 km (6 miles) north of Amsterdam. Damplein, Edam. July, August: Wednesday 9.30 a.m.-1.30 p.m. VVV Tourist Office, Damplein 1, Edam; tel. 02993-71727.
World famous for its cheese, Edam was an important port in the Golden Age. The Great Church (1602), Little Church (1561) and Town Hall (1737) dominate this rural town which seems to have remained unaltered for three centuries.

ENKHUIZEN train from Central Station
50 km (31 miles) north of Amsterdam. VVV Tourist Office, Tussen Twee Havens 1, Enkhuizen; tel. 02280-13164. Zuiderzee Museum, Westerstraat 122, Enkhuizen; tel. 02280-10122. April to 21 October: daily 10 a.m.-5 p.m. Admission: adults f 11, under-18s f 6. (NS excursion ticket costs about f 27 and includes admission to Zuiderzee Museum).
In the 17th century, the Golden Age of Amsterdam, Enkhuizen was among the most important Dutch ports after the capital. Ships from the

WALKS, TOURS AND DAY TRIPS

Dutch East and West India Companies anchored here. This rich past can still be seen in Enkhuizen. The main attraction is the Zuiderzee Museum, comprising an indoor section (on shipping) and an outdoor reconstruction of a 17th-century village.

FRISIAN SKATE MUSEUM   train to Workum then 🚌 102 to Hindeloopen
100 km (62 miles) north of Amsterdam (turn off the E10 at Bolsward). Kleine Weide 1-3, 8713 KZ Hindeloopen. March to October: Monday to Saturday 10 a.m.-6 p.m., Sunday 1-6 p.m. Admission: adults ƒ 1.50, 6-15s ƒ 1.
The museum has an extensive collection of ice skates, sledges, old advertising posters and information about ice clubs. There is also fascinating documentation about the 11-City Tour (an ice-skating event held only during cold winters), with photos, statistics and trophies.

GOUDA CHEESE MARKET   train, direct from Central Station
29 km (18 miles) south of Amsterdam. Markt, Gouda. July, August: Thursday 9 a.m.-1 p.m. VVV Tourist Office, Markt 27, Gouda; tel. 01820-13666.
The cheese market is held in front of the 17th-century Waag (Weighhouse), but Gouda has more to offer than cheese. The town where Erasmus was born is famous for its clay pipes, cheeses, *stroopwafels* (thin waffles with syrup) and earthenware. Sights include: the St. Janskerk, with its unique stained-glass windows; the Catherina Gasthuis, which was a hospice from 1320 to 1910; the Moriaan Museum; and the Goutse Librij.

DE HAAR   train to Utrecht and 🚌 to Haarzuilens
30 km (19 miles) south of Amsterdam. Kasteellaan 1, Haarzuilens; tel. 03407-1275. March to mid-August, mid-October to mid-November: Monday to Friday 11 a.m.-4 p.m., Saturday, Sunday 1-4 p.m. Admission to castle and grounds ƒ 7.50 adults, ƒ 3 under-13s.
The largest castle in Holland dates from 1391. It was destroyed several times before being restored to its present state around the turn of the century. The luxurious interior comprises fine Gobelins, Louis XIV-XVI furniture and Oriental art. The castle grounds cover 100 hectares (250 acres) and include an English-style landscape park, French and Roman gardens and two deer parks.

DAY TRIPS OUTSIDE AMSTERDAM

HAARLEM train from Central Station
20 km (13 miles) west of Amsterdam (on A5). VVV Tourist Office, Stationsplein 1, Haarlem; tel. 023-319059. Frans Hals Museum, Groot Heiligland 62, Haarlem; tel. 023-319180. Monday to Saturday 11 a.m.- 5 p.m., Sunday 1-5 p.m. Admission f 4. Teylers Museum, Spaarne 16, Haarlem; tel. 023-319010. Tuesday to Saturday 10 a.m.-5 p.m., Sunday 1-5 p.m. Admission f 6.50.

Haarlem deserves more attention than it gets. This peaceful city looks like a living museum and has the highest concentration of old Dutch courtyards in Holland. The St Bavo Basilica (early 16th century) has been immortalized by many painters such as Ruysdael. It dominates the imposing Grote Markt. The Frans Hals Museum in the Old Men's Home (1608) has an extensive collection of works by Frans Hals, but also contains unique pieces by artists such as Adriaan van Ostade. The Teylers Museum is also a must. It is the oldest museum in Holland, dating from 1778 and has a hoard of scientific instruments, fossils and minerals. The Teylers also boasts a notable collection of Dutch, French and Italian drawings from the 16th to the 20th centuries, including work from Michelangelo, Rafael and Rembrandt.

THE HAGUE train from Central Station
50 km (31 miles) south west of Amsterdam.
VVV Tourist Office (at Central Station), Koningin, Julianaplein, The Hague; tel. 070-3546200.
Mauritshuis, Plein 29, The Hague; tel. 070-3469244. Tuesday to Saturday 10 a.m.-5 p.m., Sunday 11 a.m.-5 p.m. Admission f 6.50.
Panorama Mesdag, Zeestraat 65, The Hague; tel. 070-3642563. Monday to Saturday 10 a.m.-5 p.m., Sunday noon-5 p.m. Admission f 4.
Mesdag Museum (closed until 1993), Laan van Meerdervoort 7f, The Hague; tel. 070-3635450. Tuesday to Saturday 10 a.m.-5 p.m., Sunday 1-5 p.m. Admission f 3.50.
Haags Gemeente Museum, Stadhouderslaan 41, The Hague; tel. 070-3381111. Tuesday to Sunday 11 a.m.-5 p.m. Admission f 7.

The Hague, known in Dutch as Den Haag or even formally as 's Gravenhage, is the greenest city in The Netherlands, with countless parks, woods and nearby sand-dunes. Add this to the grandeur of aristocratic mansions, palaces and the Binnenhof Parliament complex and the result is as far removed from Amsterdam as you can get.

Sights include the Ridderzaal (Knights' Hall), the Binnenhof (Parliament Buildings) and the Gevangenenpoort (the only surviving gate of the medieval town). Lange Voorhout is the most splendid avenue in Europe and there is exclusive shopping in Noordeinde and the Passage shopping precinct. All these attractions are in easy walking distance of each other.

WALKS, TOURS AND DAY TRIPS

The same can be said of the Mauritshuis (1644) which houses a fine collection of 14th- to 17th-century paintings by the likes of Van der Weijden, Holbein, Rembrandt, Vermeer, Steen, Hals and Van Eijk. The Mesdag Panorama is one of the eight remaining painted panoramas in the world, providing a fascinating view of Scheveningen in 1881. The nearby Mesdag Museum is closed until 1993 for renovation. It is a 19th-century house which has been preserved intact with a large collection of works from the Hague and Barbizon Schools (including Mauve, Mesdag, Israels, Delacroix and Gericault). The Haags Gemeente Museum has one of the finest collections of modern art including many works by Piet Mondrian. (For the Madurodam model buildings, see page 136.)

HOORN
train from Central Station
33 km (20 miles) northeast of Amsterdam. VVV Tourist Office, Nieuwstraat 23, Hoorn; tel. 02290-18342.
Hoorn flourished alongside Enkhuizen in the 16th and 17th centuries. The trade with the East and West Indies is reflected in the architecture. The former town hall (1632) now houses the West Frisian Museum. A folklore market is held on Wednesdays in July and August (10 a.m.-5 p.m.). Costumes, handicrafts and local products are sold. From May to September an antique steam train runs a service to Medemblik (July, August: daily from 11.30 a.m.; May, June and September: Tuesday to Saturday from 11.30 a.m.).

KEUKENHOF
train from Central Station
27 km (17 miles) south west of Amsterdam. Stationsweg 166/a, Lisse; tel. 02521-19144. Late March to mid-May: daily 8 a.m.-6 p.m. (NS excursion ticket includes train, bus and admission).
The largest flower gardens in the world. The Keukenhof was set up in 1949 to persuade people to plant more flowers. Seven million plants are on show, most of them outdoors. Others are housed in the 5,000 square-metres (5,980 square-yards) of greenhouse space. From June to March the Bulb District Museum (Tuesday to Sunday, 1-5 p.m.) provides a survey of the history of bulb growing.

KINDERDIJK
train to Dordrecht
then 🚌 52 to Alblasserdam, then 🚌 154
60 km (37.5 miles) southwest of Amsterdam (beyond Rotterdam turn left at Barendrecht towards Alblasserdam). Molenkade, Alblasserdam. VVV Tourist Office tel. 01859-14300. April to September: Monday to Saturday 9.30 a.m.-5.30 p.m. Admission: adults f 2.50, 6-16s f 1.50.
This molengang (as it is also known in English) is a row of 19 windmills co-ordinated to drain water from reclaimed land. They can be seen work-

DAY TRIPS OUTSIDE AMSTERDAM

ing in July and August, on Saturdays from 2.30 to 5.30 p.m. Only in the second week of September are all mills rigged and illuminated. It makes for a spectacular sight.

KOOG AAN DE ZAAN
WINDMILL MUSEUM train from Central Station
10 km (6 miles) north west of Amsterdam, near Zaandam. Museumlaan 18, 1541 LP Koog aan de Zaan; tel. 288968. Tuesday to Friday 10 a.m.-5 p.m., Saturday, Sunday 2-5 p.m. Admission: adults f 3.50, 4-12s f 1.50.
This Museum houses the collection of the Zaanse Molen Association, including model windmills, tools, machines and historic documents.

LEIDEN train, direct from Central Station (four per hour)
40 km (24 miles) south west of Amsterdam (on A4).
VVV Tourist Office, Stationsplein 210, Leiden; tel. 071-146846. Monday to Friday 9 a.m.-5.30 p.m., Saturday 9 a.m.-4 p.m.
Pieterskerk, Kloksteeg 16; tel. 071-124319. Daily 1.30-4 p.m. Admission free. Lakenhal Museum, Oude Singel 32, Leiden; tel. 071-120820. Tuesday to Saturday 10 a.m.-5 p.m., Sunday 1-5 p.m. Admission f 2.50.
Rijksmuseum van Oudheden, Rapenburg 28, Leiden; tel. 071-163163. Tuesday to Saturday 10 a.m.-5 p.m, Sunday noon-5 p.m. Admission f 3.50.
Rijksmuseum voor Volkenkunde, Steenstraat 1, Leiden; tel. 071-211824. Tuesday to Saturday 10 a.m.-5 p.m., Sunday 1-5 p.m. Admission f 3.50.
Museum Boerhaave, Lange St Agnietenstraat 10, Leiden; tel. 071-214224. Tuesday to Saturday 10 a.m.-5 p.m., Sunday noon-5 p.m. Admission f 3.50, under 18 or over 65 f 2.
Leiden Pilgrim Collection (Municipal Archives), Vliet 45, Leiden; tel. 071-120191. Monday to Friday 9.30 a.m.-4.30 p.m. Admission free.
The birthplace of Rembrandt was larger than Amsterdam until the 16th century. In 1581, Holland's first university was built here. This seat of learning was later to become world famous thanks to Descartes, Boerhaave, Linnaeus, the U.S. President Adams, Lorenz and Einstein. Today students still dominate the streets. Leiden otherwise remains a characteristic small Dutch town, with canals, patrician houses, courtyards and alleyways. Interesting sights include the Burcht (Fortress), the Pieterskerk and the Lakenhal Museum with its collection of Dutch Masters (including Rembrandt, Gerard Dou, Jan Steen and Jan van Goyen). Among the other renowned venues are the Rijksmuseum van Oudheden, an archaeological museum filled with rare finds from Egypt, Greece, the Roman Empire and the Low Countries; the Rijksmuseum voor Volkenkunde, an anthropological museum with an extensive collection

WALKS, TOURS AND DAY TRIPS

from the non-western world; and the Boerhaave Museum with a fascinating array of maritime instruments. The Pilgrim Fathers departed from Leiden, having sojourned there from 1609 to 1620. The Pilgrim Collection provides a survey of this period.

MARKEN
🚌 111 from Central Station; or 🚌 110 to Volendam, then boat to Marken
15 km (9.5 miles) north east of Amsterdam. VVV Tourist Office, Zarken 2, Monnickendam; tel. 02995-1998.
Since it was linked to the mainland by a causeway, Marken is officially no longer an island. Yet evidence of its centuries of isolation can still be seen in the traditional costumes worn by its inhabitants and in the fine wooden village. The fishing port provides panoramic views of the IJsselmeer and the coast of North Holland. Cars are banned from the village centre. Many people combine a visit to rural Marken with one to touristic Volendam (see below). If you have to choose between them, choose Marken.

MUIDERSLOT
train to Amstel, then bus 136
12 km (7.5 miles) east of Amsterdam. Herengracht 1, Muiden; tel. 02942-1325. April to September: Monday to Friday 10 a.m.-5 p.m., Sunday 1-4 p.m. October to March: Monday to Friday 10 a.m.-4 p.m., Sunday 1-4 p.m. Admission: adults f 4, under-18s f 2.50.
Strategically situated at the mouth of the River Vecht, Muiderslot Castle was built in 1280 by Count Floris V who was murdered here in 1296. The Dutch poet and historian P.C. Hooft made the castle famous in the 17th century with his Muider Circle of poets, painters and musicians.

NAARDEN VESTING MUSEUM
train, direct from Central Station
20 km (12 miles) east of Amsterdam. Naarden tel. 02159-45459. Easter-October: Monday to Friday 10 a.m.-4.30 p.m., Saturday, Sunday noon-5 p.m. Admission: adults f 3, 5-12s f 2.
Naarden Vesting is a fortified town, built around 1675. It has splendid star-shaped ramparts and is surrounded by a double moat. Admission to the Museum allows you to explore the bastions and includes a boat trip on the moat.

PURMEREND CHEESE MARKET
🚌 100 from Central Station
direct train from Central Station
26 kilometres (15 miles) north east of Amsterdam. Kaasmarkt, Purmerend. July, August: Thursday 11 a.m.-1 p.m.
VVV Tourist Office, Kaasmarkt 20, Purmerend; tel. 02990-52525. tel. 02990-52525.

DAY TRIPS OUTSIDE AMSTERDAM

Women in traditional costume and folk dancing accompany this cheese market, which takes place in front of the Renaissance Town Hall. There is a cattle market on Tuesdays (see also page 135). Deals are often agreed by clapping hands. The Purmerend Museum provides a survey of local history.

ROTTERDAM train from Central Station
73 km (45 miles) south of Amsterdam (A4 then A13).
VVV, Coolsingel 67, Rotterdam. The Rotterdam Tourist Office is only prepared to take phone calls on a surcharged phone number: 06-34034065 (50c per minute—be warned, using this number could prove expensive, especially if you find yourself put on hold). Monday to Thursday 9 a.m.-6.30 p.m., Saturday 9 a.m.-5 p.m., Easter to September: also Sunday 9 a.m.-5 p.m.
VVV, Central Station (no phone). Daily 9 a.m.-10 p.m.
Leuvehaven Outdoor Maritime Museum, Leuvehaven 50-72, Rotterdam; tel. 010-4048072. Daily 9 a.m.-4 p.m. Admission free.
Prins Hendrik Maritime Museum, Leuvehaven 1, Rotterdam; tel. 010-4132680. Tuesday to Saturday 10 a.m.-5 p.m., Sunday 11 a.m.-5 p.m. Admission f 3.50.
Spido Boat Tours, Willemskade, Rotterdam, tel. 010-4135400. Easter to September: daily.
De Dubbele Palmboom, Voorhaven 12, Delfshaven; tel. 010-4761533. Tuesday to Saturday 10 a.m.-5 p.m., Sunday 1-5 p.m. Admission f 3.50.
Boymans-van Beuningen Museum, Mathenesserlaan 18-20, Rotterdam; tel. 010-4419400. Tuesday to Saturday 10 a.m.-5 p.m., Sunday 11 a.m.-5 p.m. Admission f 3.50.
National School Museum, Nieuwe Markt 1a, Rotterdam; 010-4045425. Tuesday to Saturday 10 a.m.-5 p.m., Sunday 11 a.m.-5 p.m. Admission f 2.50.
Toy Toy Museum, Groene Wetering 41, Rotterdam; tel. 010-4525941. September to June: Sunday to Thursday 11 a.m.-4 p.m. Admission f 5.
The restored Laurenskerk (1646) and the 17th-century Schielandshuis (now the city museum) are the only tangible remains of the Rotterdam's past. The present is expressed in experimental housing projects, such as Blom's cube dwellings; the very un-Dutch skyscrapers by Central Station; and the Euromast (180 m/600 ft high). In The Leuvehaven Outdoor Museum and the Prins Hendrik Museum, the maritime history of The Netherlands and especially of Rotterdam are brought to life. Today's shipping can be seen at close range with Spido Boat Tours. The industrial activity of the past is the theme in De Dubbele Palmboom. The Boymans-van Beuningen Museum provides a selection of art from

WALKS, TOURS AND DAY TRIPS

the 14th to the 20th centuries (including Breughel's famous *Tower of Babel*), while focusing on contemporary art. The National School Museum provides a survey of Dutch education through the ages. Mechanical and tin toys (1890-1930) and antique dolls (1700-1920) can be found in the Toy-Toy Museum. The Netherlands Railways organizes a day trip to Rotterdam and Europort for about ƒ 50 including a boat trip around the harbour.

SCHERMERHOORN MUSEUM MILL — train to Alkmaar then 🚌 126, 127, or train to Purmerend then 🚌 127

35 km (22 miles) north of Amsterdam (on the E10, towards Alkmaar). Noordervaart 2, (1636 VL) Schermerhoorn; tel. 12202-1519. Schermerhoorn. 1 April to 30 September: Tuesday to Sunday 10 a.m.-5 p.m. 1 October-31 March: Sunday 10.30 a.m.-5.30 p.m. Admission: adults ƒ 2.25, 4-14s ƒ 1.

Along with two adjacent mills, the Schermerhoorn Mill was responsible for draining the Schermer polder in 1634. The Museum, housed in the 17th-century structure, screens a slide show (in five languages) about the significance of mills in the Dutch landscape.

DE VALK WINDMILL MUSEUM — train from Central Station

Tweede Binnenvestgracht 1, (2312 BZ) Leiden; tel. 071-254639. Tuesday to Saturday 10 a.m.-5 p.m., Sunday 1-5 p.m. Admission: adults ƒ 3; 6-16s, over-65s ƒ 1.

De Valk is a seven-storey grain mill that was built in 1743. The ground floor is a miller's home with an original interior dating from 1900. Everything can be examined closely: grinding, pour, stone and roof lofts. The vanes turn every afternoon (weather permitting).

VECHT RIVER TOUR — boat from the De Ruyterkade behind Central Station

Rederij NACO, Pier 7, De Ruyterkade (1011 AA); tel. 6262466. Mid-April to early October: Monday, Wednesday, Friday and Saturday 9.30 a.m.-6 p.m. Admission: ƒ 37.50, 4-11s ƒ 22.50.

The cruise takes you through Nederhorst den Berg past a series of castles such as Guuterstein (rebuilt in 1681), Nijenrode (15th century), Oudam (1303), Sypesteyn (1580) and Slot Zuylen (about 1300) to the picturesque village of Loenen and includes a visit to a cheese farm or a guided tour of Loenen. On Sunday, Tuesday and Thursday, there is a boat trip to the island of Pampus and Muiderslot castle.

DAY TRIPS OUTSIDE AMSTERDAM

VOLENDAM 🚌110 from Central Station or boat trip from Pier 7, De Ruyterkade behind Central Station

18 km (11 miles) north-east of Amsterdam. Volendam Museum, Zeestraat 37, Volendam; tel. 02993-69258. Daily 10 a.m.-5 p.m. Admission f 2.50, f 1.25 under 18. VVV, Zeestraat 37, Volendam; tel. 02993-63747. Boat trip: Rederij NACO, Pier 7, De Ruyterkade (1011 AA); tel. 6262466. Mid-May to early October daily 10 a.m. Cost: f 57.50, 4-11s f 27.50.

The Volendam traditional costume, along with the windmill and the tulip, became the international emblem of Holland abroad. The Volendam Museum has recently been opened to house a collection of paintings, costumes, and interiors reflecting the traditional village. Almost all tourists find their way here, by bus, car or boat. There is a daily boat trip to Marken, followed by a bus trip to Volendam and back to Amsterdam through the province of North Holland. Volendam is not the only town in The Netherlands where people still wear traditional costumes in everyday life. In Schagen, Marken, Medemblik (north of Amsterdam), Bunschoten, Spakenburg (east of Amsterdam), Staphorst (in the province of Drenthe), Zuid Beveland (province of Zeeland) and Scheveningen (near The Hague), people in *klederdracht* can still be seen on the street. In Schagen (48 km/30 miles north of Amsterdam) traditional dance shows are given on Thursdays in July and August.

WATERLAND

The area to the north of Amsterdam, bordered by Edam, Purmerend and Zaandam, is known as Waterland. It is a unique piece of Old Holland, filled with rare polder-scapes and sleepy villages. Durgerdam, Ilpendam, De Rijp and Broek in Waterland are especially attractive. Waterland is ideal for an afternoon's cycle tour (get a cycle map from the VVV Tourist Office).

ZAANSE SCHANS train from Central Station to
MUSEUM VILLAGE Koog-Zaandijk. Then an 8-minute walk

14 km (9 miles) north of Amsterdam. Kalverringdijk, 1509 BT Zaandam; tel. 075-162221. April to October: daily 10 a.m.-5 p.m. November to March: Saturday, Sunday 10 a.m.-5 p.m. Admission free.

This museum village comprises houses, mills and shops from the 17th and 18th centuries. The area used to have hundreds of mills for paint, wood and grain; mustard is produced in one of the five still operating. There is also a copper-smith, a cheese-maker, a tin-smith, a traditional bakery, a clock and a costume museum. The NS excursion ticket to Zaanse Schans includes a cruise on the River Zaan, admission to the windmill museum and a pancake (for f 22.40).

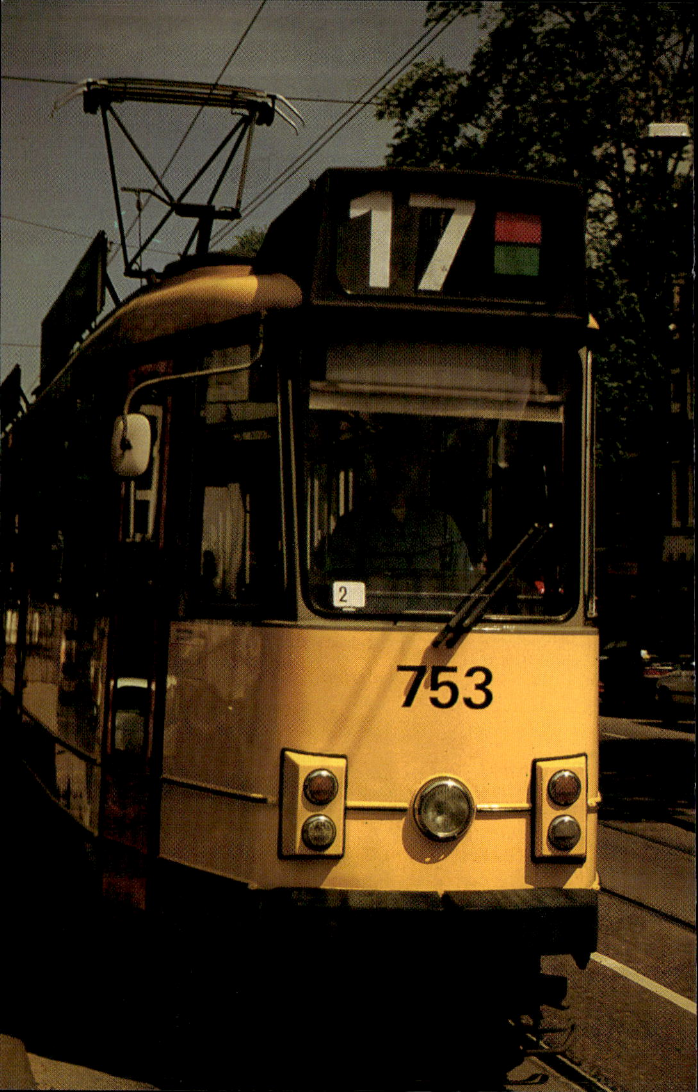
17
2
753

PRACTICAL INFORMATION

Airport
Amsterdam's Schiphol Airport is one of Europe's most important air-traffic hubs. It is located about 15 kilometres (9 miles) south of the city. Schiphol is most easily accessible by train. There is a station next to the main terminal and trains linking it to Central Station depart at least four times an hour (also at night, but less frequently). Journey time is about 20 minutes. There are also bus services to other parts of Holland. A taxi into town costs about ƒ 55, with a 25 per cent surcharge at night.
Airline Information. Information about flights and arrivals can be obtained by phone on 6010966. Charter flight information: 5110666.

Climate
The average temperature in Holland in January is 4° C (39° F) and in July 20° C (68° F). Temperatures in Amsterdam are usually slightly higher. It can be very rainy in the autumn and winter months.

Consulates
Most countries have their embassies in The Hague (The Dutch seat of government), but usually have a consulate in Amsterdam. If you lose your passport or get into trouble, your consulate can usually help.
Australia: Koninginnegracht 23, The Hague; tel. 070-3630983
Canada: Sophialaan 7, The Hague; tel. 070-3614111
Ireland: Dr. Kuyperstraat 9, The Hague; tel. 070-3630903
New Zealand: Mauritskade 25, The Hague; tel. 070-3469324
U.K.: Koningslaan 44, Amsterdam; tel. 6764343
U.S.A.: Museumplein 19, Amsterdam; tel. 6645661

Crime and Petty Theft
While Amsterdam is quite a safe city, tourists are favourite prey for pickpockets and thieves. Be especially vigilant on public transport, in stations, tourist haunts and markets. And don't leave any valuables in your car. A foreign number-plate tends to attract thieves. The Red-Light District may seem to some uninviting at night, but it is probably one of the safest areas in town. Beware around metro stations and alleyways.

If you are the victim of a crime, call the police (the emergency number is 06-11) or report the theft at a police station (call Police Headquarters on 5599111 to find the address of the nearest district office). The police usually let you fill in your own report form (also available in English, German and French). Make sure you report all thefts and obtain a copy of your report from the police as evidence for insurance.

PRACTICAL INFORMATION

Customs and Immigration
Visitors from the EC and most English-speaking countries do not need visas. Check with your travel agent. Holland has no currency restrictions on import or export of cash. There may, however, be restrictions in your own country.

Disabled Visitors
Amsterdam is not the easiest of cities for the disabled traveller. New buildings and the larger film theatres and museums have facilities for wheelchairs and easy access. But smaller theatres, bars and older hotels are often not equipped to cope with wheelchairs. The staff are usually willing to help. Most pavements have ramps on the corners, but chaotic parking can make this sensible provision useless.

Driving in Amsterdam
Traffic regulations. If you bring your car to Holland, you need a valid driving licence, your car papers and a national identity sticker on the back. You also need a green card to demonstrate your insurance also applies abroad and you are obliged to have a red warning triangle in the car.

Speed limits in Holland are 120 km/h (75 mph) on motorways unless indicated as 100km/h (62 mph) by small yellow boards on the central crash barrier. Otherwise the speed limits are 80km/h (50 mph) outside built-up areas and 50km/h (30 mph) in towns. Vehicles coming from the right have right of way, unless you are crossing a major road (shark's teeth markings across the road indicate you have to give way).

In a city like Amsterdam, junctions can be confusing, with separate lanes for bicycles, private vehicles and public transport. Beware when turning right: a cyclist on your inside going straight on has right of way. You should also be careful opening the car doors—cycling into an open car door can cause a lot of physical and material damage. Trams always have right of way. Taxis can usually share their special lanes.

The wearing of front seat-belts is compulsory. Children under 12 must sit in the back of cars.

Parking. Parking can be a major headache in Amsterdam (for car drivers and others). There are meters throughout the inner city where you can park for a couple of guilders an hour. In some suburbs you are expected to buy a ticket from a machine on the pavement and stick it behind your windscreen. If the time runs out or the meter is defective, you may return to find a wheel-clamp. If so, call 5233111 and go to the nearest *Parkeerpolitie* office to pay. It will cost you at least ƒ 120. If you park your car where you shouldn't, it is fairly likely to get towed away at a cost of at least ƒ 250. The parking authorities accept credit cards.

PRACTICAL INFORMATION

The major car parks in the city are: Bijenkorf Garage, on Beursplein (1012 JW) tel. 6218080 ext. 434; Europarking, on Marnixstraat 250 (1016 TL) tel. 6236694; Het Muziektheater, on Waterlooplein 22 (1011 PG) tel. 5518100/5518068; and Victoria Parking, near Central Station, on Prins Hendrikkade 20a (10) tel. 6385330.

Accidents and Breakdowns. The ANWB, the Dutch automobile association (called confusingly the Dutch Cycling Club) can help you if your car breaks down. Call the "Wegenwacht" (the ANWB breakdown service). The freephone number is 06-0888 or locally in Amsterdam 6268251. If you are a member of an affiliated organization (AA or RAC) you will be helped free of charge.

Fuel. There are plenty of petrol stations dotted around town selling *Euroloodvrij* (95-octane unleaded), *Super Plus* (98-octane, unleaded), *Super* (98-octane leaded), *Normaal* (95-octane leaded), *Diesel* and *LPG*. There are a few 24-hour service stations; on Sarphatistraat by the Gooier windmill (East), on Marnixstraat by Europarking (see PARKING) and behind the windmill on Haarlemmerweg (only with a credit card).

Car Hire. Cars can be hired at the airport from the internationally-known firms. They usually also have branches in the city, but these tend only to open during normal office hours. You need a driving licence and usually a credit card. Drivers need to be over 21 or even 24 and to have had a licence for at least a year.

Drugs
While Holland (and Amsterdam in particular) has a tolerant policy towards soft drugs, possession and use is technically illegal. You can however buy hash and marijuana over the counter in countless coffee shops and clubs (such as the Melkweg). This is safer than buying on the street from pushers who may be selling henna or Oxo cubes.
The tolerant attitude to drugs seems to have helped the city solve its hard drug problem. But local heroin can be extremely pure and potent; most deaths these days are of foreign addicts who overdose. Information and advice is available from the City Drugs Prevention Centre, tel. 6265115.

Electric Current
The electric current in Holland is 220 volt AC. Sockets differ from those in the U.K. and the U.S.A. Your hotel may be able to provide an adaptor, otherwise buy one before your departure.

Emergencies
The central alarm phone number is 06-11, for police, fire brigade or ambulance.

PRACTICAL INFORMATION

Festivals

Ice Skating (cold winters). During severe winters, the whole country is seized by skating fever. The high point is the *Elfstedentocht* (11-City Tour), a freezing 200-kilometre (125-mile) marathon through 11 Frisian towns. When the canals of Amsterdam and ditches in the surrounding countryside are also frozen over, you can make special tours on skates (see the newspapers).

Carnival (six weeks before Easter). Catholics in Holland celebrate Carnival. Most Catholics can be found in the south of the country and the atmosphere of Carnival is best tasted in Den Bosch and Maastricht. But even Amsterdam has a (Calvinist) carnival of sorts.

Floriade 1992 (April to October, 1992). The Floriade is an enormous garden festival held once every ten years. A myriad blossoms, plants and trees flourish on the huge festival site. After the Amsterdam festivals (held in 1972 and 1982) Zoetermeer near The Hague is the location for the fourth Floriade. It will be held from 10 April to 11 October 1992, 9.30 a.m.-7 p.m. (9.30 a.m.-6 p.m. from 1 September). Admission *f* 20, children *f* 12.50, family *f* 60.

Queen's Birthday (30 April). The traditionally straight-laced Dutch drop their Calvinist reserve on 30 April and join in the massive celebrations throughout the country. All street-trading laws are suspended as market traders are joined by children selling their old toys and comics, students selling T-shirts, hippies selling hash cake and shopkeepers moving their tills out into the street. The festivities in Amsterdam centre on Rokin, Spui, Leidseplein, Jordaan and Vondelpark.

Remembrance Day (4 May). Remembrance Day, marking the German invasion in 1940, is still strictly observed in Holland. Flags fly at half-mast and a two-minute silence is observed throughout the country at 8 p.m. (all the trams and buses stop, if not private cars). The Queen herself usually leads the memorial service in Dam Square.

Liberation Day (5 May). The mourning for the victims of war soon gives way to revelry, as Holland celebrates the liberation in 1945 only a day later (with a public holiday every five years). The day is gradually developing into a retake of 30 April, with a free market and festivities in the Vondelpark.

Holland Festival (1-30 June). The Holland Festival is an annual festival of the dramatic arts. From 1 to 30 June, the theatres of Amsterdam and to a lesser extent The Hague, are filled with a variety of music, dance and theatre. Phone 6276566 for details.

PRACTICAL INFORMATION

Flower Parades (September/October). Bulb growing is concentrated along the coast between Amsterdam and Rotterdam.
Last Saturday in April: Haarlem–Bennebroek–Hillegom–Lisse–Noordwijk.
First Saturday in August: Rijnsburg (11 a.m.)–Leiden (1 p.m.)–Noordwijk (4 p.m.).
First Saturday in September: Aalsmeer (9.30 a.m.)–Amsterdam (4 p.m.).

Sinterklaas (5 December). The Dutch Santa Claus arrives in mid-November on a white horse from Spain, instead of in a reindeer sleigh from the North Pole. He stays around until 5 December when gifts are exchanged, usually with poems which are blunt and can be very personal. Presents at Sinterklaas still tend to be modest and everyone only gets one gift, often from an anonymous member of the group.

Christmas (25, 26 December). Dutch Christmases tend to be quiet family affairs and is not the best time to be traipsing around Amsterdam. Most bars and restaurants are shut and those that are open usually need to be booked and concentrate on large family groups.

Libraries
If you need reference or reading material in English, the local public library (see the Amsterdam Yellow Pages) can help. Alternatively, try The America Institute of the University of Amsterdam, Jodenbreestraat 9 (1011 NG) tel. 5254380; or the British Council, Keizersgracht 343, (1016 EH) tel. 6223644.

Medical Care
You can receive medical attention from any GP. Your hotel should be able to help, but otherwise call the Central Doctors Service (tel. 6642111) for information, or for the addresses of doctors on weekend and night duty. The Service can also help you find a dentist.

First aid. Amsterdam Medical Centre, Meibergdreef 9; tel. 5669111. Out of town in the south-eastern suburbs.
Eerstehulp Kruispost, Oudezijds Voorburgwal 129; tel. 6249031. A first-aid centre in the Red Light District.
Onze Lieve Vrouwe Gasthuis, 1e Oosterparkstraat 179; tel. 5999111. To the east of the centre.
St Lukasziekenhuis, Jan Tooropstraat 164; tel. 5108911. To the west.
VU-Ziekenhuis, De Boelelaan 1117; tel. 5484831. To the south.

Pharmacies. Pharmacies are open from Monday to Friday 8.30 a.m.-5.30 p.m. In the evenings and at weekends, each district has one or two pharmacies open on a rota system. For information, phone 6948709.

PRACTICAL INFORMATION

Money Matters

Currency. The unit of Dutch currency is the guilder, divided into 100 cents. There are coins of 1, 2.50 and 5 guilders; and of 5 (stuiver), 10 (dubbeltje) and 25 cents. Bank notes are denominated: ƒ 5, ƒ 10, ƒ 25, ƒ 50, ƒ 100, ƒ 250 and ƒ 1,000.

Exchanging Money. Banks and post offices give the best rate of exchange with the lowest charges. Banks are open Monday to Friday 9 a.m.-4 p.m., often until 7 p.m. on Thursdays. (Some banks open later on Mondays.) The GWK Bank at Central Station is open 24 hours a day to exchange money and provide cash on credit cards. Beware of street-corner exchange bureaux. They are often open long hours, but impose higher charges and unfavourable exchange rates.

Credit cards and traveller's cheques. Traveller's cheques can be cashed at all banks and some hotels. Take along your passport. If you lose American Express traveller's cheques, phone 06-0220100 (free). Most hotels and restaurants and many shops accept credit cards. Credit cards are, however, in less common use than in many other countries. Credit cards can also be used to obtain cash from bank dispensers. If you lose a card, phone these local numbers:
American Express: 6424488
Diners Club International: 5573557
Eurocard/Mastercard/Access: 010-4570899 (Rotterdam)
Visa/Barclaycard: 5205911

Newspapers and Magazines

Foreign (British/German/French) newspapers are available throughout the city from newsagents, on the morning of publication. The news-stands at Central Station have a wider assortment, as do:
The Atheneum Nieuwscentrum, Spuistraat 305 (1012 VS); tel. 6242972.
Scheltema Holkema & Vermeulen Boekhandel, Koningsplein 20 (1017 BB); tel. 6267212.
Univers, Rozengracht 21 (1016 LR); tel. 6245369.

Post Offices

Post offices are open from Monday to Friday 8.30 a.m.-5 p.m. The main post office (Singel/Raadhuisstraat) is also open on Saturdays 9 a.m.-noon. You can buy postage stamps and phone cards and exchange money. Sub-post offices in the city centre are located at:
St Anthoniebreestraat 16 (1011 HB).
Bloemgracht 300 (1015 TV).
Bijenkorf Department Store, Damrak 90A (1012 LP).

PRACTICAL INFORMATION

V & D Department Store, Kalverstraat 201 (1012 XC).
City Hall, Waterlooplein 2 (1011 PG).

Public Holidays
Shops, offices and banks are closed on 1 January, Easter Monday, 30 April (Queen's Day), Whit-Monday, Ascension Day, 25 and 26 December. Museums and theatres are often open on these days.

Public Lavatories
The lack of public toilets in Amsterdam, especially for women, is a disgrace. Stations, museums, large department stores and the airport are an exception. Sometimes, however, you are expected to pay 25-35 c. The brave can enter a bar or restaurant, but even some of these expect payment.

Telephone
A phone box is never far away. Some take coins (25 c, ƒ 1, ƒ 2.50) others take phone cards (obtainable from post offices, tobacconists, stations and the Telehouse). You can also place calls from the Telehouse, Raadhuisstraat 48-50 (1016 DG); tel. 6743654. The Telehouse also has fax, telegram and telex facilities. It is open 24 hours a day, seven days a week. The international access number is 09, after which you will hear a continuous tone (also heard after trunk dialling codes). You can then dial the rest of the phone number, e.g. for the UK 09-44 etc.
In this Guide, we have assumed that visitors will be phoning the addresses from within Amsterdam. The long-distance code for the city is 020 (31 20 when called from abroad).

Tipping
Service is included on all bills. It is however common to give tips in some circumstances. From 5 to 10 per cent is usual in restaurants; 10 per cent on taxi fares.

Tourist Information
VVV Tourist Information Centres are outside Central Station at Stationsplein no. 10 (the Noord-Zuid Koffiehuis), tel. 6266444 and at Leidsestraat 106 (1017 PG). Here you can book hotels, tours and theatre tickets and find information about sights and events throughout Holland. Reservations for hotels, hiking cabins, apartments, congresses and group reservations in restaurants, etc. can also be made from the Nationaal Reserverings Centrum (BRC), Vlietweg 15, Leidschendam; tel. 070-3202500. It is open from Monday to Friday 8 a.m.-8 p.m. and Saturday 8 a.m.-1 p.m.

PRACTICAL INFORMATION

Transport

Trams are usually the most efficient way to get around town. They are frequent, operate from 6 a.m. to midnight and most start their routes at Central Station. But they can be very crowded in the rush hour. Watch out for pickpockets and drivers who start and stop abruptly. Some places inaccessible by tram have **bus** services. These are also very frequent and comfortable. There are only two **metro** lines, both running from Central Station, via Amstel Station, to the south-eastern suburbs.

Payment. You can pay for all these forms of public transport (and even trains within the city) with the *Nationale Strippenkaart*. This national public transport booklet is obtainable at stations, tobacconists, post offices, or any shop showing a small yellow board outside. The system is based on stamping a card that has been divided up into a number of horizontal strips. The idea is that you leave a number of strips free, equal to the number of zones travelled, and stamp the card on the next strip in the yellow machines on-board trams, buses or at the entrance to metro stations. The centre of Amsterdam is all one zone, so you only need to leave one empty strip and stamp the second. Several people can travel on one ticket, but each must be stamped separately. Strippenkaarten are sold with 15 and 45 strips (for about ƒ 10 and ƒ 28). You can also purchase a day ticket (about ƒ 10 per person).

Public transport information can be obtained by phoning 6272727, or by calling in at one of the GVB offices (Central Station and Amstel Station). These can also supply a free map of public transport in the city. There is also a central public transport information number: 06-9292, but it costs 50 c. per minute.

Trams, buses and the metro stop running at midnight. After this you can take **night-buses**, which only run every half hour and tend to take very circuitous routes. You can also take a **taxi**. There are taxi halts all over town, or you can ask bar staff to call one (tel. 6777777).

Trains tend to run on time. There are all kinds of reduction tickets for periods of five days or a month.

Ferries. The local public transport authority also runs the ferries across the River IJ behind Central Station. The ferry is free of charge and can only be used by pedestrians, cyclists and municipal buses. It provides one of the city's favourite free tourist attractions.

Water

"Municipal beer", as the locals call it, is always safe to drink, if not especially tasty.

MAP SECTION KEY

Scale 1:17 500

— ●— Eisenbahn, Metro/ Spoorlijn, Metro
Railway, Underground/Chemin de fer, Métro

—43— Tram/Tram
Tramway/Tram

---29--- Autobus/Bus
Bus/Autobus

Schiffslinie – Anlegestelle/Rondvaartboot – aanlegsteiger
Shipping route - quai /Route maritime - Embarcadère

Autofähre/Autopontveer
Car ferry/Bac pour autos

Fussgängerzone/Voetgangersgebied
Pedestrian zone/Zone pour piétons

Öffentliches Gebäude/Openbare gebouwen
Public building/Bâtiment public

Park, Sportplatz/ Park, Sportterrein
Park, Sports ground/Jardin, Terrain de sports

Wald/Bos
Forest/Forêt

Parkhaus, Parkplatz/Parkeergarage, Parkeerterrein
Car park, Parking place/Parking couvert, Parking

Informationsbüro, Polizei/Toeristen informatie kantoor, Politie
Tourist information center, Police/Syndicat d'initiative, Police

Post, Taxi/Postkantoor, Taxi
Post office, Taxi/Bureau de poste, Taxi

Campingplatz/Kampeerterrein
Camping place/Terrain de camping

Flughafen/Luchthaven
Airport /Aéroport

Schloss, Ruine/Slot, Ruine
Castle, Ruin/Château, Ruine

Kirche, Denkmal/Kerk, Monument
Church, Monument/Eglise, Monument

Windmühle, Leuchtturm/Molen, Vuurtoren
Windmill, Lighthouse/Moulin à vent, Phare

Hallwag

2

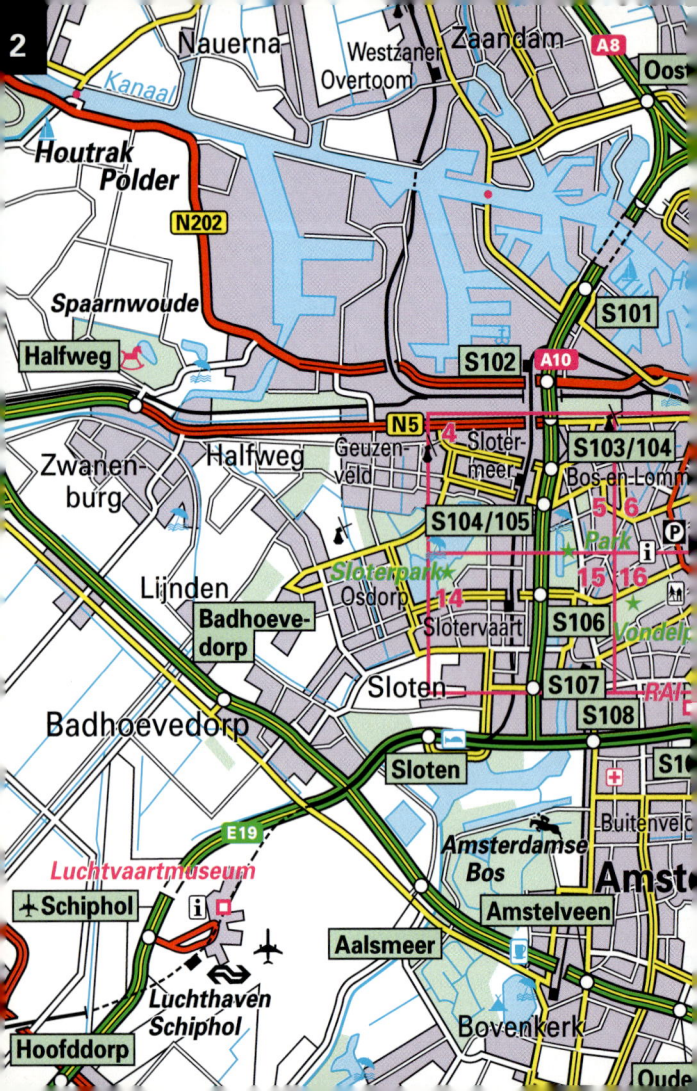

Nauerna Westzaner Overtoom Zaandam A8
Kanaal Oost
Houtrak Polder
N202
Spaarnwoude
Halfweg
S101
S102 A10
N5 Sloter-
Halfweg Geuzen- meer S103/104
Zwanenburg veld Bos-en-Lom.
S104/105 5 6
Sloterpark P
Lijnden Osdorp Park i
Badhoevedorp 15 16
14 Slotervaart S106 Vondel
Sloten S107 RAI
S108
Badhoevedorp Sloten S1

E19 Amsterdamse Bos Amst
Luchtvaartmuseum
Schiphol i Amstelveen
Aalsmeer
Luchthaven Schiphol Bovenkerk
Hoofddorp Oude

AMSTERDAM

3

Den Ilp
Broek in Waterland
Zuiderwoude
Landsmeer
S117
E35
S116 Volendam
Zunderdorp
Holysloot
zaan
Buiksloot
Nieuwendam
S114
Ransdorp
Schellingwoude

0   2 km
1 : 125 000

13
Pampus
IJmeer

18   19
A10
Oosterpark
Stadion
Watergrafsmeer
A1
Diemen
Muiden
Muiderslot
S110   S113
S112
S111
E231
Muiden
Muiderslot
Weesp
Amsterdam Zuidoost
A9
Gaasperplas
erkerk
derkerk
Bijlmermeer
Bullewijk
Aetsveld

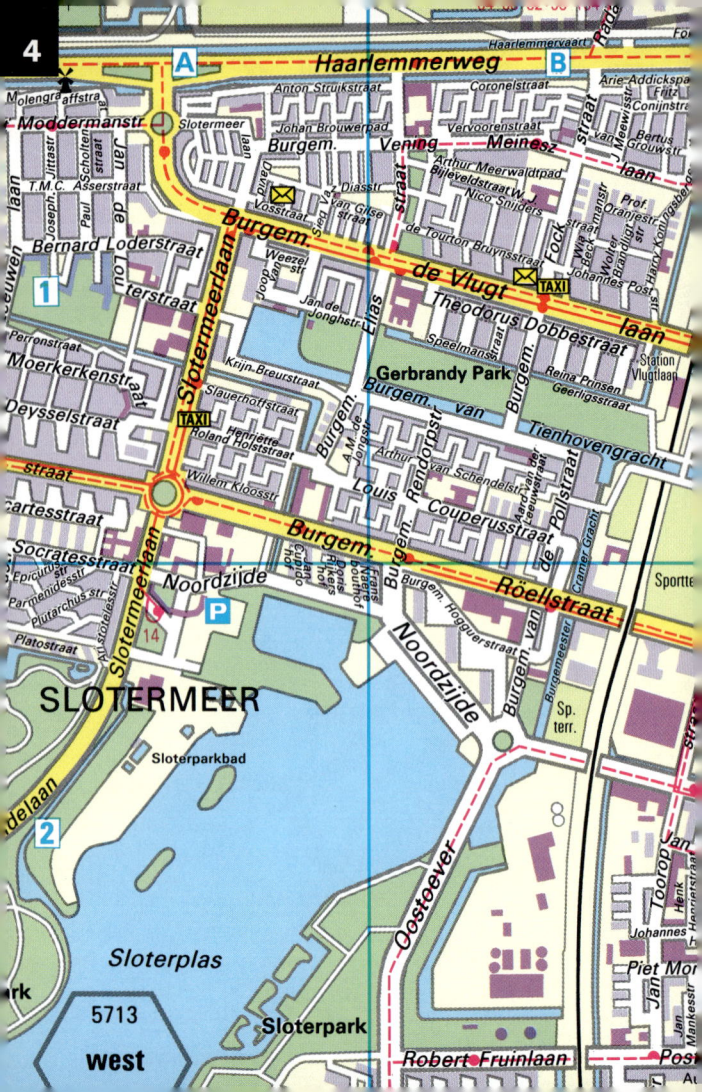

4

Slotermeer

Sloterplas

Sloterpark

5713 west

Streets and features

- Haarlemmerweg / Haarlemmervaart
- Moddermanstr
- Molengraaffstr
- Jan Jittastr
- T.M.C. Asserstraat
- Joseph Haydnlaan (Jac. Joseph / Paul Scholtenstraat)
- Bernard Loderstraat
- Jan de Louterstraat
- Perronstraat
- Moerkerkenstraat
- Deysselstraat
- Cartesiusstraat
- Socratesstraat
- Epicurusstraat
- Parmenidesstr
- Plutarchusstr
- Platostraat
- Aristotelesstr
- Anton Struykstraat
- Johan Brouwerpad
- Burgem. Vening Meineszlaan
- Slotermeer
- Burgemeester Slotermeerlaan
- Vosstraat / Sieg. Van Gelse straat
- Diasstraat
- Arthur Meerwaldtpad
- Bijleveldstraat / Wessel Nico Snijders
- de Tourton Bruynsstraat
- Burgem. de Vlugtlaan
- Weezelstr
- Jan de Jonghstr
- Eliasstraat
- Theodorus Dobbestraat
- Krijn Breursstraat
- Slauerhoffstraat
- Speelmansstr
- Gerbrandy Park
- Henriëtte Holststraat
- Burgem. A.M. de Jonghstraat
- Arthur Lehning
- Louis Couperusstraat
- Willem Kloosstraat
- Burgem. Rendorpstraat
- Arthur Schendelstraat
- Burgem. van Tienhovengracht
- Burgem. de Polstraat
- Burgem. Röellstraat
- Noordzijde
- Crispijnhof / Doris Rijkershof
- Frans Douwehof
- Burgem. Hogguerstraat
- Burgemeester
- Cremer Gracht
- Oostoever
- Sloterparkbad
- Robert Fruinlaan
- Coronelstraat
- Vervoorenstraat
- Arie Addickspad
- Fritz Conijnstraat
- Bertus van Meewenstr
- Grouwstr
- Prof. Oranjelaan
- Wouter Brandligtstr
- Johannes Postlaan
- Focke Winkelaan
- Kon. Wilhelminastr
- Reina Prinsen Geerligsstraat
- Station Vlugtlaan
- Jan Toorop straat
- Johannes Henk Hennestraat
- Piet Mondriaanstr
- Jan Mankesstr

A **B**

[1] [2]

P 14

TAXI TAXI

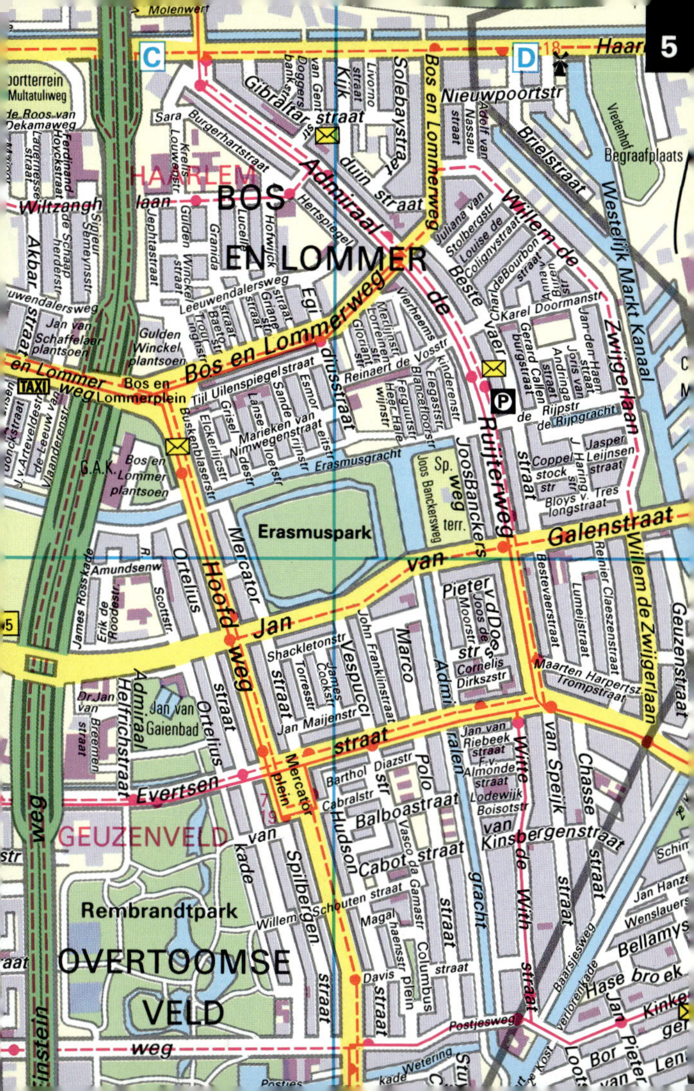
Molenwerf
C
D
Haarl
Sportterrein Multatuliweg
de Roos van Dekamaweg
Sara Burgerhartstraat
Gibraltar straat
Doggersbankstr
van Gent str
Kijk duin straat
Livorno straat
Solebaystraat
Bos en Lommerweg
Nieuwpoortstr
Nassau straat
Adolf van
Brielstraat
Vredenhof Begraafplaats
HAARLEM
BOS EN LOMMER
Admiraal de Ruijterweg
Hertspiegel
Wiltzangh laan
Ferdinand Hoyckstraat
de Schaap herderstr
Sigjeur Semeynsstr
Akbar straat
Lauernessestraat
Kreilsstraat
Louwerstr
Jephtastraat
Gulden Winckelstraat
Granida
Lucelle
Hofwijck
Juliana van Stolbergstr
Louise de Colignystraat
Willem de Zwijgerlaan
Westelijk Markt Kanaal
Charlotte de Bourbonstraat
Anna v. Buren str
Beste vaer straat
Karel Doormanstr
Gerard Callenburgstraat
Jan den Haen straat
Andringa straat
Joris van
Leeuwendalersweg
Egidiusstraat
Vierheemskinderenstr
Merlijnstr
Torreienstr
Gloriantstr
Reinaert de Vosstr
Blancefloorstr
Elegaststr.
Ferguutstr
Heer Halewijnstr
Jan van Schaffelaarplantsoen
Gulden Winckelplantsoen
Bos en Lommerweg
Bos en Lommerplein
TAXI
Tijl Uilenspiegelstraat
Esmoreitstr
Sander
Lanseloetstr
Griselstr
Marieken van Nimwegenstraat
Frijnstr
Elckerlijcstr
Buskenblaserstr
Erasmusgracht
Rijpstr
de Rijpgracht
Jasper Leijnsenstraat
Coppelstockstr
J. Haringstr
Bloys v. Treslongstraat
Joos Banckersweg
Sp. weg terr.
Bos en Lommerplantsoen
G.A.K.
Vlaanderenstr
J. v. Arteveldestr
de Leeuw van
Hoochstraat
Erasmuspark
Mercator
Hoofdweg
Ortelius
Amundsenw
Scottstr.
James Rosskade
Erik de Roodestr.
Jan van Galenstraat
Pieter v.d. Doesstr
Joos de Moorstr
Cornelis Dirkszstr
Bestevaerstraat
Lumeijstraat
Reinier Claeszenstraat
Geuzenstraat
Shackletonstr
John Franklinstraat
Marco Polo str
Vespucci
Torresstr
James Cookstr
Jan Maijenstr
Admiralengracht
Maarten Harpertsz Trompstraat
Dr. Jan van Breemenstraat
Admiraal Helfrichstraat
Jan van Galenbad
Ortelius straat
Evertsen
Mercatorplein
Barthol Diazstr
Cabralstr
Balboastraat
Jan van Riebeekstraat
F.v. Almondestraat
Lodewijk Boisotstr
van Kinsbergenstraat
Witte de With straat
van Speijkstraat
Chassestraat
GEUZENVELD
van Spilbergenstraat
Hudson
Cabotstraat
Vasco da Gamastr
Schoutenstraat
Magalhaensstr
Columbus plein
Rembrandtpark
OVERTOOMSE VELD
Willem
Davis straat
Postjesweg
Baarsjesweg
Jan Hanze
Wenslauerstr
Bellamystraat
Hasebroek
Jan Pieter
Kinker
Verlorenkade
Lootsstraat
Einsteinweg
Wetering
kade
Postjes
weg

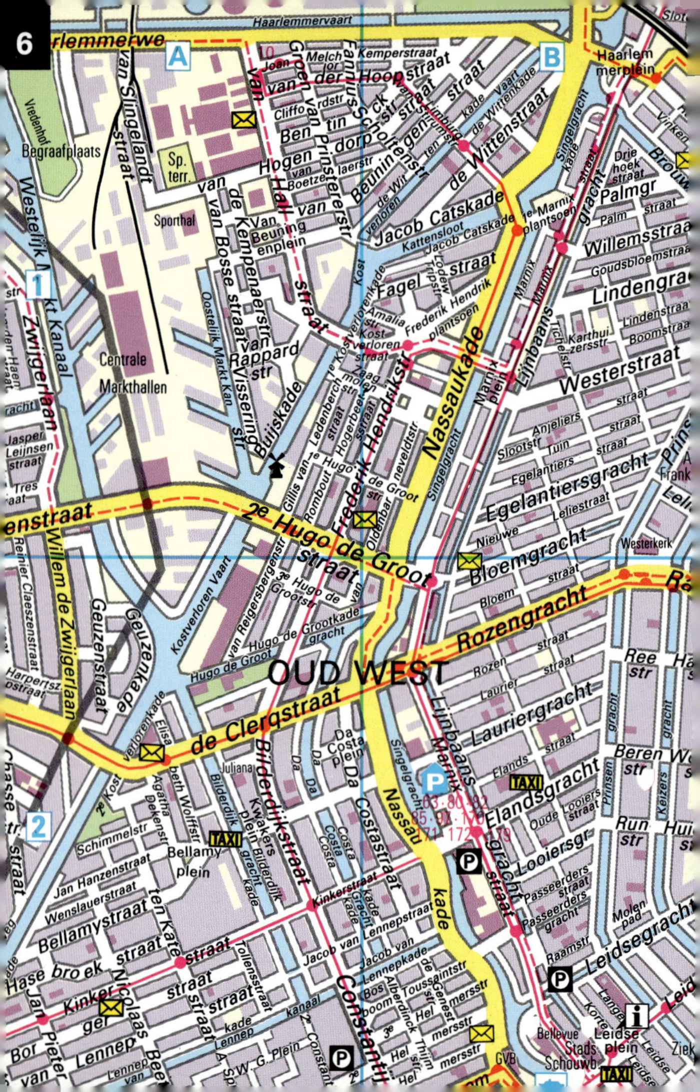
6
A
B
1
2
Haarlemmervaart
rlemmerwe
Haarlem merplein
Vredenhof
Begraafplaats
van Slingelandt straat
Sp. terr.
Sporthal
Centrale Markthallen
Westelijk Markt Kanaal
Oostelijk Markt Kan
van Hall straat
Van Beuning enplein
van Bosse straat
de Kempenaerstr
van Rappard str
Vissering str
Bullskade
Groen van Prinstererstr
van der Hoop straat
Kemperstraat
Fannius Scholtenstr
Hogendorp straat
Ben tin ck straat
Cliffo rdstr
van Boetze laerstr
van Beuningenstr
Wittenstraat
de Wittenkade
de Wittenstraat
Jacob Catskade
Kattensloot
Jacob Catskade
Fagel straat
Lodew Tripstr
Frederik Hendrik plantsoen
Kostverlorenkade
Kostverloren straat
Zaagmolen str
Amalia str
Nassaukade
Frederik Hendrikstr
Ledenberch str
Hogerbeets str
Gillis van Ledenbergstr
Rombout Hogerbeetsstr
Hugo de Groot str
Oldenbarneveldtstr
Singelgracht
Marnixstraat
Marnix plantsoen
Marnix plein
Lijnbaansgracht
Singelgracht kade
Drie hoek straat
Palmgr
Palm straat
Willemsstraat
Goudsbloemstraat
Lindengracht
Lindenstraat
Boomstraat
Karthuizersstr
Tichelstr
Westerstraat
Anjeliers straat
Tuin straat
Slootstr
Egelantiers straat
Egelantiersgracht
Nieuwe Leliestraat
Prinsengracht
Westerkerk
Bloemgracht
Bloem straat
Rozengracht
Rozen straat
Laurier straat
Lauriergracht
Elands straat
Elandsgracht
Oude Looiers straat
Looiersgr
Passeerders straat
Passeerders gracht
Raamstr
Leidsegracht
Leidse plein
Bellevue
Stads Schouwb.
GVB
Beren str
Run str
Ree str
Molen pad
2e Hugo de Groot straat
Westerstraat
Willem de Zwijgerlaan
Reinier Claeszenstraat
Harpertsz. straat
Geuzenstraat
Geuzenkade
Kostverloren Vaart
van Reigersbergenstr
Hugo de Grootkade
Hugo de Groot gracht
OUD WEST
de Clerqstraat
Bilderdijkstraat
Bilderdijk kade
Da Costa plein
Da Costastraat
Da Costa kade
Nassaukade
Juliana
Elisabeth Wolffstr
Agatha Dekenstr
Schimmelstr
Bellamy plein
Jan Hanzenstraat
Wenslauerstraat
Bellamystraat
ten Kate straat
Kwakers plein
Kinkerstraat
Jacob van Lennepstraat
Jacob van Lennepkade
Tollensstraat
Nicolaas Beets straat
Bosboom Toussaintstr
Albardingk Thijmstr
De Genestetstr
Helmersstraat
Hasebroekstraat
Jan Pieter
Bor
Lennep kade
Lennep kanaal
2e Constantijn
W.G. Plein
Constantijn
Zwijgerlaan
Jasper Leijnsen straat
Tres
Chasse straat
Lijnbaansgracht
Marnix
63 · 80 · 82
85 · 97 · 170
171 · 172 · 179
TAXI
P
i

7

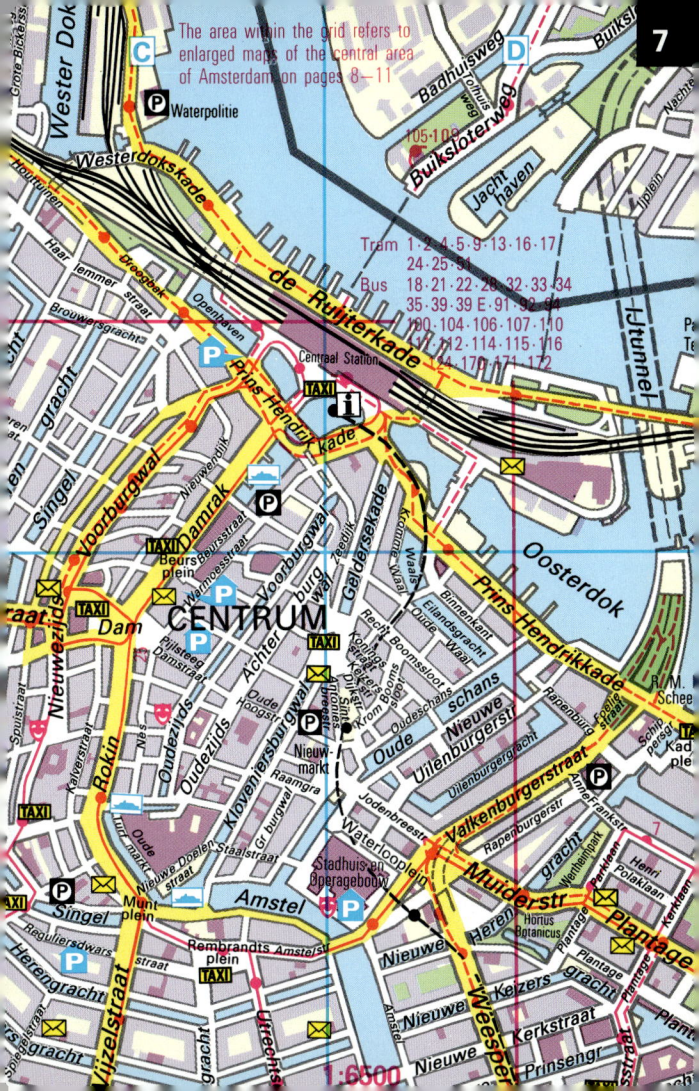

The area within the grid refers to enlarged maps of the central area of Amsterdam on pages 8–11

Tram 1·2·4·5·9·13·16·17
24·25·51
Bus 18·21·22·26·32·33·34
35·39·39 E·91·92·94
100·104·106·107·110
111·112·114·115·116
154·170·171·172

CENTRUM

1:6600

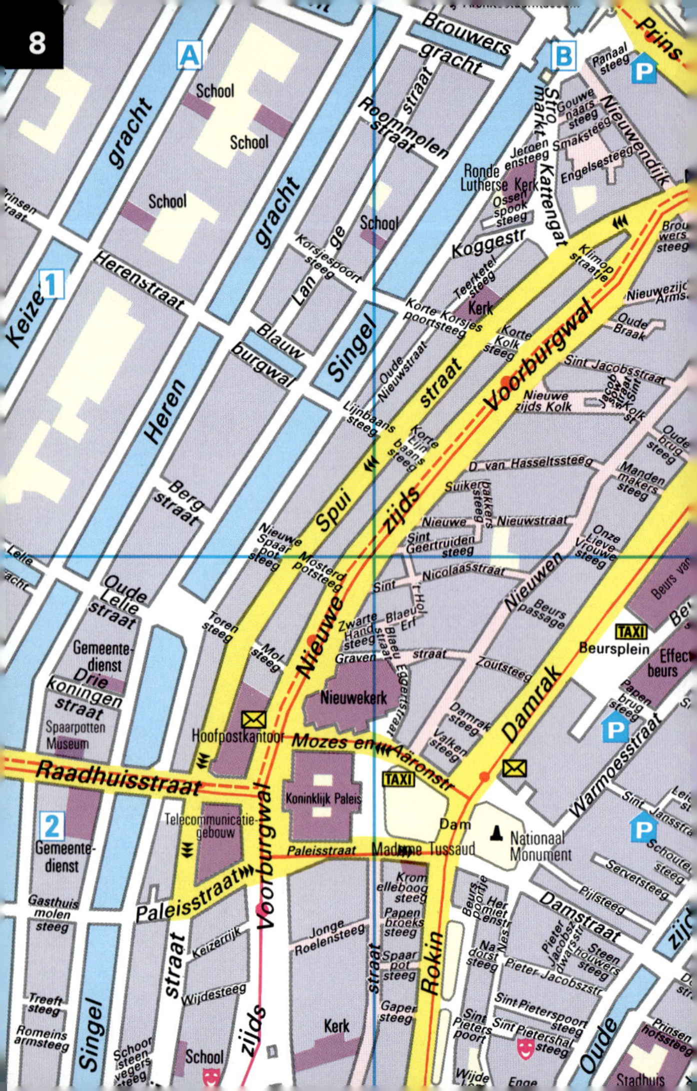

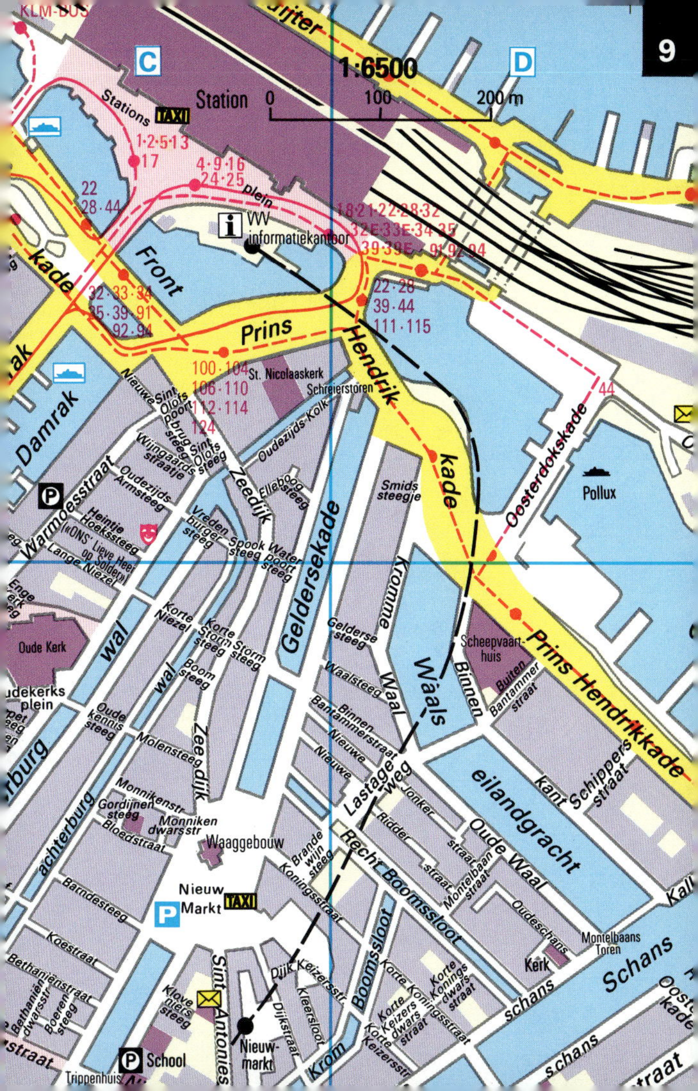
KLM-BUS
C
D
1:6500
0
100
200 m
Station
Stationsplein
TAXI
1·2·5·13
17
4·9·16
24·25
22
28·44
VVV informatiekantoor
18·21·22·28·32
32E·33E·34·35
39·39E·91·92·94
22·28
39·44
111·115
32·33·34
35·39·91
92·94
Front
Prins Hendrik kade
100·104
106·110
112·114
124
St. Nicolaaskerk
Schreierstoren
Damrak
kade
44
Oosterdokskade
Pollux
Nieuwe Sint Olofspoort
Sint Olofs steeg
brug steeg
Wijngaardsstraatje
Oudezijds Kolk
Oudezijds Armsteeg
Warmoesstraat
Heintje Hoeksteeg
("ONS' Lieve Heer op Solder")
Lange Niezel
Zeedijk
Elleboogsteeg
Vredenburgersteeg
Spooksteeg
Waterpoortsteeg
Geldersekade
Smids steegje
Kromme Waal
Oude Kerk
Oudekerksplein
wal
Korte Niezel
Korte Stormsteeg
Stormsteeg
Boomsteeg
Gelderse steeg
Waalsteeg
Waals
Binnen
Scheepvaarthuis
Buiten Bantammerstraat
Prins Hendrikkade
Oude kennissteeg
Molensteeg
Zeedijk
Binnen Bantammerstraat
Nieuwe
Lastage weg
Jonker
Ridder
straat
eilandgracht
kant
Schippersstraat
achterburg
Monnikenstr
Gordijnensteeg
Monniken dwarsstr
Bloedstraat
Waaggebouw
Brandewijnsteeg
Recht Boomssloot
Oude Waal
Montelbaanstraat
Oudeschans
Montelbaans Toren
Barndesteeg
Nieuw Markt
TAXI
Koningsstraat
Koestraat
Bethaniënstraat
Bethaniëndwarsstr
Boerensteeg
Kloveniersteeg
Sint Antonies
Dijk
Keizersstr.
Dijkstraat
Kleersloot
Boomssloot
Korte Koningsstraat
Korte Konings dwarsstraat
Korte Keizers dwarsstraat
Korte Keizersstr
Krom
Kerk
Schans
schans
s.chans
Nieuwmarkt
School
Trippenhuis
Kall
straat

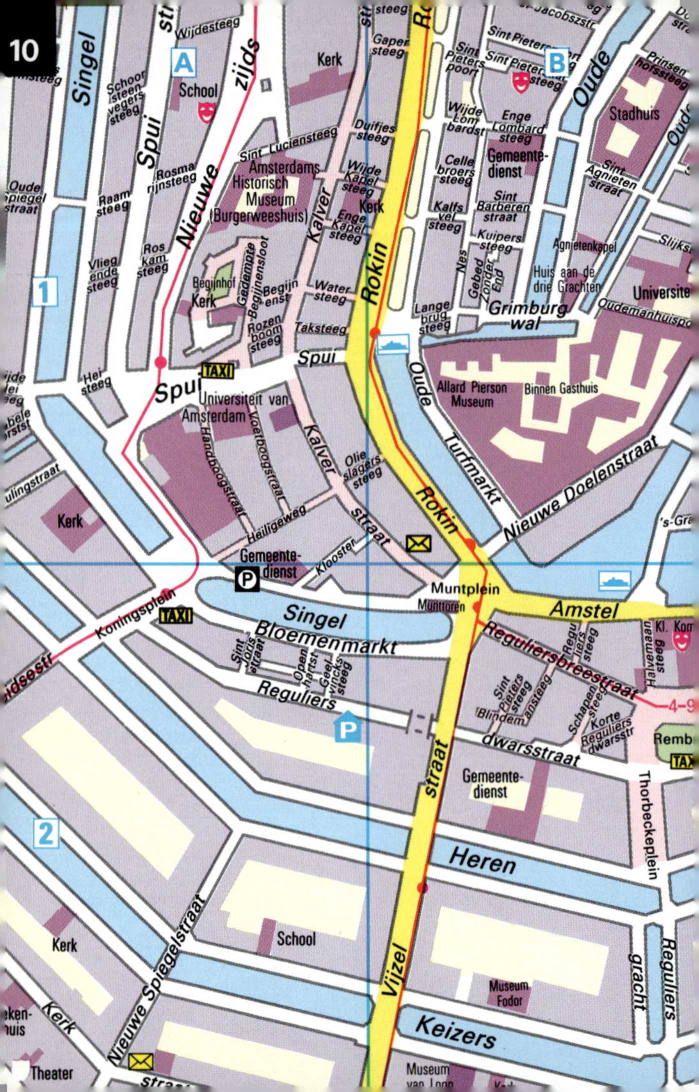

11

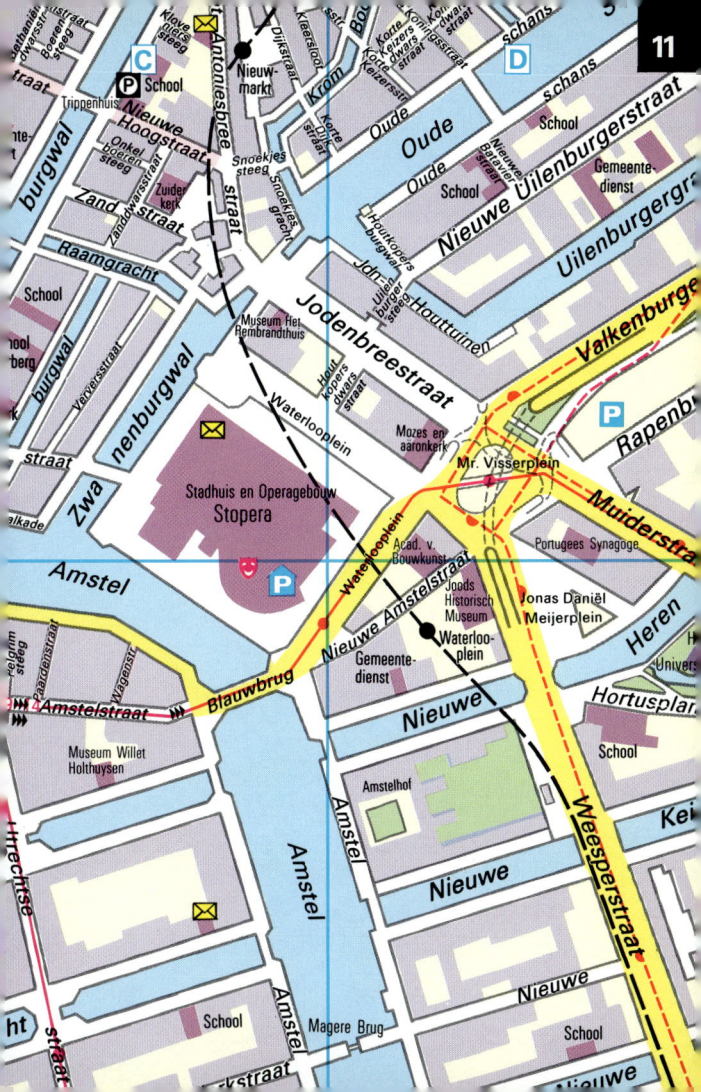

C D

Streets and places:

- Kloveniersburgwal
- Klovenierssteeg
- Kreeksteeg
- Kromme Kolk-steeg / Korte Koningsstraat
- Keizers-straat / Keizersstraat / Kolkj
- s. schans
- Nieuwmarkt
- Dijkstraat
- Nieuwe Hoogstraat
- Trippenhuis
- P School
- St. Antoniesbreestraat
- Onkel-boeld-steeg
- Snoekjes-steeg
- Krom Boomssloot
- Kromme Snoekjes gracht
- Korte Koningsstraat
- Oude Schans
- Oude Waal
- Nieuwe Uilenburgerstraat
- School
- Gemeente-dienst
- Uilenburgergracht
- Zandstraat
- Zuiderkerk
- Zandhoekerwarsstraat
- Raamgracht
- School
- Houtkopersburgwal
- Jdn-Ullrer-steeg
- Jodenhouttuinen
- Schoolberg
- Verversstraat
- Zwanenburgwal
- Museum Het Rembrandthuis
- Houtkopers-dwars-straat
- Jodenbreestraat
- Valkenburgerstraat
- P
- Rapenburg
- Waterlooplein
- Mozes en aäronkerk
- Mr. Visserplein
- Stadhuis en Operagebouw **Stopera**
- Acad. v. Bouwkunst
- Portugees Synagoge
- Muiderstraat
- Amstel
- Waterlooplein
- Nieuwe Amstelstraat
- Joods Historisch Museum
- Waterloo-plein
- Gemeente-dienst
- Jonas Daniël Meijerplein
- Heren...
- Univers...
- Pazzadsteeg / Belgiumsteeg
- Waggenstraat
- Amstelstraat
- Blauwbrug
- Nieuwe Kerkstraat
- Hortusplantsoen
- School
- Museum Willet Holthuysen
- Amstelhof
- Amstel
- Nieuwe Kerkstraat
- Weesperstraat
- Kei...
- Utrechtse-straat
- Magere Brug
- School
- Nieuwe Prinsengracht
- School

A
B
1
2
Badhuisweg
Tolhuisweg
Buiksloterweg
105·109
Jachthaven
Adelaarsweg
Havikslaan
Sperwerlaan
Nachtegaalstr
Leeuwerik
Meeuwenlaan
Gedempt Insteekhaven
Bankwerkerij
IJplein
Motorkade
Motorkanaal
Spijkerkade
Gedempt Hamerkanaal
Hamerkanaal
Schaafstr
Herstraat
Ketelstr
Boorstr
IJtunnel
Passagiers Terminal
IJ haven
Piet Heinkade
Dijksgracht
Dijks gracht
5700
centrum
Oosterdok
Prins Hendrikkade
Binnenkant
Eilandsgracht
Oude Waal
Waals
Kattenburgerstraat
Kattenburgervaart
Grote Wittenburgerstraat
Wittenburgervaart
Kattenburgergracht
Wittenburgergracht
R. M. Nederlands Scheepvaartmuseum
TAXI
Kadijksplein
Schippersgr
Foeliestraat
Rapenburg
Nieuwe Uilenburgerstr
Uilenburgergracht
Valkenburgerstraat
Rapenburgerstr
Anne Frankstr
Nieuwe Vaart
Hoogte Kadijk
Entrepotdok
Oostenburgergracht
't Kromhout Werfmuseum
Conradstr
Zeeburgerstraat
Wertheimpark
Muiderstr
Henri Polaklaan
Parklaan
Kerklaan
Planetarium
Natura Artis Magistra «Artis»
Plantage Doklaan
Plantage Middenlaan
Plantage Kerklaan
Plantage Muidergracht
Hortus Botanicus
Nieuwe Herengracht
Nieuwe Keizersgracht
Nieuwe Kerkstraat
Weesperstraat
Prinsengr
Muidergracht
Aquarium
Sarphatistraat
Kazernestraat
Kazerne Oranje Nassau
Singelgracht
Pieter Vlamingstr
Von Zesenstr

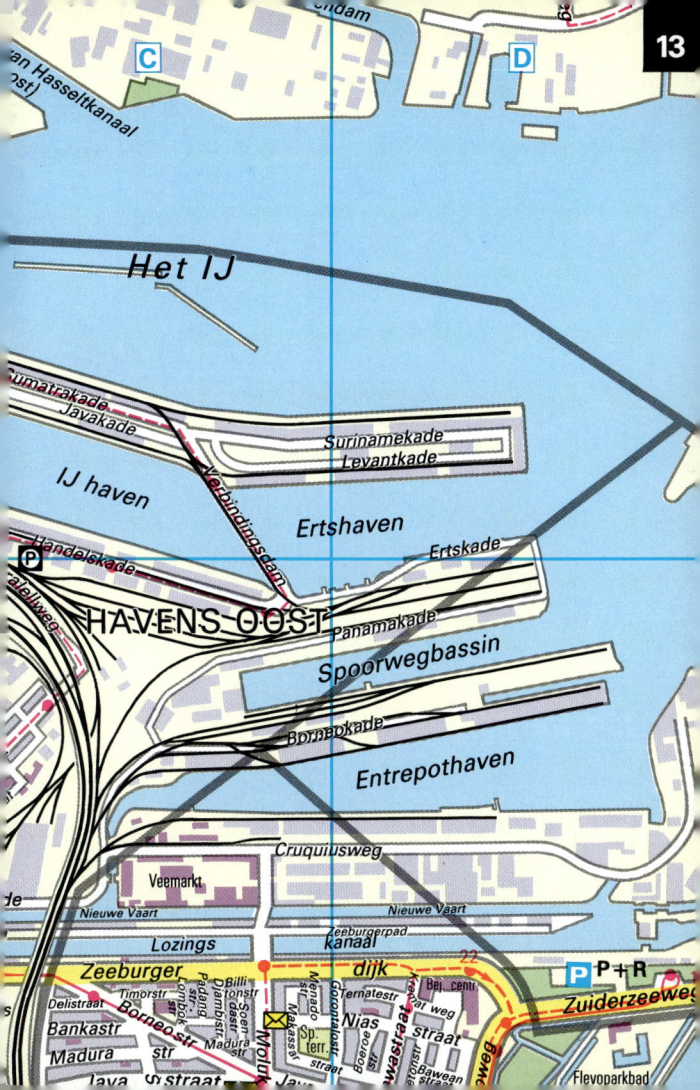

13

- C
- D

Hasseltkanaal

Het IJ

Sumatrakade
Javakade
Surinamekade
Levantkade
IJ haven
Verbindingsdam
Handelskade
Ertshaven
Ertskade
P
HAVENS OOST
Panamakade
Spoorwegbassin
Borneokade
Entrepothaven
Cruquiusweg
Veemarkt
Nieuwe Vaart
Nieuwe Vaart
Lozings
Zeeburgerpad
kanaal
Zeeburger
dijk
22
P P+R
Delistraat
Timorstr
Billi
Menado
Bej. centr
Zuiderzeewe
Bankastr
Borneostr
Djambistr
Padang
Djambistr
Ternatestr
straat
Madura
str
Bawean
Molu
Sp.
Nias
straat
weststraat
Java
str
terr
Flevoparkbad

14 5713 west

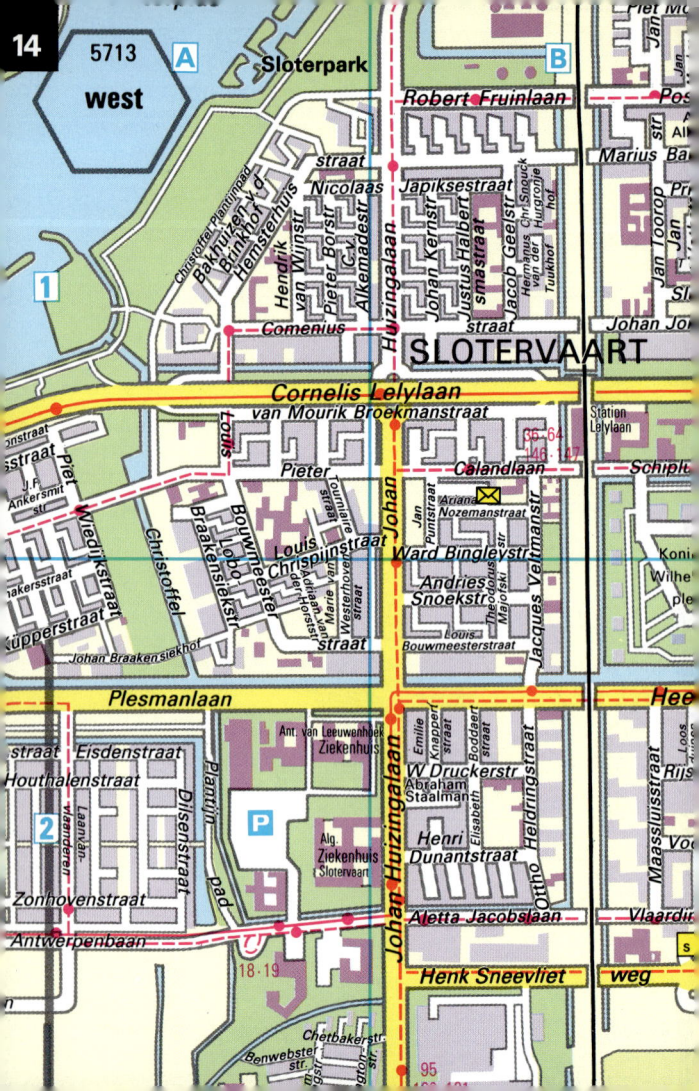

Sloterpark

SLOTERVAART

Robert Fruinlaan
Marius Ba...
Piet Mo...
Jan Toorop str
Jan Pr...

straat
Nicolaas
Japiksestraat
Hermanus Chr.Snouck
Hurgronje hof
van der Tuukhof

Christoffel Plantijnpad
Bakhuyzen
v.d. Brinkhof
Hendrik van Wijnstr
Pieter Borstr
C.d. Alkemadestr
Johan Kernstr
Justus Halbertsmastraat
Jacob Geelstr
Huizingalaan

Comenius straat
Johan Jo...

Cornelis Lelylaan
Station Lelylaan
Schiph...

van Mourik Broekmanstraat
35·64
146·147
Calandlaan
stonstraat
J.F. Ankersmit str
Piet Wiedijkstraat
Christoffel
Louis
Lobo
Braakensliekstr
Pieter
Bouwmeester
Jan Puntstraat
Nozemanstraat
Chrispinstraat
Daumarie
Marie van Westerhoven
Cornel Horst straat
Johan Huizingalaan
Ward Bingleystr
Andries Snoekstraat
Theodorus Majofski str
Jacques Veltmanstr
Koni...
Wilhe...

bakerstraat
Küppperstraat
Johan Braakensiekhof
Louis Bouwmeesterstraat

Plesmanlaan
Hee...

straat
Eisdenstraat
Houthalenstraat
Ant. van Leeuwenhoek Ziekenhuis
Emilie Knappertstr
Boddaert straat
W Druckerstr
Abraham Staalman
Loos...
Maassluisstraat
Rijs...
Vo...

2 Laamar-vlaanderen
Plantijn pad
P
Alg Ziekenhuis Sloten vaart
Henri Dunantstraat
Ortho Heldringstraat

Zonhovenstraat
Aletta Jacobslaan
Vlaardin...

Antwerpenbaan
18·19
Johan Huizingalaan
Henk Sneevliet weg
s

Chetbakerstraat
Benwebsterstr
95

OVERTOOMSE
ELD
Rembrandtpark
OSDORP
SLOTEN
Vond
Einstein
Einsteinweg
A 10
Terheideweg
Hodenpijlkade
Postjesweg
Postjeswe
Postjes kade
Corantijnstr
van Walbeeck straat
Curacao straat
Hoofdweg
Arubastr
Antil lenstr
Paramaribo straat
Bonairestraat
Cryssenstr
Stuyvesant straat
Wetering kade
Kostverloren Vaart
Kostverlorenkade
3e Kostverlorenkade
Baarsjesweg
Surinameplein
Suriname straat
ANWB
Andreas Schelfhoutstr
Andreas Ziekenhuis
wachtlaan
Nacht
Jacob van Lennep
Jan Pieter Hase
Bor
Lootsstr
Verlorenkade
Heijestraat
Staringstr
Kanaal
Wilhelmina straat
Rhijnvis Feithstr
Pieter Langendijk
Brede rode
1e
J.J. Cremer plein
Overtoom
Frederiks
Vondelstr
Anslostr
Saxenburg str
School straat
Zocher str
Koningslaan
Emma laan
Emma plein
Oranje Nassau laan
Prins Hendriklaan
Waldeck Pyrmont laan
Saxen-Weimarlaan
Sophialaan
Koninginne weg
Valerius plein
Valerius
Hendrik Jacobsz str
Okeghem str
Loman straat
Cornelis Kruseman
Lastman kade
Noorder
Bertelmanplein
Bernard
Kochstr
Pieter
Olympia weg
Olympia plein
Marathonweg
Sportstr
Turner
Hercules straat
Hygiëaplein
Achillesstr
Achillesstraat
Agamemnon
Hector
Stadionweg
Amazonenstr
van Tuyll van Serooskerkenweg
Jason
Stadion plein
Stadion
Sportterrein
Olympisch
Stadiongracht
Stadionkade
Karperweg
Karper straat
Havenstr
Vlietstraat
Vaart straat
Veer straat
Zeilstraat
Baarsstraat
Sluisstraat
Schinkel
Schinkelkade
Schinkelhavenstr
1e Schinkelstr
2e Schinkelstr
3e Schinkelstr
Amstelveenseweg
Marisstr
Jacob Marisplein
Wijsmuller str
Jacob straat
Theophile de Bockstraat
Vogelenzangstr
Leiduinstr
Groenendaalstr
Warmond straat
Haarlemmermeerstr
Legmeer straat
Sloterkade
Westlandgracht
Bennebroekstr
Hillegomstraat
Hoofddorp plein
Hoofddorpweg
Leimuiden straat
Woestduin straat
Piet Gijzen brug str
Stolwijkstraat
meerweg
Rietwijkerstraat
Westland
Poeldijkstraat
Naaldwijkstr
Honselersdijkstr
Hoek van Hollandstr
Sassenheim straat
Abbenesstr
Woubrugstr
Rijnsburgstr
Aalsmeerweg
Aalsmeerplein
Spijtellaantje
Begraafplaats
Tramwegstichting
Museumlijn
Voorm. Haarl. Station
Anthony Fokkerweg
Laboratorium straat
Vetter
Slotermeer
TAXI
C
D
P
17
43
24
6
16
15 · 23 · 60
70 · 146 · 147
170 · 171 · 172
179 · 196 · 197

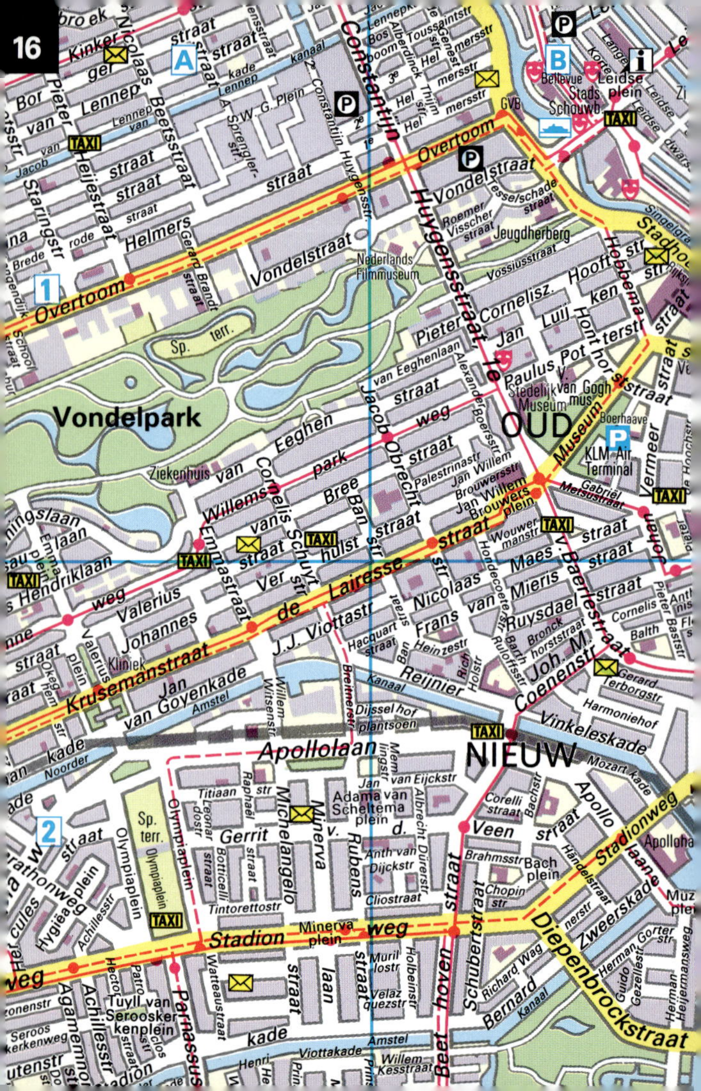

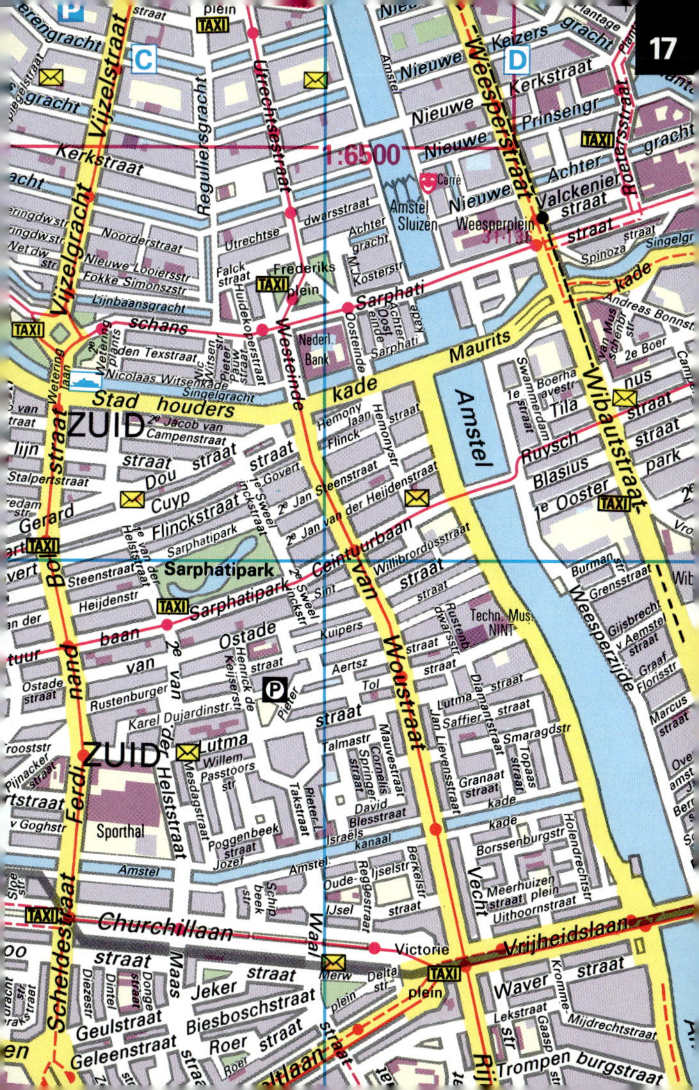
C
D
1:6500
Vijzelstraat
Vijzelgracht
Kerkstraat
Reguliersgracht
Utrechtsestraat
Utrechtse dwarsstraat
Noorderstraat
Nieuwe Looiersstr
Fokke Simonszstr
Lijnbaansgracht
Falck straat
Huidekoperstraat
Frederiksplein
Westeinde
Sarphati
Achter gracht
Kosterstr
Oosteinde
Achter Oost einde
Sarphatikade
Nederl. Bank
Amstel
Nieuwe Keizersgracht
Nieuwe Kerkstraat
Nieuwe Prinsengr
Nieuwe Achter gracht
Amstel Sluizen
Carré
Weesperstraat
Weesperplein
Valckenierstraat
Roetersstraat
Plantage
Spinozastraat
Singelgr
Mauritskade
Andreas Bonnstr
van Muschenbr str
2e Boer
Swammerdamstraat
1e Boerhaavestr
Tilanusstraat
Wibautstraat
Ruyschstraat
Blasiusstraat
1e Oosterparkstraat
Stadhouderskade
Singelgracht
Nicolaas Witsenkade
Jan van Texstraat
Nic Witsenstr
Pieter Pauwstraat
Weteringschans
Wetering plantsoen
2e Weteringdwarsstr
ZUID
2e Jacob van Campenstraat
Hemonylaan
Hemonystraat
Govert Flinckstraat
Stalpertstraat
Gerard Doustraat
Albert Cuypstraat
Flinckstraat
2e Jan Steenstraat
2e Jan van der Heijdenstraat
1e Sweelinckstraat
1e van der Helststraat
Sarphatipark
Ceintuurbaan
Willibrordusstraat
Burmanstraat
Grensstraat
Weesperzijde
Steenstraat
Heijdenstr
2e Sweelinckstr
Sint Willibrordusstraat
Rustenburgerdwarsstr
Techn. Mus. NINT
Gijsbrecht v Aemstelstraat
Graaf Florisstr
Marcusstraat
Van Woustraat
Ferdinand Bolstraat
Ostadestraat
van Ostadestraat
2e van der Helststraat
Henrick de Keijserstr
Kuipersstraat
Aertszstraat
Tolstraat
Pieter Aertszstraat
Rustenburgerstraat
Karel Dujardinstr.
Lutmastraat
Diamantstraat
Saffierstraat
Smaragdstr
Jan Lievensstraat
Topaasstraat
Granaatstraat
Willem Passtoorsstr
Mesdagstraat
Talmastr
Springerstraat
Cornelis Mauvestraat
David Blesstraat
Takstraat
Pieter L. Takstraat
Roostr
Pijnackerstraat
Sporthal
Poggenbeekstraat
Jozef Israëlskade
Amstelkanaal
Borssenburgstr
Holendrechtstr
Meerhuizenplein
Uithoornstraat
Vechtstraat
Berkelstr
IJsselstr
Oude Reggestraat
Schipbeekstr
Amstel
Churchillaan
Victorieplein
Vrijheidslaan
Scheldestraat
Maasstraat
Waalstraat
Merwedeplein
Deltastr
Dintelstraat
Diezestr
Dongestraat
Jekerstraat
Geulstraat
Biesboschstraat
Roerstraat
Geleenstraat
Waverstraat
Krommestraat
Lekstraat
Gaaspstr
Mijdrechtstraat
Trompenburgstraat
Rijnstraat
TAXI
P
31·136

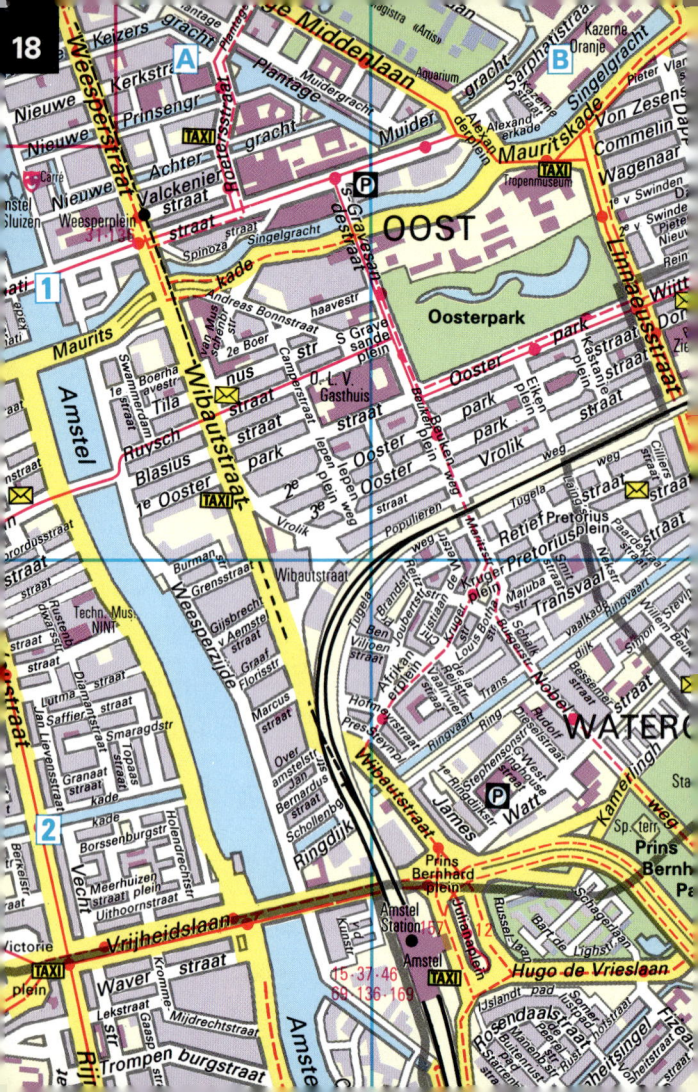

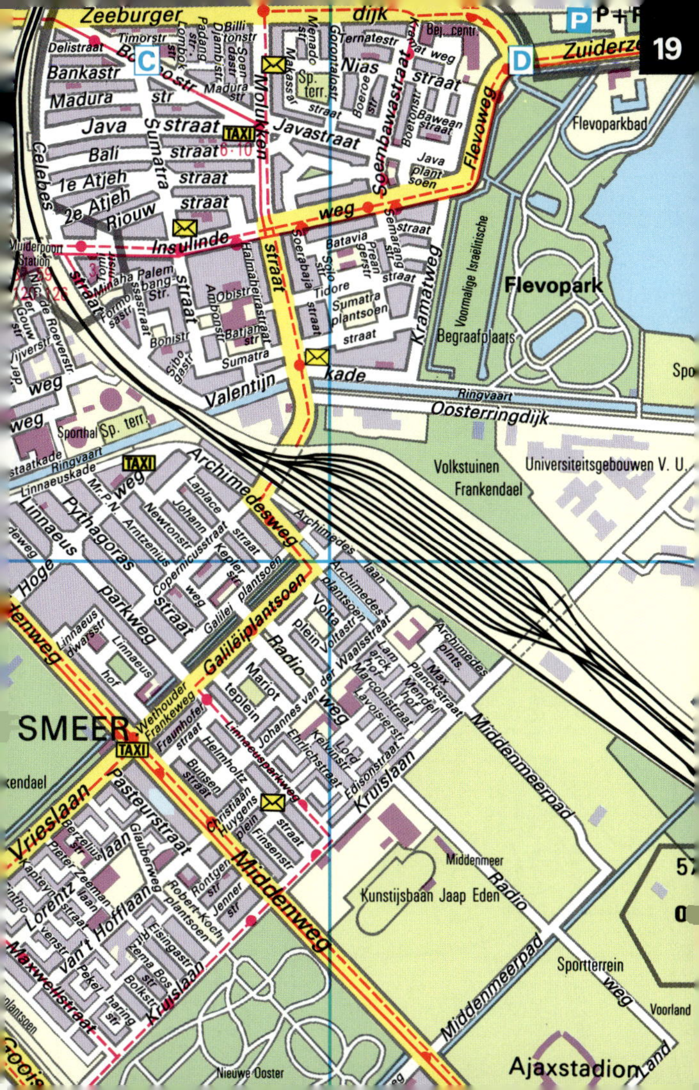
Zeeburgerdijk
Zuiderzeeweg
Flevoweg
Flevoparkbad
Flevopark
Voormalige Israëlitische Begraafplaats
Molukkenstraat
Javastraat
Soembawastraat
Sumatrastraat
Insulinde weg
Celebesstraat
Valentijnkade
Ringvaart
Oosterringdijk
Volkstuinen Frankendael
Universiteitsgebouwen V. U.
Archimedesweg
Archimedeslaan
Galileiplantsoen
Pythagorasstraat
Linnaeusstraat
Linnaeuskade
Linnaeusparkweg
Hogeweg
Radioweg
Middenweg
Kruislaan
Middenmeerpad
Kunstijsbaan Jaap Eden
Middenmeer
Sportterrein
Ajaxstadion
Nieuwe Ooster
Pasteurstraat
Vrieslaan
Maxwellstraat
Wethouder Frankeweg
SMEER
Muiderpoort Station
Sporthal
Sp. terr.
TAXI
P+R
Bej. centr.
Voorland

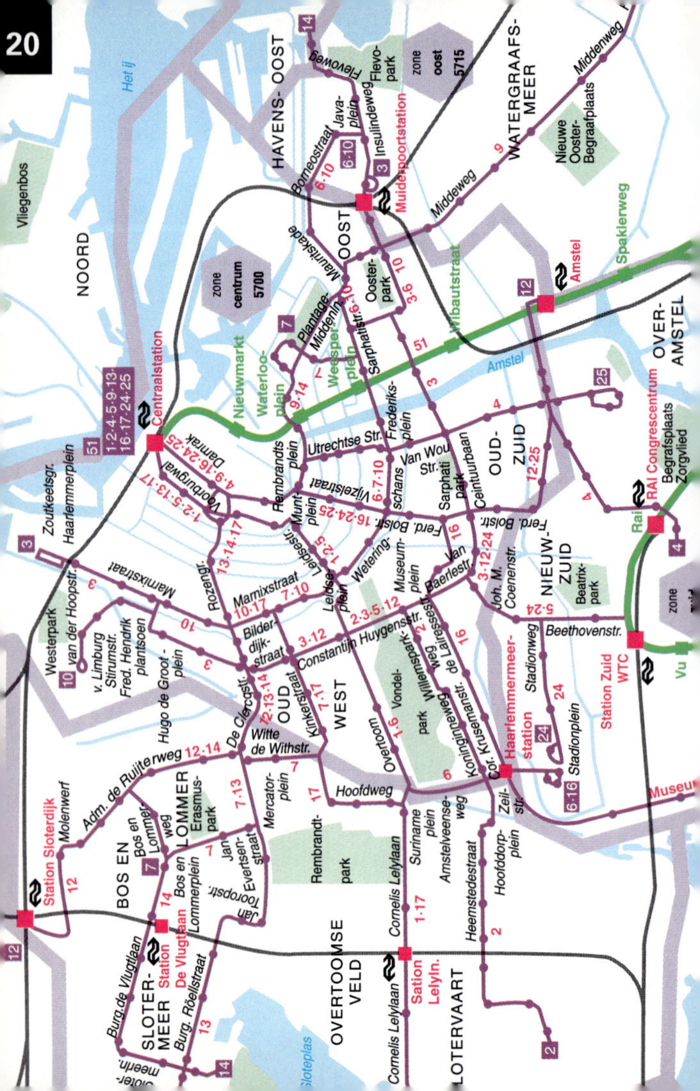
Het IJ
Vliegenbos
NOORD
zone centrum 5700
zone oost 5715
HAVENS-OOST
WATERGRAAFSMEER
Nieuwe Ooster-Begraafplaats
Flevoweg
Flevopark
Java-plein
Insulindeweg
Borneostraat
Muiderpoortstation
Middenweg
Middeweg
Spaklerweg
Amstel
Mauritskade
OOST
Oosterpark
Wibautstraat
Plantage-Middenlaan
Weesperplein
Sarphatistr.
Nieuwmarkt
Waterlooplein
Centraalstation
Damrak
Voorburgwal
Zoutkeetsgr.
Haarlemmerplein
Rembrandtsplein
Utrechtse Str.
Frederiksplein
Amstel
OVER-AMSTEL
Vijzelstraat
Muntplein
Van Woustr.
Sarphatipark
Ceintuurbaan
OUD-ZUID
Ferd. Bolstr.
RAI Congrescentrum
Begrafplaats Zorgvlied
Rai
Leidsestr.
Leidseplein
Weteringschans
Museumplein
Van Baerlestr.
Joh. M. Coenenstr.
NIEUW-ZUID
Beatrix-park
Beethovenstr.
Station Zuid WTC
Vu
Marnixstraat
Rozengr.
Westerpark
van der Hoopstr.
v. Limburg Stirumstr.
Fred. Hendrik plantsoen
Hugo de Groot-plein
Bilderdijkstraat
Constantijn Huygensstr.
Willemsparkweg
de Lairessestr.
Vondelpark
Overtoom
Koninginneweg
Cor. Krusemanstr.
Haarlemmermeer-station
Stadionweg
Stadionplein
De Clercqstr.
Kinkerstraat
OUD WEST
Witte de Withstr.
Adm. de Ruijterweg
Molenwerf
Station Sloterdijk
Bos en Lommerweg
BOS EN LOMMER
Erasmuspark
Bos en Lommerplein
Jan Evertsenstraat
Jan Tooropstr.
Mercatorplein
Hoofdweg
Rembrandtpark
Suriname plein
Amstelveenseweg
Zeilstr.
Hoofddorpplein
Heemstedestraat
Cornelis Lelylaan
Station Lelyln.
OVERTOOMSE VELD
LOTERVAART
Station De Vlugtlaan
Burg. de Vlugtlaan
Burg. Röellstraat
SLOTERMEER
Sloterplas
Museum

INDEX

A
A La Carte 66
A. Kok & Zoon 65
Aalsmeer Flower Auction 144
Abal 60
Acacia Hotel 123
Accidents 157
Adam & Eva 122
Adams, Dr 57
Admiraal, De 99
Agora Hotel 127
Airport information 155
Akitsu 90
Albert Cuypmarkt 62
Alkmaar Cheese Market 144
Allert de Lange 66
Altea Amsterdam Hotel 127
Alto 115
Ambassade Hotel 127
America Today 55
American Discount Book Center 66
American Hotel 101
American Hotel 129
Ams Hotel Holland Hotel 126
Amstel Church 20
Amstel Taveerne 118
Amstelpark 23
Amstelveld Square 25
Amsterdam Weichmann Hotel 127
Amsterdam Windmills 144
Amsterdamse Bos 23
Amsterdamse Bos Open-Air Theatre 109
Ankara 94
Antigua 64
Apollofirst Hotel 129
April 118
Argos 118
Art Galleries 43-51
  Akinci 43
  Amazone 43
  Amsterdams Beeldouwers Collectif 43
  Andre Coppenhagen 51
  Animation Art 44
  Apunto 44
  Art Gallery Comic Sense 44
  Art Unlimited 50
  Arti et Amicitae 44
  Asselijn 45
  Atelier Artiglas 50
  Barbara Farber 46
  Brinkman Amsterdam 45
  Canon Image Centre 45
  Eendt, D' 45
  De Appel 44
  De Expeditie 45
  De Haas Art Nouveau-Art Deco 49
  De Looier Antique Market 50
  De Selby 47
  Droomdoos 51
  Eble/Aziatica 49
  Espace 45
  Fons Welters 48
  Forum Gallerie 46
  Guntur Holland 51
  Institute of Contemporary Art 46
  Italiaander Galleries 49
  Jurka 46
  Kalpa 49
  Kunsthandelaar en Antiquair Frides Lameris 49
  Lemaire 50
  Living Room, The 46
  Matelski Muziek Galerie 51
  Montevideo 46
  Nanky de Vreeze 48
  Out of Africa 51
  Paul Andriesse 44
  Pebble Rock Shop 51
  Petit 46
  Pieter Brattinga Print Gallery 45
  Printshop 47
  Pulitzer Art Gallery 47
  Ra Sieraden 51
  Reflex Modern Art Gallery 47

INDEX

Siau 47
Signaal 47
Steendrukkerij Amsterdam 47
Steltman 48
Suzanne Biederberg Gallery 45
Swart 48
Thom and Lenny Nelis Antiques 50
Torch 48
Toth Ikonen 49
Tramlijnmuseum 40
Tropenmuseum 40
Tropical Museum 40
Van Dreven Toebosch Antiquairs 49
Van Gelder 46
Van Paridon Brothers 51
Van Rossum & Co 50
Vlaams Cultereel Centrum (Brakke Grond) 48
Wetering Galerie 48
Art Shop Rulot 60
Artis Zoo 133
Asian Caribbean Restaurant 93
Asian Fashion Shop Himalaya 55
Asp, De 60
Asterisk Hotel 123
At Mango Bay 84
Atheneum Boekhandel 66
Atlas Hotel 129
Avondmarkt 72

B

Babysit Centrale Babyhome 139
Backbeat 68
Bali 75
Balie 109
Bally for Men 57
Baltus-Sterk 72
Bamboo Bar, The 104
Banketbakkerij Lanskroon 70
Barco, El 92
Bark 82
Bastille, La 104
Beaches 144
Beatrixpark 23
Beddingtons 75
Begijnhof 24
Belga Hotel 124
Bell Tree Toys & Games 137
Bellevue Theatre 109
Berend Botje 137
Berlage, Hendrik Petrus 13
Berry, De 104
Betondorp 18
Beurs van Berlage 112
Beurs van Berlage Blauwbrug 13
Bierkoning, De 70
Big Shoe 57
Bijenkorf, De 53
Bimhuis 115
Black and White 104
Blaffende Vis, De 104
Blauwe Hollander, De 79
Blauwe Theehuis, 'T 105
Blue Bridge (Blauwbrug) 13
Boetiek Belle Fleur 55
Bojo 83
Bolhoed, De 97
Bolle Jan 100
Bols Taverne 76
Bonaparte, Louis 15
BookTraffic 64
Bordewijk 85
Borgmann Hotel 127
Botte, La 89
Boudisque/ Blackbeat 68
Brakke Grond 110
Brakke Grond, De 84
Breakdowns 157
Brit, De 105
Broeker Auction 145
Brouwersgracht Warehouses 27
Burgerweeshuis 14
Bus- of Tuighuis 14

C

Café Pacifico 91
Cafécox 80
Caffe Panini 89
Cajun 91

INDEX

Canal Bike 141
Canal House Hotel 127
Capri 89
Car Hire 157
Caramba 91
Caransa Karena Hotel 129
Carel's Café 1 105
Carnival 158
Cartouche 76
Casa Di David 89
Casa Molero 95
Casa Rosso Erotic Theatre 117
Cattle Market 135
Centra 92
Centraal Station 14
Centro José Marti 66
Château P.C. Hooft 70
Cherubijn 58
Chez George 85
China Corner 83
Christmas Festivities 159
Christmas World 60
Christophe 76
Ciel Blue, Le (Okura Hotel) 76
Cinderella Schoenen 57
Circus Elleboog 133
Cirelli 90
City Theater 107
Claes Claeszhofje 24
Classic Western House 55
Climate 155
Coc 118

Cock-Ring 118
Collectors 61
Concertgebouw, Royal 114
Concerto 68
Condomerie "Het Gulden Vlies" 72
Consulates 155
Coster Diamonds 58
Country House Boerderij Meerzicht 136
Credit cards 160
Crignon, Le 85
Crime and Petty Theft 155
Cristofori 68
Cul-De-Sac 117
Customs and Immigration 156

D
Dam Square 26
Dansen Bij Jansen 115
Dantzig 102
Dappermarkt 62
Datscha Alexander 92
Decorent Silk Flowers 63
Delft 145
Delicious Traiteur 95
Delphi 85
Delta Hotel 127
Desmet 108
Desmet Gay Cinema 118

Dikker & Thijs Hotel 129
Diridas Puppet Theatre 134
Dirk Witte 69
Disabled Visitors 156
Djanoko 87
Djawa 87
Doelen Karena Hotel 129
Doffer, De 80
Drie Fleschjes, De 99
Drie Grachtenhuis 27
Driving 156
Drugs 157
Druif, De 100
Dutch Chamber Orchestra 13
Dutch Design in Fashion 55
Dutch Museum Year Card 31
Dynasty 93

E
East of Eden 102
Eben Haezer 122
Echhardt & Leeuwenstein 59
Edam Cheese Market 145
Edha Interieur 59
Eenhoorn, De 78
Eetsalon van Dobben 96
Eettuin, De 80
Efteling, De 135

INDEX

Eichholtz 70
Eijlders 100
Electric Current 157
Emergencies 157
Engeland Hotel 124
Engelbewaarder, De 105
English Bookshop, The 66
English Church 20
English Hatter, The 55
Enkhuizen 145
Entrecôte, L' 76
Escape 115
Esperance Hotel, L' 124
Esprit Café 105
Exchanging Money 160

F

501 54
Fame Music 69
Fantasia Hotel 124
Feduzzi 70
Felix Meritis 27, 113
Ferries 161
Festivals 158
Filosoof Hotel, De 124
Firma J. Vlieger 73
First aid 159
Flemish Frites 96
Flipper Hotel 128
Floriade Festival 158
Flower Market 62
Flower Parades 159
Focke & Meltzer 61
Forever Changes 69
Former Main Post Office 14
Former Rijks-Entrepôt 15
Fornhuis, 'T 79
Fox Hotel 124
Frank Govers 55
Frankendael 24
Frascati 81
Frascati Theatre 110
Fred de la Bretonnière 57
Frisian Skate Museum 146
Frozen Fountain 59
Fuel 157

G

Gaasper Camping 121
Gaffa 105
Garage, Le 76
Garden Hotel 130
Gay and Lesbian Switchboard 119
Gelaghkamer 105
Geparkeerde Mossel, De 88
Gerstekorrel Hotel, De 124
Gieter, De 100
Giftshop Tendenz 61
Golden Bend, The 28
Golden Temple 97
Gollem 100
Goochem Wooden Toys 138
Gouda Cheese Market 146
Gouden Bocht, De 28
Graaf, De 76
Grand Café Berlage 102
Grand Café 1e Klas 88
Groenhof Hotel 124

H

Haar, De 146
Haarlem 147
Haesje Claes 79
Hague, The 147
Halvemaan 77
Hampe Musical Instruments 69
Hanky Panky 73
Hans Brinker 122
Hatshop Chapeau! 56
Havana 119
Heeren Van Aemstel, De 102
Heineken Hoek, De 102
Hema 54
Hemelse Modder 88
Herman Kwekkeboom 70
Het Kantenhuis 61
Het Molenpad 81
Het Tuinhuys 77
Het Sienjaal 67
Heuft's First Class Nightshop 72

INDEX

Hilton Hotel, Amsterdam 130
Hilton International, Schiphol 131
Hoi Tin 84
Holland Festival 158
Holland International 143
Holland International Tours 142
Hollandse Schouwburg 15
Homolulu 115
Hoorn 148
Hoppe 101
Hortus Botanicus 24
Hotel de L'Europe 131
House on Three Canals 27
Huiszutten Weduwehof 24

I
Ice Skating 158
Ijsbreker 113
Imperial Continental Gas Association 15
Impressionist, De 85
Indonesia 87
Inpakwinkel 61
International Institute for Social History 19
International Theatre and Film Bookshop 67
Intratuin Wielinga 63
It 116

J
Jacob Hooij 72
Japanse Winkeltje, 'T 61
Jaren, De 102
Jazz Inn 69
Johannes and Ursula Begijnhof Church 20
Joseph Lam 115

K
Kabul 106
Kaiko 91
Kalfje, 'T 106
Kantjil & De Tijger 87
Kapitein Zeppos 81
Kasstoor, De 59
Keijzer Koffie en Theehandel 71
Kersentuin, De 77
Keuken Van 1870, De 78
Keukenhof 148
Kinderboekwinkel 138
Kinderboerderij de Dierenpijp 134
Kinderboerderij de Uylenburg 134
Kinderdijk 148
Kinderkledingwinkel, De 138
Kinderkookcafé 137
King Hotel 125
Klaas Compaen 93
Kleine Komedie 110
Kleine Vleeshal 18
Kloof, De 65
Knijp, De 83
Koninklijk Paleis 15
Koog aan de Zaan Windmill Museum 149
Kookboek Handel, De 67
Kooning van Siam 94
Korsakoff 116
Krakeling, De 134
Kriterion 108
Kroon, De 103

L
Lac, Du 103
Lach, De 65
Lady Day 56
Lambiek 138
Land Van Ooit 135
Land Van Walem 106
Lankamp & Brinkman 138
Leiden 149
Leidseplein 26
Lelie, De 78
Leonidas 71
Liberation Day 158
Libraries 159
Lido 103
Lieve 85
Linnaeushof 136
Lisboa 92
Lucius 94
Lucullus 81
Luwte, De 88
Luxembourg 103

INDEX

M

Maagdenhuis 16
Maas Hotel 128
Madurodam 136
Magazines 160
Maison de
  Bonneterie 54
Manchurian 84
Marken 150
Marowijne 93
Marrakesch 91
Mateloos 56
Mayur 86
Mazzo 116
Mechanisch
  Speelgoed 138
Medical Care 159
Mee in Mokum Tours
  142
Meervaart 110
Melkweg, De 114
Metz & Co 54
Miles 116
Milieu Winkel 67
Minds, The 106
Moeders 78
Molen Hotel, de 128
Money 160
Montelbaan Tower
  16
Morlang 106
Moses and Aaron
  Church 20
Movies, The 108
Moy Kong 78
Mucho Mas 81
Muiderpoort 16
Muiderslot 150
Munck Hotel, De 125
Muntplein 26

Museum van Loon
  28
Museums 31-41
  Agnietenkapel
  Allard Pierson
    Museum 34
  Amsterdam
    Municipal
    Archives 36
  Amsterdams
    Historisch
    Museum 35
  Anne Frankhuis 35
  Aviodome 36
  Bible Museum 36
  Bijbels Museum 36
  Bosmuseum 36
  Dutch Press
    Museum 39
  Electric Tram
    Museum 40
  Fodor Museum 32
  Geels & Co Coffee
    and Tea Museum
    36
  Gemeentearchief
    36
  Hash Info Museum
    37
  Jewish Historical
    Museum 37
  Joods Historisch
    Museum 37
  Kattenkabinet 37
  Kromhout Wharf
    Museum 41
  Madame
    Tussaud's
    Scenerama 37

Maritime Museum
  (Scheepvaart
  Museum) 39
Max Euwe
  Centrum 38
Museum
  Amstelkring 38
Museum Jaarkaart
  31
Museum van Loon
  32
National Aviation
  Museum 36
National Piggy
  Bank Museum 38
National
  Spaarpottenmus
  eum 38
Nederlands
  Filmmuseum 38
Nederlands
  Persmuseum 39
Nederlands Piano
  en Pianola
  Museum 39
Nederlands
  Scheepvaart
  Museum 39
Nederlands
  Theaterinstitut 39
Nint Museum of
  Technology 39
Open Harbour
  Museum 40
Open Haven
  Museum 40
Rembrandthuis 32
Resistance
  Museum 41
Rijksmuseum 32

INDEX

Schriftmuseum J.A. Dortmond 40
Sex Museum 40
Six Collectie 33
St Agnes Chapel 34
Stedelijk Museum 33
Surinaams Historisch Museum 40
Theatre Museum 39
Tramlijnmuseum 40
Tropenmuseum 40
Tropical Museum 40
Van Gogh Museum 34
Verzetsmuseum 41
Vrolikmuseum 41
Werf 'T Kromhout Museum 41
Werkspoor Museum 41
Zoological Museum 41
Musikado 62
Muziektheater 113
Mykonos 86

N
Naarden Vesting Museum 150
Naranjo, El 92
Narrowest House 28
National School Museum, Rotterdam 151
Nederlandse Handelsmaatschappij/ABN 16
Nederlandse Stoomkoffiebranderij Geels & Co 71
Netherlands Philarmonic Orchestra 13
Newspapers 160
Nico Israel 65
Nieumarkt Square 26
Nieuwe de la Mar 110
Nieuwe Oosterbergraafplaats 29
Niewe Kerk 20
Nightbuses 161
NMB Bank Head Office 19
Noi, Da 90
Noorderkerk 21
Noordermarkt 62
Noordermarkt Square 26
Nova Hotel 128

O
O'Henry's 83
Odeon 116
Oesterbar, De 94
Olofspoort, In de 100
Olympic Stadium 16
Oosterkerk 21
Oosterpark 25
Oostindisch Huis 17
Open-Air Theatre in Vondelpark 111
Opera, L' 103
Oppascentrale Kriterion 139
Orkestje, 'T 81
Oud Holland 79
Oude Kerk 21
Oude Lutherse Kerk 21
Oudemanhuispoort 17
Owl Hotel 128

P
Padi Mas 87
Pakistan 86
Pancake Bakery, The 137
Pancake Corner 79
Papillon, De 56
Paradiso 114
Park Lane Hotel 125
Parking 156
Parkzicht Hotel 125
Paul Lijfering 58
Paviljoen de Carroussel 137
Pecheur, Le 95
Pentagon 19
Pied à Terre 67
Pier 10 89
Piet de Leeuw 80
Piet Hein Hotel 125
Pompadour 71
Ponte, Del 79

INDEX

Poppendokter, De 138
Port Van Cleve, Die 80
Portugees Israëlische Gemeente Synagogue 22
Poseidon 86
Post Offices 160
Postzegelmarkt 63
Prins Hendrik Hotel 128
Prins Hendrik Maritime Museum, Rotterdam 151
Prins, De 82
Public Holidays 161
Public Lavatories 161
Puccini 96
Pulitzer Hotel 131
Punch 57
Purmerend Cheese Market 150

Q

Quatre Canetons, Les 77
Queen's Birthday Celebrations 158

R

Raephofje 25
Ramada Renaissance Hotel 131
Rederij D'Amstel 143
Rederij Lovers 143
Rederij P. Kooij 143
Rederij Plas 143
Reiger, De 82
Rembrandt Hotel 125
Rembrandt Karena Hotel 130
Rembrandtplein 27
Remembrance Day 158
Reuter Diamonds 59
Rialto Filmhuis 108
Richfield for Prestige 56
Rob Van Reijn Theatre 111
Robert Pemsela 67
Rokin Hotel 125
Ronnie Hotel 126
Rose's Cantina 91
Rosenthal Studio-Haus 62
Rotterdam 151
Roxy 116
Royal Carré Theatre 111
Royal Palace 15
Rum Runners 83

S

S. Emmering 64
Saarein 119
Sama Sebo 87
Sandwichshop Sal Meijer 96
Saul Groen 69
Scandic Crown Victoria Hotel 130
Scarabee 84
Scheepvaarthuis 17
Scheltema 101
Schermerhoorn Museum Mill 152
Schiller 104
Schiller Karena Hotel 130
Schilling Juwelier 58
Schooltje, 'T 139
Schreierstoren 18
Schutter 101
Sea Palace 84
Seven Bridges Hotel 126
Shelter, The 122
Shoebaloo 58
Shorts of London 106
Simon Levelt 71
Sinterklaas Festival 159
Sisters 56
Sisters Restaurant 97
Sjaalman 106
Sleep-in Mauritskade 123
Slegte, De 65
Sluizer 95
Smalle, 'T 101
Soeterijn 114
Soul Kitchen, The 116
Sound of the Fifties 69
Spanjer en van Twist 82

INDEX

Speciaal 87
Speelmuis, De 139
Spetters Kindermode 56
Spinoza Antiquariaat 65
St Andries Hofje 25
St Antoniespoort 17
St Nicholas Church 22
Stadsdoelen (YHF) 123
Stadsschouwburg 111
Stalhouderij, De 112
Steeple Climbing 134
Stempelwinkel Posthumus 139
Stephan Kelian 58
Stern Hotel, De 126
Stock Exchange, The (Beurs van Berlage) 13
Strada, La 119
Studio 19c 60
Sukasari 88
Swissotel Amsterdam Ascot 130
Szmulewicz 85

T

Tandoor, The 86
Telephones 161
Tempoe Doelgoe 88
Ten Katemarkt 63
Theehuis Vondel 79
Thermos Day 119
Thorbecke Hotel 126
Tipping 161
Tis Fris 96
Titus Hotel 126
TM-Junior 134
Toko Sari 96
Tom Yam 94
Toren Hotel 128
Torre di Pisa, La 90
Toscanini 90
Tourist information 161
Tout Court 77
Toy-Toy Museum, Rotterdam 151
Traffic Regulations 156
Trains 161
Tramlijn Begeerte 82, 106
Trams 161
Transport 161
Travellers' cheques 160
Treasure Restaurant 77
Trippenhuis 28
Trust Theater 112
Turkiye 94
Tuschinski 108
Twee Prinsen, De 107
Twee Zwaantjes, De 101

U

Upstairs Restaurant 137

V

Valk Windmill Museum, De 152
Van Bienenhofje 24
Van der Laan's 62
Van Doorneveld 72
Van Gennep 64
Van Gogh Giftshop 61
Van Haalen Hotel 125
Van Hale 81
Van Moppes Diamonds 59
Van Puffelen 82
Vasso 90
Vecht River Tour 152
Verbunt 89
Vertigo 89
Victorie Hotel 126
Vijff Vliegen, D' 77
Vliegenbos 122
Vliegende Schotel, De 97
Vogelmarkt 135
Volendam 153
Vondel Hotel 128
Vondelpark (YHF) 123
Vondelpark 25
Vondelpark open-air theatre 111
Vrolijk 67, 119
Vroom & Dreesman 54
Vrouwenboekhandel Xantippe 68, 119
VVV Amsterdam 142

INDEX

W
Waag Building 17
Waalse Kerk 22
Wampie 139
Warung Swietie 93
Water 161
Waterland 153
Waterlooplein 27
Waterloopleinmarkt 63
Weber 107
Weisse Rose, Die 68
Welling 107
Westelijk Entrepôtdok 19
Westerkerk 22
Westindisch Huis 18
Westmans Winkel 65
Wildeman, In de 100
Wildschut 104
Willemspoort 18
Willet-Holthuysen Museum 28
Witte Tandenwinkel, De 73
Witteveen 80
Wonen 2000 60
Wouda, B. 96

Y
Yab Yum 117
Yama Food Produkt 71
Yamazoto (Okura Hotel) 78
Yellow Bike Tours 142
Yoichi 78

Z
Zaanse Schans Museum Village 153
Zeeburg 122
Zeeburg Jewish Cemetery 29
Zeezicht 123
Zon's Hofje 25
Zorba the Buddha 117
Zorgvlied 29
Zuiderkerk 23